'A book of elemental passion, written with an exact elegance and a remarkable range of reference. It is a book of profound loss, intense joy, and a hard-earned wisdom. It possesses the strange beauty of a real work of art.' GWYN THOMAS

'This may be a book about grief but don't expect misery: *West* pulses with life's vitality, is shot through with resilient spirit. Perrin, a writer peerless when mapping landscapes, now turns his attention to inner lands, to the empty plains of loss. He then fills them with memories of two people who were as dear to him as breath, a son and a lover who left chasms in the heart on their departure. This may be his last book, a testament therefore. What does it tell us? That life goes on, and thrillingly so. And that grief is the deepest lesson, if you're willing to learn.' JON GOWER

West

West

A JOURNEY THROUGH THE LANDSCAPES OF LOSS

Jim Perrin

Atlantic Books
London

First published in hardback and trade paperback in Great Britain in 2010 by Atlantic Books, an imprint of Grove Atlantic Ltd.

The author and publisher would gratefully like to acknowledge the following for permission to quote from copyrighted material: *The Savage God: A Study of Suicide* by Al Alvarez, published by Weidenfeld and Nicolson, an imprint of the Orion Publishing Group, London; *The Widower's House* by John Bayley by permission of Gerald Duckworth & Co Ltd; *The Uses of Enchantment* by Bruno Bettelheim. Copyright © 1975, 1976 by Bruno Bettelheim. Reproduced by kind permission of Thames & Hudson Ltd. *The Gamble, Bobok, A Nasty Story* by Fyodor Dostoyevsky, tr. Jessie Coulson © 1966, reproduced by permission of Penguin; *On Murder Mourning and Melancholia* by Sigmund Freud, tr. Shaun Whiteside © reproduced by permission of Penguin; *The Uncanny* by Sigmund Freud, tr. David McLintock © 2003, reproduced by permission of Penguin; lines quoted from 'Ripple' by Robert Hunter © Ice Nine Publishing Company. Used with permission; 'Rocky Acres' in Robert Graves, *Collected Poems* © 1965, reproduced with permission from A. P. Watt on Behalf of the Trustees of the Robert Graves Copyright Trust and Carcanet Press; '*Darn o Gymru Biwritanaidd y ganrif ddiwethaf ydoedd hi*', a line from 'Rhydcymerau' by D. Gwenallt Jones from *Eples*, reproduced by kind permission of Gwasg Gomer; 'Funeral Music' by Geoffrey Hill reproduced by kind permission of the author; 'Erntezeit' ('Harvest-time') by Friedrich Hölderlin in Leonard Forster (ed.), *The Penguin Book of German Verse*, 1957, reproduced by permission of Penguin; 'Distance Piece', 1964, by B. S. Johnson © reproduced by permission of MBA Literary Agency; lines from 'On Raglan Road' by Patrick Kavanagh are reprinted from *Collected Poems*, edited by Antoinette Quinn (Allen Lane, 2004) by kind permission of the Trustees of the Estate of the late Katherine B. Kavanagh, through the Jonathan Williams Literary Agency; reprinted with the permission of Simon & Schuster, Inc., from *The Drowned and the Saved* by Primo Levi. Translated from the Italian by Raymond Rosenthal. Copyright © 1986 by Giulio Einaudi Editore s.p.a. Torino. English translation Copyright © 1988 by Simon & Schuster, Inc.; 'Braken Hills in Autumn', in *Complete Poems* by Hugh MacDiarmid reproduced by permission of Carcanet Press; 'I saw you among the apples', in *Hymn to a Young Demon* by Aonghas MacNeacail reproduced by kind permission of the author; 'Leaving Barra' by Louis MacNeice reproduced by permission of David Higham Literary Agency; lines from *Detholiad o Gerddi* by T. H. Parry-Williams reproduced by kind permission of Gwasg Gomer; *Mourning Becomes the Law: Philosophy and Representation* © Gillian Rose 1996, reproduced by permission of Cambridge University Press; *Autobiography of Bertrand Russell* © 1967 Bertrand Russell, published by George Allen and Unwin and reproduced by permission of Routledge and the Bertrand Russell Peace Foundation; *The Rings of Saturn* and *The Emigrants* by W. G. Sebald, translated by Michael Hulse, published by Harvill Press. Used by permission of The Random House Group Ltd; *Lights Out For the Territory* © 1997 Iain Sinclair, reproduced by permission of Granta Books; 'The Rock', in *Collected Poems of Wallace Stevens* © The Estate of Wallace Stevens and reprinted by permission of Faber and Faber Ltd; 'Yn Yr Hwyr' by Gwyn Thomas, published by Gwasg Gee, reproduced by kind permission of the author; *Blue Sky July* © Nia Wyn, 2007, reproduced by permission of Seren Books.

Every effort has been made to trace or contact all copyright holders. The publishers will be pleased to make good any omissions or rectify any mistakes brought to their attention at the earliest opportunity.

10   9   8   7   6   5   4   3   2   1

A CIP catalogue record for this book is available from the British Library.

Hardback ISBN: 978 1 84354 611 5
Export and Airside Trade Paperback ISBN: 978 1 84354 986 4

Printed in Great Britain by the MPG Books Group Ltd

Atlantic Books
An imprint of Grove Atlantic Ltd
Ormond House
26–27 Boswell Street
London
WC1N 3JZ

www.atlantic-books.co.uk

*For Joe Brown, who is kind, and was always there,
and for Jan and Elizabeth Morris, in friendship.*

And so it ends.
Some parch for what they were; others are made
Blind to all but one vision, their necessity
To be reconciled. I believe in my
Abandonment, since it is what I have.

Geoffrey Hill, 'Funeral Music'

Contents

BOOK ONE

The Aftermath

I

Furthest West

The tide had drained from Omey Strand. I stopped on the road south of Claddaghduff and looked across. Flashes of water still gleamed among the sand. Under a mercury sky their surfaces were scumbled into pewter texture by a cold east wind that funnelled and blustered out of Streamstown Bay. A solitary turnstone picked among clumps of seaweed by the quay, its tortoiseshell colouring merging into the khaki. From over on Omey a flock of knot, late as the spring itself and several hundred strong, took off in swirling flight, flickering dark and then silver against a slate-hued northern sky before scattering down into ebb channels around Skeaghduff, their low, muttering call drifting back just audibly against the wind. The hummocky green island crowded in against the coast. I started the engine of the old black Citroën. It had been Jacquetta's favourite. She called it our 'gangster car' (and in it, daredevil and subversive to the last, she'd collected a speeding ticket that had arrived days after her death. This time I was spared the need for tactics or argument to save her licence). My son

Will had borrowed it from time to time, for the style of the thing, to cruise along the quiet roads of Dyffryn Tanat and up to the waterfall, winding the windows down as he pulled away from the house to jet the bursts of gangsta rap at me that completed the pose, the laconic familiar grin on his face, the sideways and backwards toss of the head to acknowledge the joke of it all. The car creaked up on its suspension. I pointed it west down a narrow, pot-holed lane with brilliant green-bladed leaves of a few early flags in the fields to either side, and jounced and groaned across the wave-ribbed sand on to Omey itself. This was where my instinctive flight had led, to Iar Connacht, the westernmost province of Europe and historically one of the poorest and most tragic. There was psycho-geography at work here – the primal instinct Thoreau expressed in his journals and essays:

> there is a subtle magnetism in Nature, which, if we unconsciously yield to it, will direct us aright. It is not indifferent to us which way we walk. There is a right way... which is perfectly symbolical of the path which we love to travel in the interior and ideal world... My needle is slow to settle, varies a few degrees... but it always settles between west and south-southwest.[1]

For me, on impulse I had fled, and fetched up in the furthermost west with a clutch of Irish words to offer some definition and explanation: *Iar*, which signifies not only 'west' but also 'the end, every extremity, everything last, after, backwards, blank and dusky'; *iarsma*, 'after-effects, remainder, remnant'; *iartharach*, 'furthermost'; *iartestimin*, 'conclusion of a period'; *iartaige*, 'unhappy consequence'... As far as I was able at the time to understand from my state of shocked grief, all that seemed to fit and resonate. And it was hazed too with folkloric texture and the salving charge it always carries. A sad child will slip the leash of a brutal contingent and escape into story, and so did I. I knew the myths that led me here to the west: of Goll, a giant and leader of the Fir Bolg, defeated by the Tuatha De Danann but allowed by them to remain in the rough, far exile of Iar Connacht. Goll's one eye was the westering sun. In the tales he embodies a wisdom that looks askance at triumphalism and can only come from defeat. He represents too the universality of these native tales, the currency of which is loss, grief, mourning, and a background that is elemental, a deemed-sacred continuum of the orders of nature.

There is an enabling quality in this apparently primitive matter, and instinctively I was seeking it out. It allows you to loosen the halter of specific and individual sadness, is a lost and crucial necessity at times of the deepest anguish. I was seeking out the landscapes that correlate. In these first instants of my own journey into loss, for me too the treeless barrens and the wrack-rimmed coasts of Connemara seemed right. Yet I had come here by chance and at unexpected behest.

In the caravan where I was living among the Welsh moors of Hiraethog, two days after Jacquetta's funeral, my mobile phone had rung. It was an Irish writer – I'll call her Grainne – whom I'd long known, and been involved with for a time some years ago; tempestuously, disastrously, before Jacquetta and I had come back together:

'Come across to Galway, Jim – I'll mind you – you need

minding now. There's the spare room. You'll be all right here. You can work. We can talk. I'll not bother you.'

As she rang off, she repeated that formula about minding me. The prospect of being cared for after two years of caring for Jacquetta, often under the most difficult circumstances, had an undeniable appeal, sounded like rest and relief. I considered whether I should go. The westward pull that I had felt with increasing intensity since the evening of Jacquetta's death-day was near-irresistible now. There is no logic and a continual charge of magic running through your thinking after bereavement, in equal and opposite degree to your being unwitting of the practical and the predictable. To go west was to follow her – the version of thinking my mind had installed under these circumstances on that point was quite clear. To lose her twice in my life was unbearable. She had gone west and I would go that way too. There was nothing to detain me in the caravan by the stream where she and I had mostly lived for the last eighteen months. To continue there was clearly going to become increasingly difficult and inconvenient as well as painful, for pathological savagery circles after a death, breeding in families, seeking a focus and seeking a target, the guilt of those who neglected and exploited and abused fixing invariably *post mortem* on those who cared for and provided. Autonomous human love is always a threat to those whose claims on affection are based not on right behaviour but through propinquity. In the aftermath of a death, the close and caring bereaved are often made homeless, their joint belongings pillaged, whilst the erstwhile-negligent blood-tied ones are emotionally and materialistically merciless in their reappropriations of the deceased.

My Irish friend's invitation was in accord with my own desire. I phoned her back, accepted her offer, said she could expect me the following evening. And as I did so, it was with the faint, pained recognition that it was in accord too with Jacquetta's premonition that after her death this is where I would go:

'You can talk about poetry and literature with her, and those things excite you and they matter to you.'

'But I don't need to talk about them. You and I can be together without the need to talk. We know each other's thoughts, and are quiet and peaceful, and delight in what's around us. I wouldn't change that for anything or anyone. I wouldn't change you for the world.'

She looked at me in her calm way as I spoke, and when I'd finished she turned to the window of the bedroom in the house into which the last weeks of her illness had forced her to take refuge. We were silent together in the attentive stillness of mutual belonging. Two barn owls were hunting along the stone wall that traversed the moor, the pair of them ghosting pale against brown rushes and grey rocks, close-bound, returning to their roost. Re-attuned, we turned to each other again, and to the sweet ease and right fit of our embrace. Her lips parted and her head tilted back in the habitual way of her arousal. She led me to the bed, the unspoken plane of knowledge between us haunted by the sense of her imminent leaving. I might not have changed her for the world, but the world was one from which she would soon be gone.

*

No more than a bare space of weeks had passed since that moment. Now Jacquetta was smoke and ashes. Will's ashes too were in their urn in the caravan shrine, waiting on release, myself not yet knowing where or when to bestow them, my grieving for him nine months on hold whilst I'd cared for my woman in her time of dying. And I'd accepted a proposition that Jacquetta had surely foretold:

'When I'm gone you'll go to Grainne – she's more your equal than I am.'

'You're my equal in every way, and you are wise and beautiful and desirable to me.'

'You'll go to her. I can tell. Make love to me now. I want to feel you inside me...'

*

There are many things, in the first days of grieving, that you do not notice. The neurologist Antonio Damasio writes that 'consciousness and emotion are *not* separable', and goes on to note that 'when consciousness is impaired so is emotion.'[2] In this frozen state, things pass you by unobserved. You remain for many reasons at best only partially aware. The mind has lost any forward view and your whole focus is minutely backwards. It even blanks out matter that it might be sensible to register with regard to any plans you somehow summon the attention to make. Even the instinct for survival is attenuated, or even unwelcome. Perhaps, in a more alert and circumspect state, I might have thought back to my last meeting with Grainne. I'd picked her up from Manchester airport and driven her back to Wales. At my house, though it was still afternoon, she'd

straight away insisted on our fucking. In a frenzy of unzip-
pings and writhings she had me down on top of her on the
black sheepskin in front of the hearth. Afterwards, sitting by
the fire with my cat Serafina purring on my lap, dizzily post-
coital and relaxed, suddenly Grainne launched out of her chair
and with a full sweep the back of her hand cracked across my
mouth. On the return arc she caught the cat, sent her flying ten
feet across the room and sliding under a chair, from beneath
which her wide green eyes stared in fearful astonishment as I
wiped away the blood that was trickling from my lip and
asked Grainne what that was for?

'You weren't paying attention to me, only to that fecking
cat...'

'So that merits a smack in the teeth?'

'What's the point of having a temper if you can't use it?'

As with many of Grainne's sallies, I had no response to
that one, nor to the arch, acid sweetness of its west-of-Ireland
delivery. The rest of the visit did not go well. I could forgive
her the swollen lip and the loose tooth, but not the striking my
cat, to whom I was particularly attached. She was large and
slender, white with black markings and a lopsided moustache.
She'd arrived on my doorstep as a two-year-old stray, had
moved in and stayed. My bossy, good-hearted, elderly Welsh
neighbour Mair had spotted her across the back-garden fence
and – her own cat having recently died – tried to lure her in,
but cats and dogs generally bond most closely cross-gender,
and she was having none of it. 'Call her Buddug, then,' com-
manded Mair, but I pointed out to her that the Jack Russell
at the end of the terrace was a Buddug and we'd not want
forever to be inviting her around. Also, I'd already taken to

calling the new stray Serafina, after the good witch Serafina Pekkala (a name apparently taken from the Helsinki telephone directory) in the first part of Philip Pullman's great fantasy trilogy *His Dark Materials*. For Mair's sake, I added on the assonant Welsh 'Seren Haf' – 'summer star' – which appeased her, and I could often hear her whispering the full-version septosyllabics through the slate fence those summer evenings. The next week I went out and found Mair a sleek and biddable tom cat who soon grew round as a football, and down upon whom Serafina, by now fiercely territorial, glowered from high perches with sovereign contempt. She was thin and ill, and had a habit of vomiting in the most inconvenient places – computer keyboards, vegetable baskets, white duvet covers – but a diet of trout fillets, boiled chicken and rice, fillet steak gently fried in butter, and medication from the vet had eventually cured her. One day she'd been sitting in my lap purring like a small rasping bellows, I'd met the languid gaze of eyes the colour of sunlit sea over clean sand seen from a high cliff, and had convinced myself that she was a revenant, was the ghost of my own little Jack Russell, The Flea, on the exact second anniversary of whose death at the age of seventeen she had arrived. The tendency towards magical thinking had long been present in me, the deaths of my loved ones serving only to amplify it.

Grainne and I on this occasion years before had parted on furious terms when, after more nights of angry fucking that had left us exhausted and ill at ease with each other, I'd refused to drive her to her Manchester publisher's and dropped her at Chester station instead, as heartily glad to be rid of her presence as no doubt she was to be free of mine. It was several years since I'd seen her, though she would email me or ring from time to time to gossip about poets she knew; to talk about her latest book or translations she was working on, or plays she'd seen in Dublin or Paris; to slant in acerbic questions about how 'the great romance with that girl' – this despite the fact that Jacquetta was very close to my age and several years older than Grainne – was going; to suggest meetings in Dublin, Paris, Cape Cod, to none of which I agreed. And now, at the most vulnerable I had ever been, I was accepting Grainne's offer, and hoping it was in good faith. My comic innocence puts me in mind of John Bayley's in *Widower's House* – the last of his trilogy about the death of his wife Iris Murdoch and its aftermath. Had I read that in time, and relished the delicious comic absurdities of it, I might have been forewarned:

> Why had Margot come to my bed in the night? Why had Mella become so different so suddenly when she knew that another woman had been in the house? Surely no deep strategy was involved in these actions; they were just a part of human behaviour, its diversions, as one might say, bringing about both troubles and rewards.[3]

Whatever diversions were to come, I needed to pack, get ready to catch the early ferry from Holyhead, make provision for Serafina's being fed; and before I left and before the moment left me, I needed to write something, to set down a marker of the time Jacquetta and I had had together, to establish its *mythos* as a sustaining point of reference for the coming journey into a double grief that the shocks of the last nine months and its terrible gestation had left me too numbed yet to acknowledge. I stayed up that night, shaping the feelings and memories that surfaced in my mind, shading the transition from idyll to tragedy, prefacing the piece with quotations from Simone Weil and Shunryu Suzuki.

The title that came to my mind for the essay thus produced was 'Coming to Rest', in recognition of what Jacquetta had brought me. It seems proper to have it at the starting point of this book.

We tell ourselves stories in order to go on living...[4]

2

'Coming to Rest'[5]

To find perfect composure in the midst of change is to find nirvana.

Shunryu Suzuki,
Zen Mind, Beginner's Mind

Love is not consolation, it is light.

Simone Weil,
Gravity and Grace

It could simply be that I am idle by nature, or that my old legs are giving out. Whatever the reason, these last two years what has given me most pleasure in the outdoors has been coming to rest within a landscape rather than racing through it in pursuit of some distant objective. There has been an additional factor at work here too, a crucial dimension that has brought with it new realizations and ways of seeing. John Berger wrote in one of his essays – important and insightful reading for anyone with a care for wild landscapes and what they reveal to and of us – that 'the utopia of love is completion to the point of stillness'. Since Jacquetta – my lover, wife, and friend of forty years – and I came together, the truth of that is what we sought, and what we found in the wild places through which we travelled.

Before meeting up with her again, crossing by chance the chasm of a twenty-eight-year sad divide, I was, I suspect, in the state that Robert Louis Stevenson describes in his 'Night Among the Pines' chapter from *Travels with a Donkey in the Cévennes*:

> even while I was exulting in my solitude I became aware of a strange lack. I wished a companion to lie near me in the starlight, silent and not moving, but ever within touch. For there is a fellowship more quiet even than solitude, and which, rightly understood, is solitude made perfect. And to live out of doors with the woman a man loves is of all lives the most complete and free.[6]

So we lived for a time what Matthew Arnold calls 'the ideal, cheerful, sensuous, pagan life'. We married in a pagan ceremony down by the well in the cliffs at Braich y Pwll, with the raven, the seal and the chough as our witnesses. From my house at Llanrhaeadr ym Mochnant in the Tanat valley, in May-time before the bracken was long and the blossomy blackthorn trees confettied every hillside, we walked up to the *pistyll* four miles above the village, marvelled at the water efflorescing across dark strata before climbing on into the long strath of the Afon Disgynfa above and seeking out a bed in the heather from which to watch the stars come out and the moon sail from behind the bounding, low ridges. We were not going anywhere. We were coming to rest. Clung close under whatever covering of blanket or coat we had with us as the dew fell and the last hovering kestrel scythed valleywards. We watched the mottlings of shadow deepen and the rifflings of the breeze among the sedge, the jagged dartings of snipe, and we murmured minimally to each other of these things and snuggled a little closer and half-wakeful dreamed away the hours of the dark, and dozed in the sun of morning – this often and often, for the waincrat[7] life was our joy and neither of us had found such sharing or such mutual joy before.

Many other such times in other places: one night on a Shropshire hillside, on a salient of sweet grass caverned into a thicket of gorse and facing west, from which we could see the sun's descent, rolling along a Welsh hill horizon before it finally was drawn down into the elastic earth and the liquid of its fire spilled across the sky. As response to which I cut and lifted squares of turf, gathered sticks from the copse beneath and soon the bright flames illuminated the beauty of her face as it turned attentive to the sounds of the night: the last creaking flight of the late raven across indigo sky, hush of an owl's wings, scurry of mouse and vole through dry leaf litter, and the snuffle and scrape of a lumbering badger among the trees.

Light and colour were her métier. From glass she created designs of exquisite simplicity, drawn from the gentle attention she bestowed continually upon the world. To be in her company was to enter a kind of trance of the consciousness of beauty. One morning we awoke in a little, sandy cradle we had discovered in the falling cliffs by Hell's Mouth. We had lain there nightlong listening to the soft susurrus of small waves upon the sand. The grass of the overhanging dune that sheltered us caught at rays from the sun's rising, and its matter became light, a latticed and filigreed gleam of silver, cross-hatching the azure. Later the same day, walking the beach at Porth Oer, stretched prisms before the crystal waves gave us gleaming, transfigured patterns in the sand under ultramarine water, momentarily, repeatedly. 'It's all in the stilling, in the moment, and the moment's eternal,' she breathed, turning to me and back to the water again, watching with her artist's eye this blessing of sight being obscured and renewed by each rolling wave.

In the stilling was where she found herself. I learned from her truly to come to rest within a landscape, open my eyes, and see. She had no interest in haste or achievement or distances, sought simply for the peace that comes when we are at one – with each other, with natural creation. I remember a day when I had been south to walk unfrequented hills, then drove back to meet with her again. We took bread and wine to a beautiful little river spilling down from the moors of longing, very quiet and unknown.

In its oakwood glen we sat on a shingle bank in the sunset, and I was communicating to her a picture from the morning's paper of an armless, burned and bandaged child in Iraq – who had wanted to be a doctor, to help and heal, and who might now never master those skills, might never delight in the feel of his lover's skin or the cool lightness of spring flowers, who would never hold in his own arms his firstborn child or dangle his fingers in a stream like the one by which we sat – the flyers who dropped the bombs that had maimed him invulnerable;

the press snapping away in a sort of exultation, capitalizing on all his shock and loss...

She heard me out, my hand in her strong one, and through her quietude, her still presence, over a space of hours these things we saw: a dipper working the stream feet in front of us; the sun setting as a great red and rolling orb; a sturdy horse with a white blaze that came to the far bank and communed; a little owl that alighted on a branch within arm's reach and peered, unperturbed. A bright half-moon shone down, a badger travelled across the field upstream in its gleam and two ducks scolded until it had passed; there was no human sound, no unnatural light; the stream pulsed on, the air very still, and a glimmer of frost settled across the moss and the bladed leaves from which more bluebells would soon rise. We felt the evil and the beauty of the world – no one kind and omniscient god, but an energy that splinters into these manifestations, and both perturbs and heals.

On a July day we drove down to the Radnorshire hills and by one of the mawn pools[8] above Painscastle, remote from roads, on as calm and clear a night as I can remember, we made a simple camp and built a fire. So windless was it that the flame of a candle we had placed by the trunk of a Scots pine rose unflickering to map the seamed shadows of the bark. To her, these, and the green hachurings of the weed in the shallows of the pool, and the whiskery croziers of new bracken, and the streaked carmines and tangerines of the sky, were the palette where her imagination mixed and dwelt so lovingly. I have known magic in my life, but no woman so magical as this.

When we returned to Llanrhaeadr late on a Sunday evening after this night out on the Black Hill, we poured a glass of wine and came out of the house to walk down into the old, circular churchyard of the village. She stepped on a rock in a low wall around the forecourt and it rolled away from her. A previous man in her life had beaten her savagely about the head, and her corrective balance was gone. Her feet flew in the air, she smashed down on the rock, and shattered two ribs. Six months later another fall, in which she cracked a lumbar vertebra. After that, her skin took on an ashen pallor. Our going into the outdoors was curtailed, but still, whenever we could, we would enter the margins of wilderness and come to rest there, to observe and to see: in the rainforest of La Gomera, on the wild western coast of Vancouver Island, or at bluebell and scurvy-grass time along the Pembrokeshire Coast Path, the sea a shimmer beneath. With the death of my son, whom she dearly loved, our joy was crowded out by grief. To be in each other's arms in the outdoors was our solace still, but she was forlorn and tired, physically and emotionally pained.

A fortnight after Will's passing she was diagnosed with cancer, began chemotherapy, and bravely endured its discomforts and indignities and the loss of the glory of her long and auburn hair, which she, so womanly, took hard. The shrinking of our physical horizons focused her attention ever more acutely into the splendour of detail, and its meditative power. Tint and pattern of a fallen beech leaf of autumn consumed her for an hour and more, turning it this way and that, finally letting it fall. We went to the Caribbean, away from the rigours of home weather to give her warmth, and the towering cloudscapes and scintillating emeralds of humming birds and visitant presence of the blue-crowned motmot and a scampering, comical agouti, and brilliant, fractured trajectories of fireflies absorbed her in glimpses of the joy of this jewelled world.

Always the prognosis was darkening. In March, she stood at the end of the bed and our eyes met as my face registered anguish:

'Why are you looking at me like that?' she asked.

'Because you are so very beautiful to me,' I replied, and the unspoken knowledge passed between us that she was dying. She had surgery and was told that the chances of recurrence were overwhelming, of survival beyond a very few years minimal. In the event, mercifully, it would only be weeks. On a Tuesday night, I supported her to a crystalline, mottled rock where we would often sit, water in front, west-facing across waves of tawny, cloud-shadowed moorland. Next day she went into hospital for a regular cancer clinic, but was admitted immediately, put in a small room at the end of a ward on morphine and a drip, with blackbirds singing in the cherry blossom outside. On her last night she ordered me peremptorily to stop messing about tidying things, get on the bed and cuddle her as we listened to the evening chorus. I held her, caressed her, told her how dearly I loved her as she slipped into sleep, and beyond that, deep unconsciousness. Next day, peacefully, almost imperceptibly, she died.

That evening, sitting on the crystalline rock, the little lilac helium balloon that had floated above her bed was released. There was not a breath of wind, the curlews were calling from the marsh, and courting redstarts flitted in and out of the leafless branches of the ash. The balloon rose straight up for fifty feet, and then at great speed and on an unwavering course, it took off westwards. At the exact point and moment of its disappearing from view, a star came out, blinked once, and was gone.

3

Beach of Bones

Two hours' drive, the fast ferry to Dún Laoghaire, and the long miles across Westmeath and Kildare brought me to Grainne's house in Galway at that dangerous time of late afternoon. Years on from our last meeting, there was still the disconcerting glitter in her eyes, the dark hair, the conquistadores' West-of-Ireland profile, the music of the accent, the rhythmic sway of body to words voiced almost as sacrament, and the rustle and glisten of her favoured silks. All of which I registered remotely somehow, as the stirrings of dim memory, something of the distant past from which I was now entirely dissociated, no longer either threat or allure. We went out to eat in a busy Italian restaurant in Salthill, drank wine and brandy into the small hours as she probed and compared my losses, always using the one as detriment to the other:

'As a mother, Jim, I know how you must feel about Will. That's the big one. Your partner dying – if she was your partner – that's nothing. But to lose your child, and your first-born too, what's worse than that...'

'She was my wife, and it doesn't work like that, Grainne – the loss becomes cumulative, you can't separate out – or I can't begin to yet. Maybe it's different for a woman, with the child growing in her body those nine months and often more the end of biological imperative than of love and connection. But remember that I had the care of Will from his being three weeks old, sole legal custody of him from when he was two. I doted on him and had a passionate care for him; and yet I still can't say, as you've done, that this loss is worse than that loss. There's a different intimacy with your lover, a different communion, and its being taken away is just as desolating. I can't see how comparisons are relevant. My loved ones are dead – that's all I know.'

I fretted the remnants of the night away ill at ease in the spare room. We walked the ragged coast of South Connemara in a cold east wind – the wind that in Wales is called '*gwynt o draed y meirwon*' – 'wind from the feet of the dead'. We visited graves beyond the Coral Strand; sought out brisk music that bounced off me like hailstones from frozen skin in the pubs; went to see a film – Christopher Nolan's backwards and disjunctive thriller on the nature of perception, *Memento*, with Guy Pearce as the amnesiac searching for clue and explanation to his wife's death – the trickeries of which had Grainne ranting and me pondering. And I talked much and necessarily of Jacquetta, which was not music to Grainne's ears and was received with barbed responses that could, had I been less exhausted and desolate, easily have inflamed into angry refutation and dispute. On the third night in her spare room, finally, after nine months in which there had not been a single night of unbroken sleep, my consciousness gave way to the peace of oblivion.

How long I had held to that state I do not know – perhaps hours, perhaps only minutes. What plucked me from it was awareness of urgent and wine-sodden breath panting at my cheek, and a wetness slathering rhythmically up and down my thigh. I leaped from the bed. There were words. Next morning I drove away west, circled around the mist-shrouded Twelve Bens by the shores of Lough Inagh and Kylemore Lough, and walked up Diamond Hill, which was free of cloud. From the summit I could look down Ballinakill Harbour and see Inishbofin, scan across Renvyle and the silver flash of Tully Lough to Inishturk, wildest and most remote of the Irish islands, where I'd had warm hospitality and welcome in past years, riding out there in a small island boat in a March gale from Roonagh Quay up in Mayo with The Flea tucked into my jacket as we bucked and slammed across the waves.

I came down from the hill and drank a pint of Guinness in Veldon's Bar in Letterfrack, as Jac would have done, and always did when the opportunity presented itself. I used to tease – not knowing then of the cancer's already having taken root – at how she retained her wraith-like figure whilst drinking more of the stuff than I could. And the taste of it brought the memories flooding back. Only a month before, we'd been together at the Academi Festival in Cricieth. I'd read from a recent book and interviewed a clutch of poets – Nessa O'Mahony, Chris Kinsey, Mike Jenkins. We'd dined in a rackety way with our raucous, intense, good friend Niall Griffiths and with reticent, decorous Colm Tóibín – a pairing made in comic-novel heaven. The strained and sniping interplay between the two of them, Scouse urchin and gay mandarin, was novelistic in itself, as though with hatchet wit and lancet tongues they'd battered straight out of one of Kingsley Amis's acerbic late fictions.

We'd stayed up late in the bar of the Marine Hotel. Jac locked into an intense women's conversation, concerned, anxiety-disclosing, heads bowed close, with my dear friend Sally Baker of the National Writers' Centre for Wales, whilst I warbled and slurped away in Saturday-night Welsh-pub-style with Twm Morys and Iwan Llwyd, refilling glasses when called for, holding Jac's hand all the while as our time slipped away. On the Sunday, in warm April sunshine, we'd sat on a sun-aligned bench, which is no longer there, by Cricieth's West Beach and I'd gone to fetch her the biggest ice cream I could find from Cadwalader's ice-cream parlour, which for once she couldn't finish – never anything other than the biggest of ice creams for her, who could eat a litre pot at a sitting and often did, yet still looked as slim as when I first knew her at seventeen. On one of the several honeymoons Jacquetta and I had (at least one every three months for the rest of our lives she'd decreed as part of the marriage contract, and so it worked out) – this one in Vancouver – she'd come across a kiosk in Stanley Park near the Lions Gate bridge that advertised itself as selling 'the best ice cream in the world'. So there and then she'd conducted a taste test and told the proprietor that his wasn't as good as Cadwalader's of Cricieth and he should get himself over there to try it. Also, Cadwalader's sizes were larger. He gave her an outsize free one, of course, for that concluding sally and I, recognizing the game and seeing the need for reassurance that her charm still worked – which it did unfailingly and to my frequent amusement – drifted off with a wry smile to photograph the bridge, leaving the two of them to pat the innuendo lightly back and forth.

On this warm Sunday three weeks before her death we'd left the festival and driven on down to Aberdaron at the end of the Lleyn Peninsula, one of her habitual places, thinking to make our way down to Ffynnon Fair – St Mary's Well – the secretive spring in the cliffs at Braich y Pwll where we'd married two years before. But she was no longer able to make the rocky descent, could manage only the few yards down the slipway to a perch against the sea wall of the graveyard, and I settled her there and fetched pints of Guinness from the Ship Inn to drink watching a calm sea rippling slowly on to the empty sands: 'Like as the waves make towards the pebbled shore,/So do our minutes hasten to their end.'[9] In the time we'd had together, each year at her March birthday I'd booked a room – always the same room, looking out across Cardigan Bay towards the distant coast of Pembrokeshire – at the Ty Newydd hotel here, with its terrace directly above the beach. Today, little more than a month from our last visit, it was closed. She asked me to walk her to the water's edge, paddled briefly in the tide-ripple, and – her head resting against my shoulder, my arm around her, gear-changes effected one-handed whilst my knee kept the steering wheel straight – she slept most of the way home.

In Veldon's, I slid my empty glass on to the bar and headed off past Cleggan and along the Sky Road to Claddagh-duff and Omey, the flock of knot dramatic against a sombre sky as I arrived. Leaving the car, I slung a rucksack on my back and circled around to the west of a shallow, reedy lough in the centre of the island to arrive at St Fechin's Well. It looked as grubby and unkempt as last time I'd visited here, over ten

25

years ago as a lecturer on one of the 'Island Weeks' organized by Leo Hallissey, the National School Headmaster in Letterfrack and a Connemara institution. It's little more than a trickle-fed hole in the turf above the shore. The gritty, grey, granitic sand of Omey and the votive offerings scattered around of rusting pins and the tops from Paddy bottles added to its unappetizing appearance. My mind turned to the May night when Jac and I held our pagan wedding ceremony at the cliff-well of Ffynnon Fair – the sparkle of its water, its pure and chalky taste as we stooped to drink; the purple Precambrian rock and the viridian weed that lined its sides; the continual crave and splash of the waves beneath; a seal's presence only feet away from us, peering as we sang to it; the pool triangular in all planes with its little fish and copper coins greening on the sandy bottom; the way the clouds cleared from the west and sunlight flooded beneath them to bring us illumination like a blessing; the lowering ourselves naked from the barnacle-rasp of rock into a glittering cold sea of surging swell and green depths; the stories locating here, of pilgrim embarkation and the judge's daughter's drowning[10], that I recounted as we climbed out on to rock now brilliant with slant sunlight; her face shining and her long skirt trailing across the ancient carved steps and orange glowing lichens as we climbed back from the well's perilous place into our brief future together.

On Omey, I'd no inclination to drink from Fechin's Well or formulate a wish there, though I filled a water bottle, thinking I must boil it thoroughly before drinking as I did so, and moved on to the ruined church to the north. It had been buried by sand for centuries until the priest from Claddaghduff, using a JCB to the horror of many archaeologists, had excavated it maybe twenty years ago. A watery glimmer of sun infused rather than lit up the crystalline, roughly-shaped blocks and granite erratics round an empty window, brought out subtle ochres and mauves in them, highlighted seams of quartz in a darker, slatier rock. Leaving the church behind I wandered over to another shallow, sandy, reed-girt pool, curlews circling to land on its farther side, their slow descending glide buoyed up on bubbling calls. Beyond it I slipped down to the northern beach of the island. The flock of knot were still feeding off the point to my right. Not wanting to disturb them, I turned west. Winter storms had swept and gnawed at the dunes, the winds from the ocean had carried on their work, eaten into the ancient burial ground here. Graves had opened to the urge of the elements, long bones and skulls like grey, over-sized mushrooms had rolled down on to the sand. Their presence felt more comforting to me in my state of grief than macabre. The objective correlatives were in operation again. Consumed by the presence of death, I had come to a place of the dead. And Jacquetta felt to be here with me, as she would be in this way many times in the coming months and years.

The star's brief journey that I had witnessed on her death-day, our life's journey, the sun's journey – here on a bone-beach of the uttermost west in the presence of remains from those remembered by no living soul, all felt to be co-terminous. In a hollow in the dunes close by, I found some shelter from the Siberian wind that wuthered across the crown of the island, lit a propitiatory night-light and set it in scooped sand by an adjacent skull, took the little meths stove from my rucksack, set water to boil and put coffee in the travelling cafetiere that had accompanied Jac and me throughout our wanderings. Objects and everyday rituals become infused with such texture of memory. I looked back to the July evening on which she'd broken her ribs in Llanrhaeadr. The adventitious and the contingent had asserted themselves then as they were to do again a year later with Will's death. Our intense happiness, our idyll, had come to a sudden end. The balance of our relationship changed abruptly from that of lovers who had rediscovered each other after long years of separation to that of cared-for and carer. Though I could feel the splintered ends of the ribs under her skin, she'd refused to be taken to the hospital.

Instead we'd gone down into the churchyard, its circular shape revealing its origins as Celtic *clas*, and sat where we so often sat, on a projecting shelf at the base of the church tower to see the moon drift on its slow arc behind dancing, feathery larches on the crest of the wooded hanger beyond the river. She'd rolled what she called her 'sundowner' joint of charas from Himachal Pradesh, that she smoked every night, and then allowed herself another one for the special circumstances; had finished a bottle of wine as well further to dull the pain; had insisted later, despite her injury, that as on every night we were together right to the very end we make love, because in her view twenty-eight years of absence meant there was some catching up to be done, some frenetic present re-investment. And also, because now as much as when we had known each other as young people, she was an intensely sexual and uninhibitedly sensual woman, passionately erotic and fiercely faithful:

'From now on, we kiss no one but each other on the lips,' she had instructed me when we had first lain together again after all those years of separation. And I, ever her fool, as long as she lived had gladly complied. On that first night together I'd asked her if there were any more conditions:

'Oh yes,' she'd answered, 'you have to remember and observe the first law of universal human happiness.'

'Which is?'

'That a man should cherish his woman, and keep her well fucked.'

There wasn't much that was problematical in agreeing to that. In the years after Jac's death I would put the theory to most of my close women friends, ask them how sound a maxim they thought it to be? They'd go a little misty, their expressions would grow distant and fond:

'That sounds about right,' would be the invariable gist of their replies.

The cafetiere pushed into the sand of Omey reminded me that as Jac was starting to recover her mobility after breaking her ribs, we'd gone away to a Greek island for three weeks and rented an apartment above a beach looking west across the Aegean. Each night we would sit on its balcony above 'the wine-dark sea' drinking strong and viscous Greek wines and I would read her a book from Richmond Lattimore's translation of The Odyssey. Of 'grey-eyed Athene' she always wanted more, snatching the book from me playfully, to read the passages again, to learn the roles. One morning I'd got up to make coffee as she was still sleeping, had drowsily knocked the just-filled cafetiere off a table so that the contents spilled down my thigh. I'd run out of the apartment across the beach and straight into the sea. The waves had taken the blistering skin straight off, leaving raw, weeping flesh like a map of South

America that stretched from knee to groin. Jac had known precisely what to do, as she had in Llanrhaeadr with her broken ribs. Then she'd had me comb the banks and hedge-rows around the village for comfrey – knit-bone in the old folk-name – and had made a thick, dark and unpleasant-smelling tea from the leaves, which she drank assiduously each day for weeks, washed down with sedative brandy. Here in Greece she went out and, in a small island village, found a jar of propolys – the sterile wax lining of beehives – came back and pasted it across my thigh, then dressed the burn, which healed within a week under her care. That night too she in-sisted on her making-up-for-lost-time reward, and for me, soreness aside, in being cared for there was such intensity of pleasure in seeing her sense of the balance of the relationship having been restored.

The kettle on the spirit stove coming to the boil, its lid clacking away, I poured water into the cafetiere carefully and dug the single plastic mug that it filled and that we'd always shared into the grey sand for stability. The ritual brought recol-lection of dozens of other such occasions: the time early in our renewed relationship when we'd gone to a Bruce Springsteen concert in Dublin, danced on the green turf of the stadium for four hours, for Jac would always dance. At my house in Llanrhaeadr she would play the music loud and have me on my feet to dance with her, wildly, bouncing wicked and laugh-ing off the walls of the room, or holding close for the slow ones and kissing so passionately that at certain tracks she would always turn down the music, hitch up her skirt and slip out of her knickers to sit astride me on the sofa, the droop of her lower lip, ecstatic arch of her back as she eased herself up and down upon me, my moistened finger fast and soft along the shaft of her clitoris, her breath quickening, her eyes rolling back, gasps and soft wails of her satisfied desire. In Dublin we walked back along the canal and I'd recited verses from Patrick Kavanagh to her and been teased back in return for being a stuffy old littérateur who remembered far too much:

I saw the danger, yet I walked along the enchanted way,
And I said, let grief be a fallen leaf at the dawning of
the day.[11]

We stayed in a hotel room – the only one I could find to book – so small and in such a disreputable quarter, massage parlours and pole-dancing clubs lining the street beneath, that when eventually we slept, with our feet hanging out of the window, ribald comment shafted up nightlong from the sleazy comers-and-goers and nocturnal passers-by. When we got back to Holyhead after huddling together outside on the afterdeck of the ferry throughout the crossing, there was no question of going straight home. Instead we stocked up on provisions and headed out to one of the wild western beaches of Anglesey, shrank away from the fret of rain into a tiny, rocky cove and soon were tending to the kettle's splutter and the hiss of the frying pan. She loved to be outdoors and wild, to feel the sea and the sun and the wind on her skin. When I think of Jac now, lines from Louis MacNeice's poem 'Leaving Barra' keep running through my mind:

The dazzle on the sea, my darling,
Leads from the western channel,

A carpet of brilliance taking
My leave forever of the island…

And you who to me among women,
Stand for so much that I wish for,
I thank you, my dear, for the example,
Of living like a fugue and moving,

For few are able to keep moving,
They drag and flag in the traffic,
While you are alive beyond question,
Like the dazzle on the sea, my darling.

Except that Jac is no longer alive. And these recollections, these memories?

The meeting at noon at the edge of the field seems like
An invention, an embrace between one desperate clod
And another in a fantastic consciousness.

Is Wallace Stevens' view, his notion that 'It is an illusion that we were ever alive'[12] any less legitimate than my own endless rehearsal of these memories, the underlying project of which Freud falters towards defining in his seminal essay from 1917, 'Mourning and Melancholia':

So what is the work that mourning performs? I do not think I am stretching a point if I present it in the following manner: reality-testing has revealed that the beloved object no longer exists, and demands that the libido as a whole sever its bonds with that object. An understandable tendency arises to counter this – it may be generally observed that people are reluctant to abandon a libido position, even if a substitute is already beckoning. This tendency can become so intense that it leads to a person turning away from reality and holding on to the object through a hallucinatory wish-psychosis. Normally, respect for reality carries the day. But its task cannot be accomplished immediately. It is now carried out piecemeal at great expenditure of time and investment of energy, and the lost object persists in the psyche. Each individual memory and expectation in which the libido was connected to the object is adjusted and hyper-invested, leading to its detachment from the libido. Why this compromise enforcement of the reality commandment, which is carried out piece by piece, should be so extraordinarily painful is not at all easy to explain in economic terms. It is curious that this pain-unpleasure strikes us as natural. In fact, the ego is left free and uninhibited once again after the mourning-work is completed.[13]

The temptations to 'hallucinatory wish-psychosis' were what I had to exorcize, and not always successfully. The need I recognized in myself was not immediately for detachment, but rather to celebrate and commemorate Will and Jacquetta. To do this properly demanded that, ultimately, 'respect for reality' must carry the day. But in these first weeks of cumulative loss, any desired state of achieved equilibrium was far off.

For the moment, this journey embarked upon haphazardly, instinctively, from weird and magical 'reasoning' after the deaths of my loved ones has led me solitary and at twilight to a remote beach strewn with human bones on a tidal island in the far west of Connemara. Why, apart from the distorting thought-modes of grief, had I sought out this place? What, beyond the all-consuming presence of death, was leading me to settle into it and pass here the coming hours of dark, under the hollow gaze of the ancient skulls? Hazlitt comes close to providing an answer, and one that links naturally into Freud's speculation around the libido's apparent incapacity in grief to find a substitute, in his essay of 1814, 'On the Love of the Country':

> There is, generally speaking, the same foundation for our love of Nature as for all our habitual attachments, namely, association of ideas. But this is not all. That which distinguishes this attachment from others is the transferable nature of our feelings with respect to physical objects; the associations connected with any one object extending to the whole class. My having been attached to any particular person does not make me feel the same attachment to the next person I may chance to meet; but, if I have once associated strong feelings of delight with the objects of natural scenery, the tie becomes indissoluble, and I shall ever after feel the same attachment to other objects of the same sort.[14]

Jac had gone. To counter Grainne's relativism I'd offer the simple truth that generally when searching for things lost we start in quest of the most recent. That had led me out west, by primitive impulse, to a type of landscape in which much of the relationship between Jacquetta and myself had been played out – and much of Will's upbringing too. In places like these we took delight, time and again. They had been the backdrop to Will's childhood, and the stage on which the idyllic acts of the relationship with Jacquetta took place. They played, as well, to our sense of finding our destiny in each other. One Midsummer's Night Jac and I had set off in the dusk for Traeth Gwyn, the little-visited beach at the very end of the Portmeirion peninsula in North Wales. We'd wandered around as though enchanted, as though led by the fairies, in circles in the woods, on paths that repeatedly brought us back to our starting place – a journey, as I was to find out, not unlike the endless and forlorn searchings of grief.

I look back now over the gap of years in which Jac's and Will's deaths have taken place and my rational mind, the cleaving to which has been the beacon guiding through the stages of grief, can recognize the degree to which Jac and myself invested this experience with significance, allowed it to reinforce our joint propensity for magical thinking. There is a passage from Freud's *The Uncanny* that is particularly sensible and relevant here:

One may, for instance, have lost one's way in the woods, perhaps after being overtaken by fog, and, despite all one's efforts to find a marked or familiar path, one comes back again and again to the same spot, which one recognizes by a particular physical feature... In another set of experiences we have no difficulty in recognizing that it is only the factor of unintended repetition that transforms what would otherwise seem quite harmless into something un-canny and forces us to entertain the idea of the fateful and the inescapable, when we should normally speak of chance.[15]

The single torch we carried this Midsummer's Night had given out. Innumerable times we tripped and stumbled. The fairy-tale motif of 'babes in the wood' occurring so early in our rediscovered relationship had a subconscious role to play in the extraordinary strength of our bonding, our attachment to each other. In the blank dark, moonless and drizzling, eventu-ally we'd pitched down a steep gully that led us out on to yielding sand. We'd scurried before the incoming tide on to rock ledges piled high with a springy litter of flotsam, soft as any mattress, and there we'd spread the double sleeping bag she'd insisted we have made for our adventures, and built a fire, and in glee at midnight had sent a fat rocket hissing and soaring to scatter falling stars across the estuary (rockets were another of Jac's quirky delights – she would climb out of the loft-bedroom's skylight in the house in Llanrhaeadr to launch them from a hidden recess in the roof and illuminate and arouse the sleeping village. The mischief-maker in her was strong.) So this western beach of Omey with its skulls, its reli-gious dimension linking back to the celtic-churchyard night on which our losses began, far from demanding an abandonment of the libido-attachment, acted conversely to shore it up, re-minding and reinforcing, and as Hazlitt notes, calling up the same attachment though precise location differed.

What it chiefly brought, though – and what I had been doing in every private moment and some quite public ones besides since Jac's death – was freedom to weep. I had not thought that tear ducts could generate so copious a flow. For a year I cried, and four years on from her death and five from Will's, still do at small provocation. I came to know why tears are said to scald, why those shed in grief are called 'hot tears'. Here on Omey, the wind offshore and the place at distant remove from habitation, I could make sounds I would not have believed myself capable of producing. No formal and disciplined expression of sorrow here, but primitive release. By that ancient graveyard I screamed and sobbed and wailed until finally exhaustion supervened, and I curled up foetal in a hollow in the sand and slept.

In the darkness the tide whispers over the sands of the inlet and the wind breathes. Unseen birds chatter and scold. The sea pours around Aughrus Point with a soft, audible roar. The clouded sky is darkness impenetrable. I am alone with my dead, and the grieving can begin. I am alone with my dead in a place of the dead, and I do not want to live. *This* is why I have come here – to be alone; to be in a place of the dead; to be at peace and undisturbed with my own dead. Profoundly, I no longer wish to be alive. I wish, in that way of magical thinking again, to be with them – to inhabit whatever dimension they now inhabit. To reason out where that may be is the journey I must go on. There is another option, which is to take my own life, to extinguish the pain of my own consciousness. But I cannot take it. Even at this lowest point, its inadmissibility for me is clear. Even in the past, when the desperate absurdity of the world had only registered its nature and not the necessity for its acceptance in my mind, I could not have killed myself. I came near to it at times, yes – once when I lived in the isolated shepherd's cottage in Cwm Pennant, in the seasonal grip of listless, hopeless depression I had sat with the barrels of a shotgun in my mouth and the triggers wired together. My Labrador – a young dog then – came over and licked my hand. It was the autumn of the year in which I'd arrived there, the preceding spring the one in which, after intense promises between us, I'd lost contact with Jacquetta.

The experimental novelist B. S. Johnson a few weeks earlier by chance had shambled through, seen me reading in the garden, smelt the rabbit stew simmering on the stove. The valley was one of his particular places, the last poem in his only collection a long sequence set here.[16] He ate with me, stayed, talked, left with me a batch of poems. That autumn he killed himself. Suicide is suggestible, contagious. One of the new poems he gave me, in typescript and signed, is called 'Distance Piece':

> I may reach a point
> (one reaches a point)
> Where all I might have to say
> (where all that one has to say)
> Would be that life is bloody awful
> (Is that the human condition is intolerable)
> But that I would not end it
> (But one resolves to go on)
> Despite everything
> (Despite everything)

Thirty and more years on, eerily, on a west Connemara strand in the deep night Johnson's poem was roosting in my brain. I had reached that point, arrived at its distance. Life was bloody awful, but I would not end it. Camus, in his great essay on the subject, suggests that 'Rarely is suicide committed (yet the hypothesis is not excluded) through reflection.'[17] To continue to live might be anguish, but its catastrophic bleakness was militating enigmatically against the sense of futility and pointlessness. Only by carrying on could I honour my dead. Only by being alive myself could I remember and express the joy they had brought and shared. That Will himself should have chosen to die – a choice that I can never presume to criticize or do other than respect and try to understand – that he should have perceived 'the absence of any profound reason for living, the insane character of that daily agitation and the uselessness of suffering'[18] – conversely and all the more strongly insisted on my carrying on, however unwilling or anguished I might be in doing so. Even at this earliest stage of my journey into loss, instinctively I knew this, though there was much work to be done before the assent I could give would be any more than notional.

Thus did my arguing thoughts circle in the darkness as I drifted in and out of sleep, until eventually the external gaze fastened on a slightest silvering of the sky above, a thinning consistency to the dark. To the east, a faint flush of colour even, and beyond it an accelerating shift through brightening tints of yellow, a quick atom of scarlet that ran like flame along the rim of the Twelve Bens before gathering suddenly into a fiery ball that floated free of the earth and shot out searching rays beneath a canopy of cloud retreating fast now to the west, leaving above Omey unsullied sky the blue of robins' eggs, reflecting too in water around the island that was rippling back now towards the sea, the causeway to the mainland across the strand emerging, cormorants beating past in rapid even flight, dunlin stitching their patient way along the receding edge of the tide, oystercatchers piping by and sanderlings chasing the small waves. The world was coming alive, busying itself about another day. It was time for me to head back to Wales, put my affairs in order, come to terms as best I could with the events of the last nine months and all their preceding histories. I thought of the account in Alexander Carmichael's monumental collection of folklore from the Scottish Highlands and Islands, *Carmina Gadelica*, of the man of great age from Arisaig who would recite a sun-prayer each morning:

> The eye of the king of the living,
> Pouring upon us
> At each time and season,
> Pouring upon us
> Gently and generously.
> Glory to thee,
> Thou glorious sun.
> Glory to thee, thou sun,
> Face of the God of life.

Those who were buried in the ancient graveyard of Omey would have recognized those sentiments, as perhaps also would those who had set up their circular wooden stockade on the bank of the little river in Llanrhaeadr, men and women living there in fellowship, equality and harmony. I thanked them for their company through the dark night, for the sense of spiritual guidance and respect for nature that still inhabits where they have been, turned my back on their skulls' sightless gaze, and walked on into the attempt to understand.

BOOK TWO

Pre-histories

4

Soldiers in Scapa

In the second-hand and student bookshop on Holyhead Road in Upper Bangor I fumble an early volume of Gwyn Thomas out of the twentieth-century Welsh/Anglo-Welsh poetry shelf. A meagre pamphlet with a marked and pale-green stiff-card cover, one rear corner cut quite away, comes with it, flaps to the floor, lies face-down, contents concealed, no title or clue to the author among the inkblots and the stains. I pick it up. It's open at a poem entitled 'Soldiers in Scapa':[1]

> I watch the plovers wheel low at dusk
> Over the sparse-sown grass
> Where soldiers trample with lobster-pot cricket bat
> Into the wet canteen for a last drink.

I read the stanza, the whole poem and – though it's not good poetry – through it am vouchsafed a sudden glimpse into the young life of my father, forty years dead, who spent the early years of the Second World War as a sergeant in the

Salford Regiment in charge of an anti-aircraft battery at Scapa Flow. I leaf through pages of fragile wartime utility paper to the title page, curious, a tightness in my chest, a pricking in my eyes of renewed tears: *The Van pool & other poems* by Keidrych Rhys. The dedication is to Lynette Roberts. Both names have interest and association – Rhys because he founded the review for a later incarnation of which I've often written; and Lynette Roberts for the mournful, haunting precision of her late-modernist verse. I buy the pamphlet, its original sixpence crossed out and 50p written in pencil in its place, and the Gwyn Thomas collection too, walk out into the rainy, grey little shore-town of the west with its encircling hills that I have known and loved since my teens, head down College Road with a seethe of memories disorientating me, reducing time to a jumble of recall. Beyond Love Lane a path beckons, leads on to the seaward and westerly of the two ridges between which Bangor lies. The last bluebells are blanching and curling under the shadow of the oaks, their hyacinth scent carried to me with a drift of fine rain on the west wind as I climb to Roman Camp.

A bare month before, they had been in their prime in a beechwood along a sunlit slope at Bryneglwys as I drove Jacquetta to the Chester hospital where, unexpectedly (or at least not so soon), a week later she would die. Beyond the trees as I climb the path, the bluebells encroach into clearings along the ridge, their faded blue licking out as low healing flame towards the scorched rings in the turf where students have lit fires and scattered lager cans, takeaway cartons, foil barbecue trays and shrivelled, grey condoms. A jay sears past in a flash of cinnamon and celestial blue. I sit on the bench at the top-most knoll, looking down on the straits and the town's elegant little pier. The sun breaks momentarily through cloud cover and coaxes a terracotta gleam from the mudflats of Traeth Lafan to the east. Below me the trees stretch to the banks of Afon Menai – the great tidal channel that separates Anglesey from the mainland.

> Who knows, for all the distance, but I am as good as looking at you now, for all you cannot see me.[2]

Ten years ago, on this same bench, I had sat motionless and silent, as a raven on a dead branch five yards away ran through a whole rich repertoire of call and gesture and finally – having elicited no response from me – had surrounded itself with an intense violet aura that shimmered and clung to its every movement and contour. Visiting the great American naturalist Barry Lopez in Oregon later that year, I'd recounted the experience. 'So why do you have a problem with this?' he'd asked, pointing me to the beliefs of native peoples world-wide that animals can convey meaning and illumination to attentive – a word on which he laid a ringing stress – humans. The web of connection is so fine, so delicate. I want to believe in magic. I wish for some means by which to link with my losses. Yet I suspect I know the truth, the implication, in Lopez's words. That attention – the full engagement of our human consciousness – is the all, is life itself, and our enshrining memories are the only hereafter.

The raven colony has departed these woods of Siliwen now, opting for quieter forests behind remote beaches away to the west. Rain from that direction drifting in, I descend through oaks to the shore of Menai, where a solitary young bird picks among bladderwrack of the shallows, undisturbed, oblivious to my presence. Two shelduck clatter down into a pool in the arc of a tidal bar, bobbing in time as they shovel industriously, their best dapper of chestnut and iridescent green vivid against the dull. From the little working boatyard along the shingle, a breeze tunes up the halyard music. I sit on a driftwood log foundered in the shingle and weep. For weeks, in repose or involved in other things, whilst driving or talking with friends, whilst reading or walking among the hills, involuntarily the tears have come. Who would have thought that death could release so many; or of the gasping sobs, the unmannings, the night-howling, this hunched and forlorn and shambling thing I have become, scarcely able from grief's somatic oppression to breathe? C. S. Lewis, in a text that seems through the kind intentions of friends habitually to arrive on the bookshelves of the bereaved, where I suspect it remains for the most part and perhaps wisely unread, excoriates this weeping over the lost beloved:

> On the rebound one passes into tears and pathos. Maudlin tears. I almost prefer the moments of agony. These are at least clean and honest. But the bath of self-pity, the wallow, the loathsome sticky-sweet pleasure of indulging it – that disgusts me… in a few minutes I shall have substituted for the real woman a mere doll to be blubbered over.[3]

I find this passage, and much else in the book from which it derives, as offensive as it is incomprehensible. Sorrow does not of necessity cause you to lose sight of your loved ones.

There is no 'loathsome sticky-sweet pleasure' in tears. They are inescapable, proper, respectful, cleansing. Whatever Lewis's natural habitat of the Senior Common Room or the gentlemen's club may decree, there is nothing maudlin or sentimental in weeping. The emotion is natural, wells up within and spills over, is unstoppable, manifests in a way that should invite none of the rigid pejoratives indicative more of personal limitation than kindly understanding of our proper emotional states. The great Christian proselytizer and apologist seems to me to reveal himself as rather less than compassionately human here; for the last thing you need in bereavement is to be made to feel guilty about any aspect of your sorrow.

After a while, I wipe my eyes, compose myself, take the books I've bought out of my pocket and leaf through. Again the young soldier, my father, starts out at me from the Keidrych Rhys pamphlet, asserting his place in the mourning process. I turn to Gwyn Thomas's book, remember entrancing lectures he gave on the grave and elemental beauty of early Welsh verse, putting me in thrall lifelong when I was an undergraduate here decades before and the woods of Siliwen and the hills beyond were the places to which I would slip away during the frequent freedoms of student life. Wales – the place my people came from – was a part of my losses, somewhere I had then come to find. As *Cymro colli iaith* – a Welshman who has lost his language – I had transferred to Bangor after a year of study in London, had been told by my tutor, who was already set on having me stay and continue to do postgraduate work on Blake, that it was 'academic suicide'.

'If you really are going to leave and if you must have *trees*,

49

go to Oxford,' she'd pleaded, 'there are plenty of them there *and* it's quite good academically – not as good as it thinks it is, but quite good nonetheless.'

'Fuck that,' I'd smiled back at her, determined to hold out against her humorous, exasperated and kindly persuasions. The compensations in doing so outweighed all the disappointment and disapproval – albeit for the most part friendly, and a sort of weary recognition of my pig-headed obstinacy – that I'd encountered.

And so I arrived in Bangor. Once on a morning during my first summer vacation I pulled into Povey's Garage in the old quarrying village of Penygroes and Gwyn Thomas arrived from the other direction in his old blue Citroën CX. This modest, affable son of a quarrying family from Blaenau Ffestiniog, who became a Professor of Welsh in Bangor and later the National Poet of Wales, stopped and I recall that we talked – with Mr Povey the garage proprietor joining in, and no doubt brashly on my part for it was a new-found enthusiasm, and what right had I other than that of dialogue in this company? – of the ninth-century poetry of the Heledd saga.[4] I remember with intense embarrassment how I delivered an extempore lecture some minutes in length and no doubt achingly crass and jejune on a particular line from '*Stafell Gynddylan*', one of the Heledd *englynion*, which, in its concise and echoing simplicity, sound shadowing its meaning, I thought – and still think – to be as fine as any I know: 'Wylaf wers; tawaf wedy.' ('I shall weep for a while, then be silent.')[5]

It strikes me as odd that I should have been attracted by such solemnity, such depth of sadness, in the spring years of my life. Though to scan back over the years seems to bring into focus a consistent thread of mourning. I think wryly that the melancholic post-modernist zeitgeist was infecting me long before it was the intellectual fashion, and one of the ubiquitous and proliferating '…isms' that are studied at universities these days in place of 'texts' – in place of the actual literature. The philosopher Gillian Rose – a writer of thrilling acuity and intellectuality – notes that 'Post-modernism in its renunciation of reason, power and truth identifies itself as a process of endless mourning, lamenting the loss of securities which, on its own argument, were none such. Yet this everlasting melancholia accurately monitors the refusal to let go…'[6] For sure, in a minor and personal key the letting-go of the Welsh national identity of my father's family in particular, in which I invested substantial belief about the nature of power, culture, democracy and truth, was not something then or now that I was easily prepared to do. As to 'endless mourning' and 'everlasting melancholia', I've tried on those garbs and the fit's snug enough. But there was also a psychological motivation here that it scarcely requires a detailed knowledge of Bowlby on attachment to define.

My closest childhood bond was with my grandparents, particularly on my mother's side, and through them and my father's family with Wales. Years later, in an essay inspired by returning to Wrexham one night to speak at the dinner of an outdoor club there, I wrote down the feelings and reflections that derived from this Manchester–Welsh upbringing:

My people come from those colliery terraces with the clean hills of Wales at their back that look down on Wrexham from the shoulder of Ruabon Mountain to the south-west. They come from Rhos, with its fine Welsh and its score of chapels and its great choir, and they left there in the years before the Great War, in the way that working people did throughout the ages, to find jobs in Salford, and to live among the chemicals and the effluent and the smog with which the Industrial Revolution, throughout its progress, poisoned its people and its planet. I think of my paternal grandfather and the change in his life, the decision formed of necessity to make his way from Rhos to Salford and what it entailed for him and for the millions like him over the century-and-a-half up to his time who had had to follow the same path.

For my grandfather as a youth, there would have been the heather changing colour season to season on Ruabon and Esclusham Mountains; the rare mornings when their hillside stood out above the cloud sea; the times after chapel when he and his companions might have ranged over the moor past Mountain Lodge, down into the lovely green limestone valley with the cranesbill trailing from the walls and the tang of wild garlic on the air at World's End before they clattered back, hobnails sparking, along Gwter Siani and past Llanerchrugog Hall as the stars came out to reach Rhos again.

How much of this did he miss, down there in Salford by the ooze and stench of the Irwell? He took his language and his culture with him. Each Sunday after his death my grandmother still went to the *Capel y Bedyddwyr* on Plymouth Grove in Manchester – she and it long gone – to sing the old hymns in the Tongue of Heaven. How can my grandfather not have taken also the memory of the sky and the wide moor and the clouds billowing out of Wales – all those glimpses of freedom that the tyranny of economics and maybe also the closeness and scrutiny of a small community forced him to barter?

I think of my paternal grandmother in her chapel pew singing out *'Ar lan Iorddonen ddofn'* – on the banks of Jordan deep – and wonder if ever a glimmer of her sly Welsh irony passed between these banks of imaginary promise and those of the Irwell on which she lived. And the names of her childhood – *Fron Deg, Bryn Goleu, Llwyneinion* – how did Factory Lane, Barrow Street and the East Ordsall Road compensate for the loss of those? Or for the liberty of walking on a spring morning maybe over Esclusham Mountain, the loping hare kicking rainbows from the dew, England still unknown and beneath the damp oblivion of the cloud behind her.

What I was writing about here, of course, was less personal than the more generalized sense of loss of connection to culture, home-place and the natural environment that was the common experience of a majority of the British people – my own family among them – in the 150 years before I was born. It's a theme that underpins much of the extraordinary upsurge in rural and nature writing from the early decades of the twentieth century and permeates the pages of W. H. Hudson, George Sturt, Henry Williamson, H. J. Massingham,

Edward Thomas. It was this enforced dissociation that fuelled the working-class outdoor movement in Britain, by the post-war manifestation of which in Manchester I was propelled back to a landscape that I could at last call home. There's a passage I love from Elizabeth Gaskell's 1848 novel *Mary Barton* that elliptically captures the ache for the original place, for the lost landscape of belonging and all its rich natural texture:

> There is a class of men in Manchester... who yet may claim kindred with all the noble names that science recognizes... the more popularly interesting branches of natural history have their warm and devoted followers among this class. There are botanists among them, equally familiar with either the Linnaean or the Natural system, who know the name and habitat of every plant within a day's walk from their dwellings; who steal the holiday of a day or two when any particular plant should be in flower, and tying up their simple food in their pocket handkerchiefs, set off with single purpose... There are entomologists... the two great and beautiful families of Ephemeridae and Phryganidae have been so much and so closely studied by Manchester workmen... Such are the tastes and pursuits of some of the thoughtful, little understood, working men of Manchester.[7]

My sister and I scarcely saw our parents until she was eight and I was six. I have fleeting memories of their presence, not all of them good. It is a mystery to us still where they were through that time. They were poor and unqualified I suppose, without home of their own in an impoverished and devastated part of Britain after a war, and things must have been going badly with them. Also, if later witness is reliable, they did not get on. But our grandparents were there, old country people transplanted into the city as young adults fifty years before. They believed in fairies and magic and ghosts, and through them so did I. Our upbringing by them was secure and in certain ways very rich:

> My grandfather? He had a ballerina
> Tattooed on his arm, faintly, in a green
> Like copper that's taken on the patina
> Of verdigris. There were books in his plain
> Back room – a Bible, the *Pilgrim's Progress*.
> Not till a late year did television
> Enter his house, then Nain could not undress,[8]
> By his command, lest from their side the screen
> Those watched watchers should see her nakedness.
> This fierce old man, blue-temple-veined and lean,
> Scowled at the wireless, spoke loud for good sense,
> Fought against the Boers, was sieged at Mafeking.
> Death ran him a kind race, at the last forbore,
> As he might have done, to boast itself victor.

He gave up the ghost peacefully enough in his late eighties, emaciated, flesh taut around 'the skull beneath the skin', features settling into the rictus of death, on the geriatric ward of a hospital that had formerly been the workhouse of which he'd spent his life in dread. My grandmother was of an entirely different character. Soft-bosomed in a faded brown dress, hair in a net, she was full of old stories, little rhymes, gossip from the last century:

Gertrude Charlesworth could charm warts, tell fortunes,
Palms and tea-leaves her magical domain.
To amuse me on afternoons of rain
She made laughing predictions, sung to tunes
Of her girlhood. On Fridays she baked bread –
Yeasty-warm under crazed honey-gold crust –
Gifts, and they came hot-dripping with her lust
For a kinder world than that which bowed her head
And judged her ignorant, who could not read
Nor write words but was wise. It's her merit
Is the best part of all I inherit,
Her instinctive goodness is my best lead,
So I appease her spirit and have fled
The unsouled, exiled streets where she last bled.

Their deaths, which happened within a year of each other as I was starting grammar school – my grandmother haemor-rhaging in the corridor of a new block of old people's council flats on a dreary croft in Gorton, my bereft grandfather a few months later on his geriatric ward – broke the link with an early childhood that had in many ways been idyllic. They had lived during that time in a street of red-brick terraced houses in the south Manchester suburb of Fallowfield. The flag door-step of the house was rough and granular to the touch, sandy-yellow in colour. My grandmother whitened it with a stone the rag-and-bone man gave her, from a bag that hung by the front of his cart. His pony clopped down the asphalt, harness creaking. The tar in the roadway bubbled in summer. Sometimes there was a barrel-organ with a monkey on a chain up by the main road. The street led down to Platt Fields Park, which had a culverted brook, copses of beech, sycamore and elm and a lake with gudgeon and stickleback. Some of my earliest memories are of walking through it with my grandfather to his allotment on a patch of ground behind a red-brick wall and a row of horse chestnut trees where the Elizabeth Gaskell College now stands – would she, I wonder, have preferred the trees? In those days it was one of the interstitial zones before the city stuttered out into rural Cheshire – a place of muddy paths, playing fields and neglected hedgerows where the damson trees flowered pink in the spring and there were dunnocks and noisy, combative greenfinches. Sixty years have changed it and its tenor beyond recognition, but childhood is satisfied with small marvels and pleasures and it was a kind of heaven to me then.

As it was for my father too, I think, for he came to my grandparents' house as often as he could, and, though weary, was genial to us children when there. I remember Saturday mornings when he took me with him to the UCP shop – a Lancashire institution, it stood for United Cattle Products – on Stretford Road. In the window were white trays full of animal parts, Lancashire delicacies like cow-heels and chitterlings and brawn, at which I dared not look. There were marble tables inside, cruets with fat, stoppered bottles of malt vinegar, and a sour, steamy atmosphere. He ate tripe and onions, ladled out from steaming vats behind the counter, that he laced with pepper and vinegar. I didn't want any, not even to try a mouthful off his plate. He would laugh, and afterwards buy me a penny apple from the greengrocers next door. Slivers of paint stuck to his cuticles. His hair shone with brilliantine and he smoked Senior Service, sixty a day, tapping the ends on the packet, flicking open a heavy lighter that smelt of petrol, on which the chrome had worn away to reveal the brass. 'Salubrious blast of the obnoxious weed' he would mouth, to no one in particular, inhaling deeply. Doctors in those days advised that smoking was good for the chest, and mostly did so themselves. Already the fits of coughing racked him each morning, and he would hawk and spit out thick gobbets of phlegm as we walked along the streets. He had photographs in his pocket, of when he was a soldier in the war at Scapa Flow. One set of his photographs was of Orkney: 'This is Skara Brae, this is the Old Man of Hoy.'

I study them wonderingly, little knowing the role the latter would play in my own life and that of my son. He tells of a waitress in a Kirkwall Café who would fry sausage meat and give him two eggs, even with rationing. He talks about her a lot, but not at my grandparents'. I can picture her. It was only ten years before. He had been summoned home to marry. Now he is a journeyman-decorator with a wife, two kids, bad chest, no place of his own to live. One set of photographs is of the extermination camp that he reached months after D-Day: 'Fucking Germans,' he mutters and I'm not supposed to hear. He goes quiet and puts them hastily away. We get the bus to walk the streets where he lived before the war in Salford, down by the Barton Bridge. He is searching, for his own father I think, silently, in a way that decades later I will search for him. When I remember him as he was then, I think of a passage from Iain Sinclair that could act as definition to the manner of his drift:

> Walking is the best way to explore and exploit the city; the changes, shifts, breaks in the cloud helmet, movement of light on water. Drifting purposefully is the recommended mode, tramping asphalted earth in alert reverie, allowing the fiction of an underlying pattern to reveal itself.[9]

Except that the underlying pattern here was no fiction but his personal history from before a war that had changed his life and consciousness. He used to play rugby league for Salford, was the hooker. And he boxed. Still had the athletic build, slim, muscular, keeping his head up; and his guard. He was capable against the straightforward adversaries. But I see in memory his eyes, and they are not now those of someone who expects to win. Once on Kersal Moor we go into the churchyard. He stops before one huge upright tombstone of polished black marble with a brief inscription, 'Blessed are the humble', and I catch the flicker of a sardonic grin, an incredulous shake of the head. In the February of 1971, seven years after his death, this childhood incident quite gone from my memory, I'm visiting a girlfriend, Stella Campion, a jeweller and a vital, alert, pretty young woman, tiny under a corona of tight blonde curls, humorous, her accent of the north and her tongue quick to the sharp and muttered sidelong deflating phrase, with whom I had a very intermittent relationship for fourteen years, neither of us able wholly to commit or let go, and who lived at this time in a sparse and spacious cold flat in

Kersal where the only warm place was her bed. Coming down from an acid trip and dreamy too from days of making love, we find ourselves one afternoon in the churchyard on Kersal Moor in front of the selfsame overpowering grave-marker and suddenly my father is there again to the life, dapper and physically powerful with the sardonic grin faintly flickering. This time his eyes meet mine in laughter, complicit somehow, taking in Stella before he fades from view. It is the only time I have seen him since his death.

On another excursion from my grandparents he and I fetch up in Peel Park in Salford, from which the view reaches out to moors pressing in close against the ragged margins of the city. He tells me about going there once or twice in his teens, walking for miles across the peat and the heather, camping out; stories of a mate of his from the next street, Jimmie Miller, who'd been trespassing, nearly got himself arrested. Others had gone to gaol. 'Lefties,' he snorts, scattering clues to the way through the maze of his own and perhaps all our lives. Years later, with a jolt of instant recognition, I come across the following passage from a haunting account of a Salford slum childhood by Robert Roberts, *A Ragged Schooling*. I use it in the introduction to my first collection of essays, and dedicate the book to my dad, by then more than twenty years dead:

One sunny Wednesday afternoon [my mother] took me to Peel Park. We sat on a high esplanade and looked far over the countless chimneys of northern Manchester to the horizon. On the skyline, green and aloof, the Pennines rose like the ramparts of paradise.

'There!' she said, pointing. 'Mountains!' I stared, lost
for words.

Years beyond that again, with a little help from Benny
Rothman – my friend and mentor in the Communist Party – I
recognize Jimmie Miller as Ewan MacColl the singer, some-
time husband of Joan Littlewood, writer of songs like 'Dirty
Old Town', 'The Manchester Rambler', 'First Time Ever I Saw
Your Face' and – exquisitely, elegiacally – 'The Joy of Living'.

Sometimes on these psycho-geographical rambles, these
shape-shiftings of my father into Salford Saturday *flâneur*, we
would call on his sister Elsie at her corner shop on Erskine
Street in Hulme, between the Stretford and the City Roads.
The streets there were cobbled, the terraces built of soot-
steeped brick, the air itself fumy with sulphur, that mingled
with the malted, sickly vapour drifting down from brewery
chimneys. Elsie lived with her husband Sam at a pub just
across the City Road, down by the Pomona Docks. Over a cup
of tea in the back kitchen, she offered my father the two rooms
above the shop. We went to live there in 1953. There was a
yard at the back where he could keep a dog, which he had
always wanted; an alleyway, an outside toilet. The close rows
of houses had gaps in them where bombs meant for the docks
during the Blitz had hit. Interior walls were revealed to either
side, with fireplaces, wallpaper shredding and fading, hooks
and nails from which ghost pictures hung. Paired timber
baulks rooted in piles of brick and thickets of rosebay willow-
herb shored up the survivors. When the hazy sun filtered
through the smoke, up and down the street women put
straight-backed chairs on the pavements outside the doors,

and helped to them husbands and grandfathers blinded and maimed from the Great War, in which my father's father had died. But for these brief spaces in the sun, they had lived inside for more than thirty years. I passed by one sightless man with a kind of terror, shrinking myself along the edge of the kerb. Half his face was still a raw and weeping wound, the flesh taken away by shrapnel in 1916. In the first volume of his autobiography, from a quarter-century before, Anthony Burgess recalls 'the blond, blind man who would horrifyingly appear from the living quarters of Price's cake-shop and mumble nonsense at the customers before being led back.'[10] His like still haunted my Hulme childhood. One afternoon coming home from school I saw my cousin Glyn on an old flatbed lorry down on the croft at the end of the street. A bigger kid was beating him up, all the other kids around jeering him on. I jumped up, hung on to the big kid's legs, got a boot in the mouth for my pains. We went back bloodied to Auntie Elsie's. My dad took me down to the gym behind Hulme Church after that, to start boxing: 'Bigger they come the harder they fall,' he said cheerily, waving me out to play on the streets.

We lived in those two rooms – apart from a brief and unsuccessful sojourn in Harrogate – until the slums were demolished. The acrid smell from the piles of rubble when the wrecking balls had done their work and the bricks were bulldozed into heaps caught in your throat. I returned once to look for Erskine Street, found a turning off the Stretford Road, the stub of a street, a cul-de-sac, of dreary new-build, the ground plan of that part of my childhood quite gone. When we left, we went to a flat on top of an office block of which my father was employed as caretaker in Albert Square in the centre of Manchester. In the first year there, my first year at grammar school, sometimes when he finished work early he would take me with him on the bus back to Platt Fields Park. We would get off at Old Hall Lane, walk through the gates with 'Ash Fields' inscribed on them, me holding his hand. He would play a game of crown green bowls and give me a threepenny bit, hexagonal and thick, livid yellow with a picture of thrift-flowers on it, to take out a clinker-built skiff with a single sliding seat on the lake for half an hour. The skiffs have long gone, replaced by fibreglass rowing boats. I saw Robbie Coltrane in one once, years later, being filmed for a television pro-gramme. The boat was listing so much its gunwale was a bare inch above the water. After one such evening with my father in the park, at school a senior prefect of what seemed immense height, bespectacled and with a tin leg, said to me in jeering tone during the morning break, 'Holding Daddy's hand in the park last night, were we!' I never did so again.

Albert Square was where we stayed until my father died. The strain of this shiftless existence on my parents' marriage was intense. Every night I heard the screaming, my mother railing endlessly, bitterly against him. His lack of ambition, his ease with women, the charm that drew them to him, infuriated her. She rebuffed his expressions of affection. Often I would come home from school, look for him and find him perched on the edge of a desk in the typists' pool of the insurance office, an atmosphere around him of fun and teasing and levity. Flirtation as well no doubt. In photographs from the time, my mother looks away from him, her face set in a mask of anger, frustration and disappointment. One evening I watched from a window as she and my father walked out on to the pavement to go ballroom dancing at Belle Vue with a friend. A Ford Anglia pulled up and the friend – my step-father-to-be – emerged, went around to the passenger door, opened it and tilted the seat forward without so much as acknowledging my father. He held my mother in a close embrace as my father, diminished, climbed in the back and looked intently away through the side window. Late that night I heard the voices raised again. My sister left home as soon as she could, at the age of fifteen, to train to be a nurse. It was not long before my father died. He fell badly, changing a light bulb in the bathroom, broke the washbasin. After that, something was wrong, the vitality draining away. He lost weight, stopped work, took to his bed. I'd carry him in his pyjamas, put him down on the sofa in front of the television. He was so light, proud that I could lift him and yet he weighed no more than pounds, bones protruding through the emaciated flesh. There were lumps on his back. Eventually the doctors noticed. Secondaries, metastases – they took him in to Salford Royal Infirmary. I was seventeen, in the express stream at school, doing A and S Levels a year early, went in to see him each evening. And I knew – just as I did when Jacquetta was dying.

After a time the secondaries blocked off the circulation to his legs and they became gangrenous. We still talked of what we would do when he was out of hospital. We would go to those places in Salford again, of his childhood. Perhaps we'd take another trip on the *Waverley*, the paddle steamer with the polished wooden deck and brass rails that plied from Liverpool to Menai Bridge, stopping at Llandudno pier, on summer Sundays, and see the timber hulk between the bridges across Menai that was HMS *Indefatigable*. The doctors debated above my head, within his hearing, whether to amputate the legs, but there was no point. He was delirious, sinking fast into a coma. The stink of gangrene made me gag as I sat by his bed. It was a relief when he died.

Forty years on, when they broke into my son's house and found him in that hot July in the bedroom under the eaves, decomposition well advanced, a noose from the skylight around his neck, into which he had simply knelt rather than hanged, that was the stench that pervaded the house and all his belongings even weeks or months later. I could not bear to see him dead – because of that smell, because I did not want a decayed thing to be the last sight I would have of my son, who was so beautiful – would not look even at the pictures for identification that the coroner's office sent.

Four months after Will's death, Jacquetta and I were in Tobago. She had started her chemotherapy but there was to be a break of three weeks, and on our caravan roof in Wales the November rains were hammering relentlessly. Quite early in our renewed relationship I had resolved to sell my house in Llanrhaeadr, use the equity to pay off her debts and take her to places and give her things that she had not seen, had never had. I think right from the outset we had a subliminal knowledge that our time together would be short. Things said between us make sense now that puzzled me then. She had known, as you do when the crab starts to nip. But neither of us knew that this holiday in the Caribbean would be our last. Her auburn hair had gone. She was given a wig by the hospital that I still have, keep in a drawer together with the night-gown she had sent me out into Chester to buy on her last day – simple white cotton with broderie anglaise around the bodice and cuffs, stained where a polite young Chinese male doctor had drawn off the ascites that was so distending her abdomen and causing her pain. The wig smells of her perfume, the only one she would wear – *Rive Gauche* by Yves Saint Laurent. Once when I had thought to buy perfume to give to my daughter Hannah on her birthday, not knowing what she wore, Jac had rounded on me: 'You mustn't do that – you must never buy a woman perfume without knowing what she likes. You men are so stupid at times! Do you know nothing about women after all these years!'

Sometimes I try on the wig, but mostly just bury my head in its lustre, hunting for the fading scent of her. In Tobago we stayed in a fisherman's hut on a bluff above Castara Bay – heartstone in the necklace of jewelled bays along the island's north-west coast. It was a west-facing, turquoise-watered, red-cliffed, forest-backed, surf-rimmed bight of a bay, beach-café'd, reefed and knolled and blue-roof-churched; a dozen rakish, indigo-canopied fishing pirogues, rods on either side like the antennae of some strange tropical insect, lolling at their moorings out beyond the surf, ready for the village fishermen to race one another into the water and swim out at their leisure. In the mornings, shadows of tall pines stretched across the beach and village children squealed across the sand to hurl themselves into the waves. Four pelicans perched on a rock to squabble and stab as another attempted to join them. Boobies plunged and came up with beaks full of wriggling fish. Frigate birds, fork-tailed and spectacular, spiralled ever higher on the thermals. We stayed mostly in the seclusion of our hut, for she was too tired with the effects of chemotherapy to descend the steep path to the beach. The hut was minimal and comfortable in a manner Jac loved – much like our caravan, but without the need for cosiness. Once we went out to the island capital, Scarborough, where a group of young black men teased her loudly about the bright headscarf she wore to conceal her baldness, calling her a gipsy woman, and for once she winced and had no response. We hurried away and I kissed tears from her eyes, told her how perfectly lovely she was, how utterly desirable, and held her to me, felt her wasting body against mine, her smooth skull cupped in my palm. We drove back to our fisherman's hut and its mosquito-netted bed and made love gently until the night suddenly fell and she was soothed and sat up and asked for wine and food and a candle to be lit.

In the mornings groups of apple-green parrots with rich and raucous calls flew by. Clouds of bananaquits chattered in through the window and sipped from trays of sugar-water we'd put on the sill. Sleek violet-blue tanagers squeaked from the bushes and a blue-crowned motmot visited mysteriously each day. One side of our hut was balustraded, open to the elements, facing into the sunset from among lush gardens where three-foot-long lizards sunned themselves, agoutis scuttled, and every tree was an aviary, a scene of constant activity. We watched from above as the fishermen pulled seine nets into the beach, all silver flash and heave and the men throwing the small ones back into the sea, or the waves licking in to reclaim them. I would be sent down to the village to buy limes that tasted sweeter and more piquant than ever they did in Britain, or mangoes, ginger, garlic, pawpaws, dasheen, and bread baked in banana leaves in the village's communal clay oven, which the old women took out on long wooden paddles and scraped clean of charcoaled leaf before inviting me, with much banter and teasing, to choose the shape and texture and complexion I preferred.

'I'm buying bread, not a woman,' I joked back as their shrewd old eyes laughed at me, 'I've got one of those, and she's a good one.'

'She too thin, mister – you starvin' her. We seen her. You go feed her up, fill her belly – that make a woman happy. You go get yourself some fish now – that what a man like!' And they'd send me on my way with a fat loaf and raucous laughter, dancing together with a shaking of copious bosoms and a bumping of heavy hips if I cast a look back over my shoulder.

As the days eased down towards brief tropical twilight, boats having returned, the fishermen's cooperative would lay out its wares on the beach stall and I would trip down the steep path again. Could I buy any? If the catch was good, and there was enough for the villagers and the proprietors of the beach cafés, and I waited my turn, and then pointed insistently and assertively enough at what I'd like, then yes – at which point it would be cleaned and filleted: whitefish, kingfish, grouper, tuna – which I'd take back and cook with the day's vegetables and Jacquetta and I would eat on the terrace under the tropical stars with the fireflies and the sound of the waves below. If I was unlucky with the fish, it was no matter. It just meant that Brenton and Sharon from the Little Beach Café had got there first, so Jac would lean on me down the path and we would go to sit in the velvet night at tables between which dawdled friendly dogs and cats, the sea's insistent soughing serenading us and phosphorescence augmenting our candles, and be served with heaped plates of kingfish and okra, goat curry, dasheen and dumplings, beans and breadfruit, creole style, spicy, washed down to her delight with Trinidadian double-strength Guinness. Later, back at Fisherman's Lodge, silver-filigreed moths, each wing of which was the size of my hand, flitted in; the geckos blinked and stalked staccato across the ceiling; intermittent trajectories of fireflies like sparks from a bonfire traversed the night; sheet lightning flickered along the horizon, and a steel band took its snare from the susurrus of the waves, each glassy back of which in the moment before its collapse reflected the moonlight as a thin and wavering line along the shore. It was time taken out of time.

One evening I took a shirt to wear from my bag, green and short-sleeved in seersucker fabric. As we sat in the humidity of the tropical night, I became aware of the smell, faint initially, but once the suggestion had been taken up by the senses it became overpowering. The shirt had come from Will's house, delivered to me in a bag with other of his clothes, most of which I gave away having washed. But I remember him wearing this one on the last occasion I saw him, how much he liked it and how well he looked in it. I washed it like every-thing else, and brought it with me, as a memento. In the starlit garden with the fireflies, suddenly the stench of putrefaction was all around. Not saying anything, I picked up Jac's glass from the table, hurried indoors to refill it and to strip off the shirt, throwing the latter into the shower. She looked from her glass to me when I returned to the table, in the way that she had of knowing what was not spoken, held my hand for a while before pensively rolling her sundowner. After a while we crawled behind the mosquito netting into bed and held each other close all night. The shirt was strung on the line in the sun and the wind and through tropical afternoon rain all the following day.

*

I am back on Menai shore, where my father and I, in his last days, had talked of being, and I take up the books again. The first poem of Gwyn Thomas's that I come across in *Y pethau diwethaf* – *The Last Things* – is called *Yn yr hwyr* – 'In the evening'.[11] On the shingle beach I read out the last stanza to the birds and the trees in the same way that I read so much to them all those years ago when I was a student here. But the lines are freighted now with the sense of how life is:

> Yn yr hwyr y daw'r sêr, yn yr hwyr y daw'r lloer –
> Encilion o oleuni oer – ac ehangrwydd
> Enbyd y gwacterau fel mwgwd ymennydd. Felly
> Y mae ar derfyn dydd.

> In the evening come the stars, in the evening comes
>   the moon –
> Cold desertions of light – and a fearful vast
> Of the void masks out the brain. Thus
> It is at the end of the day.

5

Reach Out Your Hand

For both Jacquetta and myself, there was a twenty-eight-year pause for reflection on the first phase of our involvement. I had my account of that period. She assessed it and incorporated her own additions and revisions into a summary version to which, through frequent reference and retrospective exploration, we both gave assent. This process at times involved re-traversing the actual landscape of our shared story, with interesting results. On one occasion we went back together at sunrise to a bench by the lake in Liverpool's Sefton Park that figured large between us – a bench I knew well from frequent pilgrimage back there through the years of separation.

'That's not the one,' she laughed, shaking her head as I invited her to join me, 'it's the next one along. Look!'

Sure enough, from *her* bench the sun was rising in exactly the right remembered alignment. The incident inclined me to trust her versions of events, and rather than challenging them, where I could not remember I would simply add in quite tentatively whatever I could glean from the half-light and possibility of memory for her verification. Thus it all became *our* mythos, held to as a kind of article of faith between us, of value, an expression of shared ideals and beliefs, and because of its coalesced structure in which two viewpoints, two sets of observations have merged, I am curiously incapable now of discerning to what degree any of the elements of the story have been fictionalized, as inevitably they must be in any writing project, where we shape, select, colour with our rhetoric or even at times wholly invent. I can say for certain that all of this story has some factual basis. Even so, I only have my memory now of Jacquetta's recollections to authenticate certain events about which my own recall is vague or absent.

Though she was the woman I loved – and I use the past tense here uneasily, because of course I love her still in my memory (but am caught on the dilemma of a belief in love as an active principle, difficult to apply when its object has gone, and not mere verbal protestation as easily rescinded as a proffered handshake) – that love does not preclude a certain puzzlement at times over aspects of her testimony as I now recall it. The past is another country, and even where intention is for lucidity and honesty, its distance from us can render clarity into degrees of blurring that range from soft focus through opalescence to total obscurity. And this is not even to take into account the deliberate scumblings a writer will practise where certain detail too finely resolved might affect the balance of a text. I am as guilty as the next author of all this. Also, I am getting old, and these memories, these events are receding from me, however passionately I desire to cling on to them.

There is, for example, Jacquetta's account of our first meeting. When she and I came back together after our long absence from each other, she told me that she had held this in her heart for nearly forty years. Even at the time – and the conversation took place on a November evening in my beautiful and welcoming little village house in Llanrhaeadr with its old warped timbers after she had driven over the high moorland road of Milltir Gerrig from Bala in a thick and drenching mist – I was aware that for her there was an imperative in the story, a necessity perhaps to hyper-invest it with meaning and value:

'I'm tired out. I'm spent. I'm going to have a nervous breakdown.'

'Don't do that – come and lean on me.'

'I am doing,' she'd responded, 'you're the only one who ever made any sense.'

She was clearly worn out, already ill, burdened and exploited and even persecuted. To be able to voice that last sentiment to me and about me – for it's one in which few of my friends would concur – was an index to the desperate straits in which she'd found herself. I have a sense that for her this seeking me out and our coming together was a last roll of the dice, and yet I cared for her immediately and instinctively and passionately – even more intensely, I have no doubt, than I had those many years before when we had first been close. She was a dear old friend with whom there had been the potential for happiness and fulfilment, who had disappeared from my life under quite mysterious circumstances, for whom I had spent much time over many years looking, about whom even decades on I thought very often still, and in comparison to whom no one else had ever seemed right. And suddenly she had reappeared, had come to be with me – though I did not

73

know this or the immense privilege it would be at the outset –
through her time of dying; and was to me more beautiful in
these last years even than in the splendour of her youth.

It could obviously have been disastrous between us, a
Flora Finching[12] scenario, a brief rapprochement homing back
into darkness. Instead it was a kind of redemption for us both.
This is how, on that November night in Llanrhaeadr, she
described our first meeting. Did I remember it, she had asked,
and had fortunately not waited for a response before going on
to describe. It happened, as she related, when she was seventeen and I was eighteen. She was in the Llanberis Pass on a
summer's day in 1965 during her first visit to Wales from her
home town of Kendal in the Lake District. She was with her
boyfriend of the time, a medical student in Liverpool whom I
vaguely knew through climbing and thought rather inept and
something of a show-off and a bore. They had driven down in
a Morris Minor van with the registration letters SLF, which she
joked stood for 'sex, love and freedom'. She told of how we
had talked for a long period over a dry-stone wall, slowly
leaning in together as the confidences flowed until our hair
mingled, and when we turned to each other our faces were
only inches apart and inevitably we kissed. I would never
have admitted this to Jacquetta, but I did not have the least
recollection of the dry-stone wall, our hair mingling, our faces
being so close, or even of this first kiss. To have owned up to
that would, I suspect, have been treasonable, so I dispensed
with my own version of our first kiss and happily accepted
hers, which was much more romantic.

What I did instead of contradicting her was to add in my
memory of the content of our first conversation, which may

have been on this occasion or it may have been a later one. I remembered how she had told me about the way in which, when women are living together, their periods begin to synchronise, and how she had laughed rather ruefully about her father's predicament, being in a house with a wife and four daughters, where one week in every month he had to walk on eggshells or retreat to his cellar workshop. What was remarkable even in retrospect about this conversation was that in those days – a decade-and-a-half before Penelope Shuttle's and Peter Redgrove's beautiful and life-changing book on the subject[13] and years before every young male novelist from Louis de Bernières to Owen Sheers felt obliged to include onset-of-period scenes to demonstrate their right-on credentials and understanding of female character – menstruation was virtually a taboo subject. It was joked about but never talked about. I could remember responding to the frankness and the humour and the mystery of Jac's exposition, and being quite entranced by the slim girl with the cloudy blue eyes, the intimate manner and the distinctive, long, elegant nose. But I truly do not remember when the conversation took place. It didn't matter, because it had happened early in our friendship on some occasion, which may have been this one, and her account and mine were now assimilated into our mutual history, were accepted as its starting point.

This first phase of our knowing each other had lasted for eight years. In that time I would see her often at weekends in Snowdonia, and call on her whenever I was in Liverpool. Sometimes on Sunday evenings I would give her a lift there on the back of my motorbike from Wales if her boyfriend was likely to be late back from his climbing, for the thrill of the ride and the pleasure of her company as much as the passionate and illicit kiss there would always be on parting. For her the major event in this time was when, at the age of nineteen and studying in Liverpool to be an art teacher, she was admitted to hospital with severe stomach cramps and it was found she was going into labour. Talking about it with me years on, she stated that until she was in hospital and about to give birth she had not had the slightest idea that she was pregnant, had assumed that her periods had stopped because of the stress of living away from home for the first time. She recounted how her boyfriend in the week after the birth, whilst she was still in hospital, had held out for the baby girl's adoption because to keep her would interfere with his medical studies and his climbing, and their families would not approve; how he had registered the birth under false names that he could not later remember, so that the child could not be traced; how the social workers too added in their pressure or even insistence on adoption, as was the savage norm at the time; how the daughter, whom she'd named Georgina, was wrenched away by force from Jacquetta's breast, and Jac was left screaming and had to be given sedation; how it was essentially the end of her relationship with the medical student, though they stayed together in a loose way for a few more years, because 'How could it be right from then on? We'd given away our baby...' Thirty-five or more years later, when Jacquetta and I were together, every morning as she awoke there would be tears in her eyes and lorn distance. Because of the false names given and then forgotten, all attempts to find her daughter were in vain. I talked about it once with her former boyfriend, with whom I'd had occasional contact over the years – about why the attempts to trace their daughter had come to nothing, and about Jac's continuing anguish. A GP now, and a professed Buddhist with a practised crinkle to his eyes, a grey ponytail and a confiding manner, though I may do him an injustice here he seemed little concerned: 'I've long since forgiven myself for the pain I caused Jacquetta.'

When I think about all this now, it seems almost trivial to tell of the brief time Jacquetta and I had together in our twenties. She was still in Liverpool, teaching art and living in a large-windowed, roomy flat in one of those vast, dilapidated Victorian houses around Sefton Park, edging towards closure with the boyfriend, who was a houseman by now and living in at the hospital. I had a room in a huge old house belonging to a friend among the quarries above Llanberis, not far from where I would later live with Will. Jacquetta and I were on frequent visiting terms. I remember two of these visits with great clarity. On the first of them – perhaps this was in 1973 – I'd found myself in Liverpool one Friday afternoon, had rung Jac and she'd told me to get around to her flat as fast as I could because she had 'some really good acid from Richard – we could spend the weekend tripping.'

'Richard' was Richard Kemp, whom she knew, and who was living with his girlfriend Christine Bott in Sefton Park at the time and already manufacturing on a near-industrial scale what was certainly the best LSD I ever had. It was not only widely available in Liverpool, but also in the North Wales climbing ghetto thanks to Kemp's distributor Henry Todd, who was a member I think of the North London Mountaineering Club – a group that stood out as bright, contemporary, mischievous and radical among the drearily staid, bigoted and conformist rock-climbing sect of the brotherhood-of-the-hills of the time (the gender-specific term was then pretty appropriate). Kemp's and Todd's enterprise, which I think it fair to say had a substantial – and substantially beneficial – effect on the consciousness of a generation, was finally busted by the police in Operation Julie in 1977, and at the subsequent trial draconian sentences of thirteen years were handed out to the main protagonists and nine years to Bott, 'for making the sandwiches', as one defendant commented, referring to her complete lack of involvement in the drug's manufacture and distribution. 'We were up against the intelligentsia – and we won!'[14] the police crowed after the judgement.[15]

At the Sefton Park flat Jacquetta and I talked for a while, she made some food, we wandered hand-in-hand around Sefton Park in evening sunshine, which illuminated the new beech leaves of May. She was wearing an Afghan coat and loose green silk trousers, I was in black velvet and a high-collared white shirt. It amuses me now to think of what a pair of exotic dandies we must have looked. And I think we emanated the love-light. People smiled on us so benignly. I remember us kissing on several benches around the lake. We drank some Guinness in the Masonic pub on Lark Lane, went back to the flat and dropped the acid.

There is a point now at which our memories begin to concur. She had put *American Beauty* by The Grateful Dead on the record player and was lying on the bed. I was sitting on a cushion against the wall. 'I saw you there in the corner of my eye and I felt completely safe for the first time in years. I wanted you to come and join me on the bed. I just wanted you to fuck me. I wanted you to become the end of your prick so that my cunt would be your entire universe. I wanted you to give me some weight, to feel you hard and hot at the door of my womb,' is how she described it years later, giggling, and watching carefully for my reaction. 'I love it when you talk dirty to me,' I quipped back, to hide how helpless I felt at giving an adequate response. But I remembered the moment perfectly. The track that was playing is called 'Ripple', and it had arrived at these lines:

> Reach out your hand
> if your cup be empty,
> if your cup is full
> may it be again.

She rolled on to her side, stretched out her hand towards me, smiled, and in that moment, which in the way of acid seemed to hang on a clear note of music throughout eternity and is resonating still, my world changed. Her beauty, of which I had been growing more and more aware in the way a photograph resolves in the developing tray through the magic of silver nitrate, imprinted on my soul. I remember lying between her legs and studying in awed fascination the labiate coral beauty of her vulva, and her laughing and knotting my hair in her fingers and whispering to me like a mantra, over and over, chuckling so deep as she did so I could see her belly shake, that a man should worship his woman's cunt, that it should be the centre of his universe. In the morning we watched the sun rise across the Sefton Park lake – from *her* bench – and heard the city coming to life around us. We stayed very close, clinging together as the glories subsided. I had encountered something holy through that night that my own recklessness would very soon cause me to lose.

What happened to us here is easily gainsaid and reduced. It was a chimera, a drug-induced delusion, there was no history to it, there was no substance – other than the chemical one of course...

Naturally, I would not accept any of those statements. Many times in my twenties and occasionally thereafter I took LSD of varying quality – Richard Kemp's was the Château Lafite of acid, and if he'd pleaded that to the mentally-strait-jacketed old Establishment toper who tried and sentenced him, a few years might have been knocked off his sentence – and am not only unapologetic about this, but consider it to have been one of the most valuable and educative influences in my life, consciousness-changing and consciousness-expand-ing. There are two crucial things that need saying about LSD, because it is not remotely comparable with other of the recre-ational drug spectrum used for the most part by the exuberant and questing young. These two things are codified by devo-tees of the acid experience into the phrase 'set & setting' – which means that before taking the drug you need a calm mindset, and having taken it you need to be in a safe and peaceful environment. Observe those precautions and the places to which you are taken, which are opened up to you, are magical, unforgettable, visionary:

I have seen the Bird of Paradise, she has spread herself before me, and I shall never be the same again.
There is nothing to be afraid of. Nothing.
Exactly.

The Life I am trying to grasp is the me that is trying to grasp it.[16]

In May, 1989 – I check in a notebook from the time and find, with that shivery acknowledgement to coincidence at which Freud jibes in his essay on 'The Uncanny', that it was exactly sixteen years before Jac would die – I sat the length of a bright spring morning on the grass under a lime tree in London's Green Park and talked with the American writer Peter Matthiessen – one of the great twentieth-century masters of English prose style. He had brought up the subject of *The Great Mystery*, which is at the heart of all the world's religions, and I, remembering back to my own acid experiences, to the sense of divine almost-knowing – *proctu vu* – that they brought, the feeling and assurance of a Blakeian and safe-guarding calm presence and centre within yourself that many might think of as God, had asked him what use drugs were in the quest for an insight into that mystery. His answer was immediate and straightforward: 'LSD can be. When it was being manufactured by a Swiss chemical company[17] in meas-ured doses in the 1960s, a group of us learned to use it in a way that was not dangerous. It's a very foolish thing to take irre-sponsibly, but taken responsibly with people who know what they're doing, it's enormously instructive and I think almost everyone could benefit from it. But now you can't buy it. It's been made an outlaw thing because of the example of people like Timothy Leary, who made it so through their own ego. It's a great shame, because it could have been a very, very useful therapeutic and also a spiritual tool… It rids you of all that litter in your brain. We're like bells that have been stuffed with sticks – there's so much preconception and prejudice in there that we lose the note entirely. LSD clears that out, lets you see clearly and believe that you're having a mystical experience...'

I don't now believe that you need LSD to get to that state of refined consciousness, and I'm aware that two other factors in my life have also helped towards its attainment. One is a quietism that throughout my life has come upon me at times when I've been alone in natural environments. The other came quite differently from the long years of intense involvement with rock climbing.

Rock climbing is manifestly an activity productive of terror in the reasonably sane. The body's natural counter to this is the production of adrenalin, which initially renders you strong, coordinated, mentally clear. When its function in controlling the catatonic reactions to fear has been fulfilled, its chemical structure changes in the body and it becomes a very close analogue to LSD, producing in mild form several of the characteristic experiences of an acid trip. In some of my climbing essays I've attempted to describe this, as typically in the following passage from thirty years ago about the after-effects from an unanticipated solo ascent of a difficult gritstone climb:

My hands are tattered and sore... I trip off down, stumbling and uncoordinated now, very shaky. By Danebridge, the sun is rolling down behind a light mist. I stop by a tree and watch, calming myself. The colours suddenly coruscate, explode. Shadows gape, weak rays of the sun flare violently, an oceanic feeling of great peace washes over my body, beatific, a well of infinite goodness. My steps float me away into a wood

and, wandering among rhododendrons savagely burst-
ing into bloom, I come across a dark glade with the
remnants of a fire. Beyond it stands B, her eyes upon
me, widening into black pools, inviting oblivion, above
her a latticework of branches. I watch. Flesh drains,
drips like melted plastic from her face. Cadaverous,
she steps aside. The black dog, Melancholy, stalks my
heel and the sun goes out with a pop.[18]

The quietism, the post-climb experiences and the frequent
acid trips together all seem combined now into a sense of
reverence for the natural environment, a desire closely to
attend to and celebrate its detail, a distinctly pagan sense of
the numinous in nature, and a curious instinctual sense of the
presence of the other, which I've pondered long and think of
as the soul-knowledge or the psychic polaroid – a helpful
survival tool that alerts you to the proximity of those from
whom you must shy away – all of which I'm unashamedly
happy to call acid consciousness, even though the experiences
have not come for years at chemical behest. What the legacy of
them did give to Jacquetta and myself when we came back
together was common ground in outlook and a mutual agreement that every possible minute spent together in the outdoors was for us the perfect good.

But it is premature to tell of our being back together when
we have not yet fallen apart. Here is how that happened. The
necessary deceits and concealments as she edged towards a
final closure with the medical student – a doctor by now – had
become oppressive: to have to tell lies or make use of ambiguous evasions is always diminishing. One Friday evening we

drove back to Wales together from Liverpool in her rickety, sit-up-and-beg Austin A40 Farina. There was a dense mist all the way across the moors by Cerrig y Drudion. We passed within a couple of miles of where our caravan would be thirty years later. Over the course of the weekend she insisted, as a forthright woman can, on all the assurances from me – commitment, babies and the rest – and I, who wanted her and those things with her, gave them. On the Sunday evening I saw her off. We drove to the brow of a ridge a couple of miles from where I lived, and I watched her hand waving from the window as she descended the hill to go back and resolve matters in Liverpool. She would seek me out again, and I knew it would be in her habitual way, without announcement, when it was done. The sky was wild over Anglesey. I turned west for home and as I did so the heavens opened. A torrential cloudburst turned the road into a river. Along by Allt Ddu the lightning flashed, without pause thunder crashed in my ears and the drenched ground was a singing blue electric flame. Splashing along soaked to the skin, scalp tingling with electricity, I was completely unafraid, laughing and dancing.

I waited for weeks, heard nothing, no one I asked knew of her whereabouts, her phone went unanswered, the flat when I called there had been re-let, every effort to find her led down blind alley after blind alley. She never came back. Or so I thought through those long years, when what had happened, as she later recounted, was this, and I find no reason to believe any of it untrue. She had taken a couple of weeks to do what she had to do, then reappeared in Wales and was told I was climbing in the Llanberis Pass. At Pont y Gromlech she asked a couple of climbers sitting on a wall – not the same wall over which our hair had mingled, she added – if they'd seen me: 'There he is...'

They had pointed up at 'Cenotaph Corner' on the cliff above – an imposing line first ascended by Joe Brown in the early 1950s that twenty years on still retained some faint vestiges of a reputation for extreme difficulty. Unroped, I was easing my way through the tenuous moves at the top of it. She saw, got back into her car and drove home to Liverpool in a rage, furious that this is what I was doing after my promises to her. One more man had let her down and betrayed her. It was the end of term, and she was leaving her job. So she packed up her flat and went to live in Turkey, in a beach shack in Bodrum before it had attained its present-day Euro-resort status initially, and then in Istanbul working for the British Council. I stayed for the most part rooted in Wales. In the coming years I was to go back to that bench in Sefton Park – the wrong one – a hundred times in pilgrimage. That was how big an impression she had made on me, how grievous the loss of her felt. I sang the lyrics of songs about lost love morosely to myself. 'If you see her, say hello'. She was the phantom that haunted my every attempt at relationships. And I was hers too. Once she saw me crossing the Piazza del Popolo in Rome, ran after me, called out, but the man who turned was a stranger. Eventually, years later, with both our lives thoroughly fragmented, she saw a poster for a reading I was to give in the International Pavilion in Llangollen one October evening, and turned up. I was standing front-of-house as the people filed in, and with something approaching bewilderment I noticed her. She looked directly back at me as she went into the auditorium and smiled. Her hair was still red. She came up to me in the interval:

'You won't remember me,' she said.

I laughed. Some time later, back at my house, I played 'Ripple'. She leaned against me.

'Did you really love me all those years?' she asked.

'All those years...' I answered. And was no longer sad.

6

A Short History of Will

Will arrived two weeks earlier than he was expected – not an unusual occurrence in his life, when the prospects for fun and entertainment and mischief were good. He was delivered by Caesarean section in the old red-brick St David's Maternity Hospital on Caernarfon Road in Bangor. I'd taken what had seemed a last opportunity to do so and had gone away for a weekend's exploration on the sea-cliffs of south Pembroke. I stood in the telephone box at St Govan's – this before the days of mobiles and text messages – on a Bank Holiday Sunday night and, after a few fruitless attempts at making contact, the wasted coins rattling away into the box, was informed by a deputed friend that I had a son.

I wish I could say, with Coleridge, that 'for the mother's sake the child was dear,/And dearer was the mother for the child'.[19] But it would not be true. His mother – a quirky, forceful and no doubt endearing woman – and I were as mismatched, as incomprehensible and antipathetic to each other, as perhaps it is possible for a man and a woman to be. A profound mutual antagonism between us that doubtless played its part in the initial sexual attraction was unmediated by the birth of Will. Far from bringing us close, we became ever more distant, both of us finding solace with others. When she had taken the decision to become pregnant, I was told the baby would be adopted if I didn't stay. By the time he was two, she was gone anyway, and a benign old Family Court judge at a hearing in Caernarfon had granted me custody of Will – an unusual decision in those days.

I doted on Will the instant I saw him – the concentrated, puckering mobility of his face, the tiny hands and feet, the bags under his eyes, the fluffily bald and perfect head, the gusto with which he fed and grinned and howled. I cannot remember such enforced insomniac weariness, such feelings of terror and abject inadequacy as when caring for him in his early weeks and months. Or such an ache of tenderness with its accompanying and transfiguring joy:

> My babe so beautiful! It thrills my heart
> With tender gladness, thus to look at thee[20]

With the advent of parenthood you go at best almost instantly from the second part of Blake's reversal:

> Love seeketh only self to please,
> To bind another to its delight[21]

And fetch up instead at its first premises, its articles of faith, wholly converted from whatever it may have been that went before by the capacity of the newborn to generate love:

Love seeketh not itself to please,
Nor for itself hath any care,
But for another gives its ease
And builds a Heaven in Hell's despair.[22]

I thought him so beautiful, so delicate. He changed for ever the nature of my life. I lived at the time in an old slate quarryman's cottage in a terrace above the little North Walian town of Bethesda, its demographic in flux then from a population centred around the great quarries to an alternative culture of students from the nearby university, Welsh rock musicians, dreadlocked or shaven cultists dedicated to a pic 'n' mix guru-assortment of sannyassins and yogis, shris, Bhagwans and Rinpoches along with surviving refugee hippies from the Summer of Love, for all of whom an atmosphere of rebellion engendered by the radical industrial history of the place, along with its cheap housing and marvellous hill setting, held an appeal. The old women of the village's indigenous and abiding community paraded up and down in front of my cottage each day, on their way back from shopping and gossiping in the cafés in the mornings, or heading out to the bingo sessions early in the evenings, and would poke their heads in through the stable door to ask to pet Will and rock him, to issue robust homespun advice or pass high-pitched, throaty, disyllabic comment on the state of his terry-towelling nappies hanging on the line after each day's wash:

'O-oh, ver-ry cle-an! Ver-ry cle-an!'

An alien and eccentric presence in the domain of women – and thirty years ago, before the era of the New Man and the House Husband it did feel thus – my life had become focused around garnering plaudits from old ladies through proficiency in the use of Milton and Napisan and the boiling tub. Instead of the incessant quest for pleasure and sensation through drugs and sex and climbing that had dominated much of my previous existence, life devolved into a daily round of caring and cooking and washing under distinctly primitive conditions. There was no bathroom, and the toilet was a shed without door or light at the bottom of the garden. In the house, if I sat in the inglenook and looked up, there were the stars. The Health & Safety Executive and Social Services would no doubt nowadays have condemned it as unfit for human habitation, and had Will taken into care, though he was never cold or dirty or unloved or ill-fed. I was beginning – in the evenings when the still-permissible-and-by-my-friendly-neighbourhood-sibyls-strongly-recommended gripe water had been administered, and the lullabies were all sung and the notes from the clockwork mobile above Will's cot had burred down into silence and peace had descended on the house – to earn a living from writing. The shift from one phase of life to a quite distinct and entirely new other carried with it a powerful charge of delight alongside the sheer laboriousness of day-to-day routine.

In our first winter, snow fell and lay to a depth of four or five feet along the terrace. The single indoors tap had to be left running lest the pipes froze, its constant trickle at odds with the quiet iron fixity of the night. A stiff curtain of icicles glinted around the door. Swathed to the roundness of an infant Buddha, I would take Will out, his head swivelling suddenly from point to point of fascination, the little gloved finger yawing between objects of fascination, grasping up for icicles to snap off and convey to his mouth, the arm craving aloft after the bright disc of the moon as though he would reach that down too. When the thaw came, in a baby-carrier on my back or in his blue-corduroy folding buggy, the paths and the small hills spread across the apron of the Carneddau, with their long views out west across Anglesey and the sunsets spilling the red glow across slopes still streaked with snow and then draining it back down into dark valleys and a grey, misted sea, became our daily exercise, my hair grasped and tugged to turn me this way and that and a continual burbling commentary poured into my ears. In the spring I would set him down among the bluebells on the wooded hillside of Braichmelyn, gently retrieve the flowers he grabbed by the handful from his mouth, distract him with the dipping, swift flight of the green woodpeckers and their screaming laughter, or with our old Labrador's efforts in retrieving sticks from the deep swimming pool under the cataracts in the Afon Ogwen. And I would watch and wonder at the quality of his infant perception, so intensely concentrated upon its object. The journalist Nia Wyn, in her exquisite memoir – one of the most perfectly expressed insights into the power and passion that maternal love can embody – of caring for and integrating into a full life her son Joe after he had suffered devastating brain damage shortly after birth, writes with sure vision:

> To understand this love, I guess,
> Is to understand the light,
> Sometimes we have to
> Touch it first.[23]

The sheer spontaneous beauty of Will's new consciousness of the world seems, when I look back on it, to have been just such an instinctive urge to connect with the emanations of light, to hold them, possess them, taste them, immerse himself in the experience of them. The world for him and every object within it seemed to possess a glow-worm capacity not of reflection or suffusion but rather of giving out a magical and self-generated illumination. His wondering, exultant, appreciative, instinctually alive responses to the world he newly inhabited were revelation to me, were a new set of eyes through which I too might see. In a photograph that I have of him from this time, these are the qualities that leap out – the trusting expression, the huge grin, the wayward blond hair, and all of this too. A part of our daily ritual from as soon as he had the understanding – before that there were nursery rhymes, nonsense poems, lullabies, anything with incantatory soothing rhythms – was the bedtime story, in which I do not know which one of us took the greater pleasure. I used to so delight in his wide-eyed expectancy, his asking again and again for favourite stories, always with magic in them: *The Magic Paintbrush, The Magic Porridge Pot, Rumpelstiltskin, The Gingerbread Man...*

Bruno Bettelheim wrote that:

Having taken the child on a trip into a wondrous world, at its end the [fairy] tale returns the child to reality, in a most reassuring manner. This teaches the child what he most needs to know at this stage of his development: that permitting one's fantasy to take hold of oneself for a while is not detrimental, provided one does not remain permanently caught up in it. At the story's end the hero [sic] returns to reality – a happy reality, but one devoid of magic.[24]

That was a world view of which I never remotely wished Will to partake. I wanted him to retain a sense of the wonder and mystery and magic of the world, to appreciate on those terms the narratives of life, from those of caterpillar and tadpole to the presence of fossil plants in the slate rocks around our home and the ways in which story, history, event and monument infused place with atmosphere. I remember a day in 1987 when Will and I walked up the springy turf of a green path leading from Llyn Tecwyn Isaf into the northern Rhinogydd behind Harlech – the most rough, wild and strange hills in Wales, the place that Robert Graves in an early poem writes of thus:

> ...this is my country, beloved by me best,
> The first land that rose from Chaos and Flood.[25]

Even the name is strange enough, *Rhinogydd*, an elision of *yr hiniog* – the threshold – and to this day I never come here without an encroaching sense of something secret, otherworldly about these hills. Seven-year-old Will and I walked on into the cloud, our sight focusing down on to the close particularities of the scene: the drop-beaded red blades of moor grass; the mist-wraiths' disorientating swirl; a ring cairn alongside the track. I remember reciting him a line from the great poet of the Snowdonia landscape, T. H. Parry-Williams: *'Mae lleisiau a drychiolaethau ar hyd y lle'*[26] – 'There are voices and phantoms throughout the place'. And there were, for both of us: soft mutterings of the wind; sounds half-heard and movement glimpsed only at the corner of an eye. Will, his hand in mine, leaned close against me in nervous apprehension of what might inhabit here, his mind full of story, as we followed the old way in its curve around above a *fign* – a morass – to join the ancient trackway that climbs in from the south-west. Suddenly, outlined on the crest of a bluff from which a breeze had scoured the mist, the ring cairn of Bryn Cader Faner, arguably the most beautiful Bronze Age monument in Britain, stood stark and clear. Crown-like, its stones pointing outwards, its intimate majesty perfectly in harmony with the cyclopean masonry of its setting, its appearance was in every sense magical, to Will and myself in equal measure. Years after Will's death, when I could finally bring myself to look through his photographs and personal possessions, there were photographs he'd taken on some of his solitary wanderings through Wales that had retraced and renewed through his own experience mine of forty years before – among them a sequence in the Rhinogydd, one of them of Bryn Cader Faner.

I suppose the feelings I have of regret that a time of innocence inevitably had to give way to an enforced requirement for the brutal and demeaning process of his integration into society are common to many parents. In the driving fatigue and confusion of that time, the backbeat always was a desire for continuance of Will's induction through natural influences into awareness of the world's incandescent beauty:

> ...all seasons shall be sweet to thee,
> Whether the summer clothe the general earth

With greenness, or the redbreast sit and sing
Betwixt the tufts of snow on the bare branch
Of mossy apple-tree, while the nigh thatch
Smokes in the sun-thaw; whether the eave-drops fall
Heard only in the trances of the blast,
Or if the secret ministry of frost
Shall hang them up in silent icicles,
Quietly shining to the quiet moon.[27]

The time we have with our children is so desperately brief.
If we shut our eyes and look away, if we daydream or concen-
trate elsewhere even for a short span, the occluding forces of
convention have grasped at the innocent and applied the
corrupting and illiberal rule of conformity. I look back on
Will's education with significant ambivalence. There were
women at the university crèche to which I took him in Bangor,
heeding the accepted wisdom about socializing the infant,
whom I remember with the fondest regard as patient, caring,
undogmatic and kind. There was a young teacher at his first
school in the village of Dolwyddelan, Miss Richards, a sweet-
natured and dark-curled young woman, pretty and shy, with
a ready and constant smile and a milky reek of fertility about
her, who would leave at the end of Will's first year to marry a
farmer in the soft shires of the Marches and no doubt bring up
her own children in the glow and abundancy of her capacity
to love. The wary and mischievous boy that Will had become
warmed to her, opened and flourished under her guidance
and tutelage. Others who came later were less than benign.
Some of them were malevolent witches determined on sucking the spirit out of him, their mouths at the mere sight of him

pursing into a cat's-arse semblance of profound disapproval. The strictures of his education were often at variance with the freedoms of his life beyond school. And I was often, by way of example, much at fault through gleeing in confrontation with authority rather than slipping its yoke whilst being mild and gracious in ironic compliance.

We were in the habit of going out on fine evenings or at weekends to the western beaches of Anglesey and Lleyn, gathering driftwood for a fire and setting the old wood-handled frying pan on it to cook sausages and the like, for food never tastes so good as when cooked and eaten outdoors. But if my world was changing, so was the broader world in that period during the 1980s when the odious personal tyrannies and mendacities of a political leader were reflected in society at large – direst aspect of the then much-vaunted 'trickle-down effect'. In one dreadful incident on a beach to which we had gone for the same purpose for years, and which I'd been visiting since my teens to sleep out in the dunes in quiet communion with nature, a uniformed, badged and Land-Rovered, scrub-bearded example of the new breed of brown-shirt countryside policemen that had proliferated since the first Thatcher administration saw from a distance the smoke of our fire, raced along the beach and swirled to a halt alongside, climbing down out of his cab, slamming the door and swaggering over:

'It's against the bylaws to light fires on this beach. You must put it out now,' he rapped.

'Since when has that been the case?' I asked with weary attention and reasonably politely, wishing to hear him out, for keeping up an informed onslaught in print on the restrictive effects of Thatcherite and post-Thatcherite countryside legislation was a cause to which I was and am deeply committed. Will took an educated interest in proceedings from the top of the nearest dune, and I went on to add that I'd responsibly been doing exactly what I was doing now for the last twenty-five years and more in this exact place – since before he was born, in all probability – and had always taken great care to ensure that there were no deleterious effects on the environment, as he might see if he looked around.

'Look, I'm ordering you to put that fire out now and with immediate effect, and if you don't do so I shall have to do so myself and then call the police and report your non-compliance.'

The quasi-policeman made as if to start kicking sand. I stood up from tending the sausages, sighed, stretched and flexed, approached very close, eyeballed him, and told him quietly that if he did any such thing I'd ram the handle of the frying pan so far up his flaccid arse it would pop straight out of his uptight mouth and wag there instead of his offensive and officious tongue. He climbed back into the Land Rover and shot away in a cloud of dire threats, and we carried on with preparing our picnic, Will stamping around the fire now chanting distinctly rude little rubrics. Though there is a certain testosterone-derived pleasure in the oppositional stance, in delivering a cool, rolling blast of intransigent semi-obscenity against overbearing officialdom and facing the bastards down, I don't remotely believe that this was good parenting on my part, or in any sense an apt example to help Will in his preparation to be an obedient and useful member of society. The problem was, that less and less did I like the direction in which that society was going, and it's very difficult to hide that irreconcileability from your child. With every passing year – and no doubt acid consciousness had played its part here – I was getting more and more like ornery old Ed Abbey, and becoming a fully-paid-up associate of the Monkey Wrench Gang:

> ...they're still building fires on the ground, with wood! Very messy, filthy and wasteful. Set up little grills on stilts, sell charcoal briquettes, better yet hook up with the gas line, install jets and burners. Better yet do away with the camp-grounds altogether, they only cause delay and congestion and administrative problems – these people want to see America, they're not going to see it sitting around a goddamned campfire; take their money, give them the show, send them on their way – that's the way to run a business...[28]

Books like Abbey's were always around the house and from his teenage years Will read them attentively, avidly, so that he could quote from them – *The Monkey Wrench Gang* was a particular favourite of his, and to add to its appeal 'wrenchers' from among the Newbury tree-protesters were often at our house. I could not but instil a spirit of rebelliousness into Will, and I don't think for a moment that it made things easy for him. Nor did the vagrant and unfixed lifestyle we led. We moved house on average once a year until he was ten years old and I came belatedly to the realization that he needed for the end of his primary schooling and the whole of his secondary education to have the security and the circle of friends that would accrue from our staying put in one place. But that staying-put also brought its problems, again associated with the way I'd led my life and the reputation for reckless, lawless behaviour that it had left behind. I bought a house in Dinorwig, high on the hillside at 1200 feet above sea level, facing west across the Celtic Sea so that the mountains of Wicklow eighty miles away would be etched across the horizon on those clear evenings – and this meant most of them – that preceded or followed rain. The huge abandoned tunnels and levels and chasms of the abandoned Dinorwig slate quarries – an ultimate adventure playground – were just along the road. The house the climber Al Harris, long my avatar in the rituals of misrule, had owned and in which his son Toby still lived was half-a-mile in the other direction. The great pit at Allt Ddu – filled in with the spoil heaps dug from it now, after an EEC Land Reclamation initiative in the 1980s – in which for years Al and I had played the chicken game[29] we'd copied from the James Dean film *Rebel Without a Cause*, was a bare 200 yards from the house I bought. In a small and incestuous community, every wild and dangerous thing I had ever done or was supposed to have done quickly became known to my son. Usually, too, it was transmitted to him in the habitually amplified and distorted way of gossip. Once in a climbers' pub in Capel Curig I'd been asked if I knew me, to which I'd given a vague and ambiguous answer that had led to spending half-an-hour being regaled with anecdotes purportedly from first-hand knowledge and told of my bad-ass tendencies by someone I had assuredly never met in my life – crazy soloing on the cliffs, drug excesses, multiple sexual peccadilloes, fisticuffs[30] and mayhem, miraculous leaps through upper-storey glass windows, motor-psycho nightmares, skin-of-the-teeth escapes from the police etc., etc. I listened in horrified fascination and left anonymously, thinking that if even half of what I'd heard had some basis in truth I'd have been behind bars for years.

The human imagination, and perhaps particularly the male-dominated world of climbing at the time I performed well within it, has a pathological and vicarious need for mythopoeic exaggeration. All this, when we moved in to the climbers' ghetto of Dinorwig and Llanberis, was matter with which Will was identified by proxy. More dangerously, it was set in the wrong position psychologically. Its misrepresentations and bizarre rebellions were not so easily rejected at his stage in the maturation process as might those more solid and worthy characteristics of the good and reliable parent have been before the needle on the scales flickered back to the individual synthesis of the young adult. The dangers and social rejections of it all had a wicked allure, and however far I might have moved on, however strongly I might disavow, my conventional moral influence was reduced, and Will had a distorted model to which to aspire: 'According to the common Shilluk tradition any son of a king had the right thus to fight the king in possession and, if he succeeded in killing him, to reign in his stead.'[31]

The climbing tribe to which I'd belonged for most of my life, which passed constantly through our house and of which Will himself would soon be an initiate, may have mirrored Shilluk tradition rather less lethally, but the essential pattern still obtained. I had, throughout Will's life, held back from ever thrusting climbing on him. I'd almost rather he had taken up golf. Too many of my friends had died in the mountains. From my early teens I had been in thrall. It was an intermittent addiction that came with a high degree of ambivalence. It could scarcely have been otherwise in the time of my most intense devotion. In those days, long before the development of modern protection equipment and techniques, at the highest levels it carried with it an ever-present risk of mortal consequence, was a lethal mind-game quite different to the safe and phenomenally athletic modern sport. The very first time I was on a Welsh cliff, on a climb called 'Lazarus' ('he who was raised from the dead' – our namings betray our obsessions) at the age of fourteen, a young Liverpool University student – I remember his name as Colin Larvor, though I'm not sure how I knew this – fell from the route adjacent to the one I was climbing. After the rescue, on the path below, I saw the efforts at resuscitation taking place, the grey flesh marbled with blood, the depressed skull, that habitual alliance among the rescuers between haste and despair. The young man was dead before he reached the road and the ambulance. I've witnessed this scene re-enacted too many times; counted once the number of people I had known – with most of whom I had actually tied on a rope – who had died on the cliffs or in the mountains. It came to more than sixty. I think few sports sustain so high a toll – three-score and more, among whom over the years were most of my close friends. Survivor-guilt came to haunt me. You do not come through losses like these without sorrow and damage, without a kind of emotional sclerosis. I desperately did not want Will to be numbered among the casualties.

Yet inevitably, living where we lived, he began to show an interest. Initially it was through Katie Haston, the daughter of a particularly wild younger acquaintance of mine. She lived a mile down the road and became Will's first girlfriend. She was a climber – an extremely gifted one too – hence he became one, and to look good in her eyes and to get her into his bed (another problematical area for paternal concern, particularly at the age they both were) he had to excel. All this was initially supposed to be kept from me, he being at that stage where the peer group decreed that fathers were deeply uncool. So though I noticed the absences and the climbing gear missing from under the stairs, I was far from wholly aware of what he was up to. The quarries where he climbed were his long-standing playground anyway. He knew their every tunnel and rickety iron ladder, blast shelter and *caban*. Often in the fine weather he'd take food and a sleeping bag and go out with his friends to build fires and I suspect to smoke dope[32] and to sleep out on their secret heathery terraces, and with none of this did I have any great problem, though on the issue of dope I did comment about the effect and insist that he never carried it, never took it to school with him, never drew attention to himself or got caught. All this was in vain, of course, and it was hard to say much when my own friends would frequently roll up a spliff by our fire and the scent would hit him when he came in, or would drift up to his room, and he'd roll his eyes in my direction and shoot me knowing looks. The first specific account I had of his climbing was through a concerned phone call from a good friend, Mick Ward, who gave me a description of what he'd witnessed by chance in the old chicken-game quarry just along from the house, which was now a popular and highly accessible climbing venue. Mick later wrote about it too, in a sensitive and heartfelt article for one of the climbing magazines:

Above, Will is tackling the runout that is 'bolder than life itself', with an indifferent, reckless aplomb. Unbidden, from memory, comes a sepia snapshot of a lone soloist [his father], a quarter of a century before, nearly fatally playing to the gallery. If Will comes off, he'll hit me. Why then am I far more concerned about him? Things go from bad to worse. Various hare-brained, badly communicated options emerge. Will starts to unrope, changes his mind, ties indifferent knots of dubious provenance around the bolt. Ten feet to one side, my stomach churns... Will mysteriously becomes untied from the rope; his second, about forty feet above, thus becomes unbelayed. In spite of both their protests, I grab the free end of the rope and grimly hang on to it until Will is back on the ground.

I would guess Will had just turned fifteen at this time, and it was crucial to do something about the situation. Every week-end, and on summer evenings after school, I started to take him out climbing, and to instruct him in the survival strate-gies, the means to safety, the values, the ways of approaching the absorbing physical and mental problems of rock. The effect of all this was to move us on from the brief phase of father–son succession–turbulence into a much closer relationship. It was fortunate at the outset that – fast approaching my fifties – I had just enough residual fitness and ability to be able to take him on climbs that would tax and hone his developing skills and bring him the desired kudos. And it was bitter-sweet pleasure to me to revisit with my son many of the memorable climbs of my own youth. When the time came for him to move on into the full possession of his own gifts, I could see him go with the confidence that his awareness of danger, his instinct for risk – in which lies the only real safety and against which the disempowering inanities of the Health and Safety Executive so militate – were finely attuned. Our parting-of-the-ways was made easier by my suffering a timely incapacity – a frozen shoulder that rendered me unable to climb for two or more years.[33] In that time Will's abilities on rock developed stratospherically. Rowland Edwards, one of the great climbers of the generation preceding mine, and his son Mark, one of the sport's contemporary stars, befriended him and he spent a summer working at the climbing school they ran in Cornwall from which he came back lean and tanned and inspired. Back in Dinorwig, he was soon climbing with the better climbers in the North Wales community. One of them, George Smith – a huge, amiable and comic character who lived just down the road from us on Fachwen – gives a good picture of Will from this and a slightly later time:

We were never equals. I was the older and more experienced belayer. Will was the leader. Our handful of trips across Anglesey [to the sea cliffs of Gogarth beyond Holyhead] were spent in deep conversation. Will would advise me, being such a master of the truth. On trying to keep up with the youngsters his view was that, 'Yeah, well, there would be nothing worse than you knocking around trying to pretend to be a good climber when you're getting on...[34]

Cheers, Will..!

We would talk about routes: 'Yes,' I'd say, 'Ormuzd

is a great laugh – you'd love it. There's this huge roof at the top with a hard bit at the lip. Take a No. 4 cam – you can bung it in a hole…'

He shook his head: 'You know, George, you really shouldn't tell people things like that.'

I was being ticked off by this teenager for failing to grasp the spirit of the sport, and in that soft collected voice of his.

At the crag Will climbed the way I'd have liked to. He didn't climb to the next runner[35] and then measure his courage for what lay ahead; rather he simply climbed passing runners. He was not reckless, he was rational – the protection was good enough so why stop? The technicalities that halted my progress rarely stopped him – he knew when to move with speed and when to pause and plan. And because it was Will, and done with grace, I did not begrudge the obvious process of the old being overtaken by the new – or at least, that was the presumed sequence of events.

By the age of sixteen or seventeen he was very much his own man, even within our tight Dinorwig community. One incident I remember concerned the Haughton brothers, a pair of young local bandits who lived in conditions of some squalor in the row of council houses and at one time or another broke into and stole from pretty well every house and car of the scattered community. Despite incontrovertible and overwhelming proof that the Haughtons were the culprits, the police shrugged their shoulders and patiently explained to one enraged householder or car-owner after another that there was no point in searching the Haughton house because the swag would already be gone. So the aggrieved middle-class incomers among the community – the Haughtons had chosen carefully who to hit hardest[36] – organized a public protest meeting at the community centre in the old school. Will volunteered – in retrospect with a suspicious degree of zeal – to go along as representative of our household. The atmosphere at the meeting was tense. Vigilantism was in the air. George Smith gave me the account of what happened:

I wandered in, and there was Will grinning in the middle of it all. I sat with him.

'This'll be interesting,' I said.

'Yeah!' He grinned a bit more. Those who wished to speak rose, one after another, united in the cause of catching/stopping/incarcerating the villains. Then William got up and raised a hand.

'I think we might all be missing something here. These lads are just unemployed and they don't have very much cash, and so it probably isn't easy for them. I wondered if anyone could perhaps find them some work?'

The murmurs and disapproving grunts of the mass of downcast faces built up to a crescendo of perfect angry silence – I mean, even I didn't agree with him – but I had to marvel at the audacity!

His conventional schooling was falling by the wayside, the climbing dominated, and I didn't much mind. There'd be time enough for all that, and it's only for a short period in life that the body responds with silken ease to the demands you put upon it. He and I were sitting in a café window in Bangor one morning, watching the street life stream past in all its unself-conscious weirdness, musing. He'd been telling me about the climbs he'd been doing – not in detail, just the impressions they'd made. He'd been going well – E7s on sight, radical stuff, especially whilst he was still a teenager.[37]

'Silk,' he said, 'that's what it feels like – silk!'

I knew instantly what he meant, even across the gap of years. And in response I did the father bit, and maybe in doing so I came on too strong.

'Listen, it doesn't matter what else you do because there's time for all of that, but you enjoy this while it lasts because there's no other feeling like it ever, and you'll remember it for the rest of your life.'

'I know that, Dad,' he replied, with all the stinging conde-scension of youth, 'I know that already.'

He was right, of course. It's one of those rare sensations that, even as you're experiencing them, you sense will live in you for ever, as though imprinted. It's the body's pure silk, spun of tuned muscle and the flowing moment, and however the body might fade and tear, its memory endures. I'd not felt it for years. Injuries come. You pay the toll for having done too much, too young. The body's wracked and wrecked. Shoulders go. Finger tendons pop. Even having your elbows shot full of cortisone doesn't stop them shrieking at you in protest against what you think they should still be able to do. Will had seen all that in me during those early climbs together. He was astute, and you can't conceal it, though I never wanted him to have the sense of that being what was to come. I remember waving him off through departures at Manchester Airport on to a flight for San Francisco, the ticket for which had been his eighteenth birthday present. He was to go climbing in Yosemite for two months. Alongside the pangs of parting, there was a gladness that he had found his métier, distinguished himself and gained confidence and ease through that. He walked off young and bronzed and tall and blond-curled, a youthful god brimful of the life-delight, and he cast a quick, shy, backward glance of glee at me as he rounded the last barrier, which melted my heart.

The next six years he spent world-wandering around the climbing venues, gaining qualifications for roped-access work in which he could put his skills to use and earn substantial amounts of money in short periods of time to finance his next long pleasure trip. His emails and postcards would arrive from Bohemia or Baja California, Spain, Cornwall or the Alps, Fontainebleau or the south of France, to tell me laconically, understatedly always, without bullshit, of what he'd been doing. The last time we climbed together in any meaningful way was in August 2001, when he led me up a climb of which I'd made the first ascent thirty years before on the south Pembrokeshire sea cliffs. We had a friend with us, Martin Crook, and when we arrived at the base of the cliff the old anarchies were clearly still at work, for we found that between us for a climb that began with a forbidding traverse across an overhanging wall above a huge sea-cave we only had two thin ropes of indeterminate length. I remember picking one up and uncoiling it on the little ledge from which the climb starts.

'I don't know if we should use that one, Dad. I had to cut a bit off it,' commented Will, enigmatically.

All three of us knew what he meant, which was that the rope had held a fall, been damaged in the process, should have been discarded or demoted to softer duties. Then, realizing the lack of options, he tied on to the proffered end and led off in a beautifully elegant and unhurried, contemplative way across the traverse, taking the same care to protect me as I had taken so few years before to assure his safety. There was a brief shower of rain. The second pitch followed a soaring crack-line up a vertical orange wall. Afterwards, in the gaps between showers we went to another cliff, climbed another route. Whenever I faltered, the rope came subtly and reassuringly tight. I remember the three of us sitting on top afterwards, and how I felt curiously pleased and proud of Will; for being so unaffected and competent and funny and decent; with his being of himself entirely, owing nothing to me. He came to specialize in the riskiest and most dangerous of climbs – 'Bobok', 'Death Trap Direct' – ones that few other climbers would go near and from which the best of other generations would back off – and he was widely recognized as the finest young adventure climber in the country. And though all this gave him a kind of validation, I don't think he ever took it very seriously. He had the clear insight into the phoney that great ability can bring. And he was questing around for some more substantial thing in his life, his conversation full of metaphysical enquiry. And of a dark realization too about the nature of the world. When he was seventeen or eighteen and coming into his gift as a climber, he wrote a series of sketches about climbs in the old slate quarries. They're fascinating. They express the ontological physicality of the sport, and something else besides:

I can't honestly remember the moves or the gear. The one thing that sticks in my mind is the burn I felt that first time. People talk about being pumped on something or other but this was beyond pumped. It just kept coming and coming, my arms on fire, skin barely strong enough to hold in the bulging veins, holds no longer had form – they were just there to be pulled on as a numbness began to spread through my whole body. I climbed straight past a bolt because I couldn't stop to clip it, climbed straight past a ledge because I couldn't stop full stop, reached the top and lay down for ages. When I finally came to, I couldn't even grip the rope to take it in.

The last of the sequence is about a climb called 'Journey to the Centre of the Earth', in a weird and frightening and difficult-to-reach pit known to climbers as the Lost World. You get to it through dark, curving tunnels with pools lying deep on their floor and great blocks fallen from the roof over which you blindly stumble (to take torches, of course, is considered unsporting, to falter into the pitch-dark unknowing is the essence of the thing.

I brought a self-styled mage who runs 'men's weekends' and 'Iron John' seminars at a nearby retreat-centre through here once, at his request to show him an itinerary suitable for his chaps. He baulked immediately, thought it wholly unsuitable, frightening and dangerously irresponsible and hasn't spoken to me since. In his early teens Will and his friends would go and spy on these men's weekends, disrupt them with unearthly howls from the woods, set tripwires, come back with ribald stories of which I did my best to disapprove.

In the hole itself a stream crashes down and trickles away across the slate to disappear under heaps of spoil. A pair of peregrines nest high on one of the walls, their falcon-wildness somehow suited to the place. If abandonment has a soul, an essence, this is it, and what follows was Will's perception of it:

Dreams – have you ever had one of those dreams where you're at the bottom of a deep, dark hole and there's no way out? Does everybody have them? They have a reality, too, you know – a physical expression. If you don't believe me, climb down into the Lost World. Maybe you don't climb there – maybe you're lured down into it by the mystery of the place, by its sequence of trashed and twisted ladders and its weird green pools among 300-foot walls of smooth dark slate. Hurt yourself down here and you're lost. Only the crows will hear your cries for help. The waterfalls will muffle them, the crags set them forever re-echoing till they're just in your head and you can no longer scream, fading away, looking up at the journey out of, not to, the centre of the earth. Do it to escape, before the dream turns nightmare.

We come to a certain prescience at times, through the metonymies of rock.

BOOK THREE

Chiaroscuro

7

Quest

At the turn of the millennium, with Will established in his own house in Cwm-y-Glo between Llanberis and Caernarfon and employed by various companies specializing in roped-access work, I decided to move away from the North Wales climbing community in or around which I had lived for most of my adult life. Will was now an established and significant member of that society in his own right. Whilst having his father around in the same social group didn't seem to cause him too much embarrassment, and it always delighted me when he called in for lunch or dinner, or to borrow clothes or books or records in the way that sons do, or simply for a pot of coffee and a dawdling afternoon's conversation whilst watching the fish in the garden pond, to put some geographical distance between us seemed to offer him more liberty, and more of the independence I had always allowed and promoted in him. Also, my own feelings about living within a small and intensely inward-looking, maliciously stultiloquent community centred on an activity about the core values of which I had long been suspicious and jaundiced, were very mixed. And in terms of work, in an interest group and circle of acquaintance where the work-ethic is not strong and the pleasure-and-leisure principles rule, those whose workplace is their home-base seem to send out an unwitting open invitation to be interrupted and treated as a drop-in centre, advice bureau or convenience café. For a writer, who must be mentally immersed in projects for long periods of time, must be disciplined in keeping to the task and to whom the reclusive may well be the ideal, the result is frustration and less than optimal productivity. I began casting around for somewhere else to live in which I would be as near as possible unknown, and hence less disturbed.

In the mid-1990s I had made a long journey on foot through Wales in company with the little Jack Russell terrier I had at the time, The Flea (so-called from her diminutive size and deft snappishness).[1] One place in particular that had stayed in my mind from the walk was Llanrhaeadr ym Mochnant in the far south-west corner of Denbighshire – the county of my father's people. It's a large village in the wide strath of Dyffryn Tanat – a long valley running westwards from below Oswestry on the Shropshire border deep into The Berwyn, which had been since my earliest teens one of my favourite hill areas. I first came to Llanrhaeadr – a place I'd inexplicably never seen before this occasion – in the following manner.

On a drenching mid-November day in 1995, from Llangollen I'd followed the route south and west taken in 1854 and described in *Wild Wales* by George Borrow. Borrow is one of the most fascinating characters in nineteenth-century literature. He was a proto-post-modernist writer of fictivized autobiography and travel, a Sebald before his time, a lover of gypsies, a pugilist and vagrant, scholar, polymath, devout Anglican and violent anti-Catholic. I'd been fascinated by him since buying a copy of *Wild Wales* – the best travel book ever written about Britain, as well as one of the most puzzling – from the bookshop that used to be by the bridge in Llangollen, when I was setting out on my first solitary journey through Wales at the age of twelve. As the early darkness foreclosed on this wet November day I had pitched up at the door of the Plas-yn-Llan guesthouse in Llanrhaeadr. The landlady, Mrs Sheila Fleming, a beautiful red-haired, middle-aged woman, took The Flea and me in unannounced, bemired and bedraggled, installed us with a pot of tea by the stove among her whippets (The Flea for once politely refrained from making war upon them and sat instead demurely on my knee) whilst she made up a bed; she fed me, entertained me and conducted us on a tour of the town's amusements that evening which ended at a significantly late hour in a particularly friendly pub in heated agreement with the socialist Mayor of Llanrhaeadr. I had even heard good Welsh spoken in one of the village's three pubs. It was in this village that the parish priest William Morgan between 1578 and 1587 had worked on his translation of the Welsh Bible – a work of scholarship, literary style and great linguistic power that more than any other single factor had ensured the survival of the Welsh language. In the lichgate of the church was a delicately-carved, bas-relief, commemorative slate tablet. It had been carved by my erstwhile neighbour, the sculptor and writer Jonah Jones, when Will and I had lived at Abergafren on the estuary of the Dwyryd, and I'd first seen it in his workshop at that time.[2]

The village of Llanrhaeadr itself, in a dip in the hills and hidden away from almost every angle of approach, crowded around a clear, swift river that flowed down from The Berwyn. It was a kind, pretty, grey-stone place of old houses grouped around three small squares, hills rising soft-outlined and bosomy all around. Somehow it felt instantly right – I don't know what the psycho-geographers would have to say about the impulse, but once I'd visited it, I returned as often as I could. Something about the place called to me; and still does. On this first visit, as the village in its relaxed country way was stirring about its business in the mist-hung and dewy morning, Sheila Fleming turned The Flea and me out, rested, Berwyn-bound and breakfasted, with the laughing comment that I shouldn't interpret too anatomically A. E. Housman's description of this area as 'A country for easy livers,/The quietest under the sun'. My liver was feeling distinctly delicate after the excesses of the previous night. The Flea and I walked up to the seventh-wonder-of-Wales cataract, Pistyll Rhaeadr, in relation to which the New Agers and Don Juanistas discourse on centres of power and earth energy and other such stuff, and from which the village gets its name.[3] George Borrow's often-quoted 'long tail of a grey courser at furious speed' description of it is loosely impressionistic. The cataract is complex in its structure. A stream of no great volume spills in three columns that pulse and mingle down a blocky, dark cliff perhaps 120 feet in height, efflorescing on the strata, rosetting white against the black rock before a right-hand mossy ridge obscures the water from view and it tumbles into an unseen pool, from which it jets out sideways through a remarkable round hole in the foot of the ridge to a series of lesser cascades beneath, the general impression being of less than the 240 feet total height. It is the hole, and the strange spirit-bridge spanning it that Borrow as a critic of scenery deplored, that gives Pistyll Rhaeadr its uniqueness and oddly disquieting atmosphere. It holds its mystery, the plunge pool of the main fall all but inaccessible and invisible. In the valley above are stone circles and a stone alignment close to the moorland stream of the Afon Disgynfa that Borrow had passed by unaware. I was to come to know this place intimately, as one of habitual resort.

The decision to move to the village came from another walk into the area several years later, again originating in Llangollen and the Ceiriog valley – a repetition that seems in retrospect an unconscious mirroring of the pedestrian Welsh journeys that were the highlights of my youth, and which always seemed to start at Llangollen – an easy place to get to by hitchhiking from the outskirts of Manchester. On some level, I think I was looking for a landscape that was seldom to be encountered after the grievous governmentally endorsed and promoted environmental abuses of the last thirty and more years and their concomitant social changes. W. G. Sebald in *The Rings of Saturn* – surely the finest and most resonant account of a walking journey written in the last twenty years – defines pretty closely the impulse from which I was acting: 'I became overwhelmed by the feeling that the Suffolk expanses I had walked the previous summer had now shrunk once and for all to a single, blind insensate spot... Several times... I felt a desire to assure myself of a reality I feared had vanished forever...'[4]

I wanted somehow to turn the life-clock back. I had on

many occasions distant and present walked out of Llangollen by way of a steep path and gully that Borrow knew well and that he called Paddy's Dingle, after the Irish tinkers who used to camp there. Nowadays it has a few yards of tarmac at the outset and a road sign renders the name into Welsh as Allt-y-Badi. Worn away to the stepped strata of bedrock in places, it slants up shady and cool in its tunnel of trees to climb a thousand feet in not much over a mile from Llangollen town to reach the Finger Farm on the watershed ridge above, between the valleys of the Ceiriog and the Dee – a ridge that leads away westwards alluringly into the high ground of The Berwyn. I had often leaned on a field gate up here and looked south-west at a faraway green hill I could not identify – a hill the distinctive profile of which I'd seen from many places in the Welsh Marches and among the hills of Wales. So one spring afternoon I set out to find it.

This time I drove from Llangollen by a steep road through woods hazed with bluebells to the top of the ridge, where lambs were careering about in skipping gangs and the curlews floated and called across the pastures, cloud muffling down their bubbling cadences to a sound soft as water. I paused by a gate looking south into the valley of the Ceiriog, which from this point appears as a steep and tree-lined gorge. Suddenly a breeze caught at a thinning of the mist, pulled it aside like a veil, and in the distance, flooded in light from a traversing shaft of sun, the hill again, crested like some grand animal in recline. Down in the Ceiriog valley I left the car by Pont-y-Meibion, 'the children's bridge' – the name of which Borrow had mused over. By the first bend in the track beyond, bees were busying themselves between their hives and the heavy clumps of blossom on a rowan tree, the flower-heads lumpen against elegance of branch and feathered leaf. Above me two ravens, with something of malicious glee in their flight, were mobbing a buzzard, and a peregrine bearing a pigeon in its talons swept in to a ledge on the nearby crag. As I stood and watched, a stocky, friendly, importunate piebald pony inspected my pockets with great dexterity, and when I took off my rucksack to look for an apple, took this as an invitation to the nosebag. We performed a brief extricating ballet together before he was happily munching away. 'No such thing as a free lunch,' I told him when he'd finished a second apple, and jumped up on his broad back, urging him on with my knees, at which he trotted, rather pleased and excited, high-actioned, up to the next gate where I rolled off and we parted company with some apparent regret on either side, and many lingering backward glances. Pheasants called from the depths of the wood, and the spikes of foxgloves were spearing through the bracken, a speckle of white circles on their purple bells leading in to brilliant, deep-yellow anthers hidden in rows on the upper side within. The detail of flowers is so miraculously perfect, so consummate. I sat on a rustic bench set in to the trackside bank and carved with the hopeful text, 'I will lift up mine eyes unto the hills', was surrounded by flowers, and felt blissfully happy and at ease in this place, which was so unlike the one where I then lived.

The valley I was following, that of the Nant Llechwedd-Gwyn, cut steeply into the 1500-foot-high moorland plateau that stretches, deeply dissected and incised, from here down to Severn Sea and the southern coastal plains of Wales. Grey giants' legs of rain marched clouds across the landscape. A grass slope opposite on to which the bracken was steadily encroaching was of that incandescent green of early June. My track reached a junction with a road. A triangular quartz-speckled boulder stood above a pool the surface of which was braided and laced with brilliant white stars, delicately toothed leaves and pale stems of water-crowfoot, so lovely that I sat there maybe half an hour in contemplation, aware of the crystalled rock, the atmosphere of long knowledge that hung about the place, and gathering strength from them. As a young teenager, before I was snared by the urge to climb rocks, these journeys south and west from Llangollen into Wales, with their objectives unknown, with these moments of suspended reflection along them, were how I first came to know the land. I believe now that they were the most crucial phase in my whole education: for the value of chance meetings along them; for the arduous solitude and the self-reliance they demanded; for their simplicity and austerity; for the thrill of moving forever forwards beyond bounding horizons into unknown country; for the heart-stopping beauties of an unknown land, and the reverence for the natural world thus inculcated; for the metonymical cast of mind all this produced, by which perspectives are gained and understanding is deepened.

From the spring pool on the hill my goal was visible now in the distance, and I set off through prairie fields of Euro-grass where once the high, natural pastures would have spread, the eyebright and the cowslip gleaming among them. Where a path was marked on the map there was none on the ground, nor stile either, so I left a trail of crushed and alien olive blades and moved across to the bridleway, traversing the moor, to jag south then east where I met it, and dawdled through flocks of sturdy, springy lambs with protuberant ears that crowded around as I walked, their mothers bawling raucously at a distance.

The way descended, came to a barbed-wire enclosure where black shreds of the polythene bale-wrapping that is now ubiquitous in our countryside clattered in the wind like baleful prayer flags for some corrupt and corrupting cere-mony. Beyond the enclosure a forestry plantation had been clear-felled, a sign standing out there from the ruin of the good land. I crossed over to read it. '218.352' it said – as incompre-hensible to me as the Welsh names given to the features of this landscape over centuries or even millennia would be to those who have drawn their profits from here at the expense of the land's despoliation – a reductive cipher, a number, a small god to those who worship material things. I passed down rather sadly through the dark forest that spreads now across the flank of the Crag of the Sow, the territorial disputes of ravens chorusing me along, and came to a reservoir, where laburnum in flower by the stream flowing into it and beech in its June glory reminded me that the alien need not be the ugly. But as I sat by the dam, opened my flask and plotted my way on, an aspect of what had happened in this place took me with pecu-liar force: the uniformity of dark trees, black water – we have taken away colour and light and variety. A place where now and again a passer-by, looking on the morning light across a hill-slope, at the liquid-silver glint of a stream coursing down its tiny falls, at the flocks of small birds swirling over the meadows, might have seen that a vision of the temporal heaven has been extinguished, robbed of light: and with it also a lovely part of our experience and understanding of the world, and all that is numinous in it:

> It was like a church to me.
> I entered it on soft foot,
> Breath held like a cap in the hand.
> It was quiet.
> What God was there made himself felt,
> Not listened to, in clean colours
> That brought a moistening of the eye,
> In movement of the wind over grass.[5]

I came down to the road, crossed it and followed an old sunken way around the shoulder of Mynydd Lledrod, nettle-grown, avenued with gnarled and aged thorns from the time of the Enclosure Acts, on which hung the last discoloured blossoms of May. Maybe no other tree has quite the associative texture of the hawthorn? *Blodau marw mam* the blossom's called in Welsh – 'the flowers of mother's death', apparently from the resemblance of its smell in decay to the stench of that widespread killer before the era of modern antibiotics, puerperal fever. The female association is right. In its first pure shimmer across the hillsides and along the old field boundaries in the May month, its scent is rich and warm and musky, like a woman fresh from love-making. But as it fades, an element from within that fragrance intensifies to the exclusion of all pleasure, and it takes on the same shocking odour of decay that I remember from my father's Salford hospital bedside, his handsome face wasted and barely conscious on the pillow; that I shied away from encountering after my son's death. I pushed through the thickets into more salubrious air and saw ahead the long ridge for which I was making, clear for the first time, and identifiable on the map now: Gyrn Moelfre – the horn of the bare hill. It was elegant, desirable, still a couple of miles distant, so I paced on quickly to the bridleway along its southern flank and started the gradual ascent. At a farm, an affable sheepdog came out to rub against my leg and turn up its muzzle to be petted. Country where even the sheepdogs are friendly is gentle country indeed. A mile beyond, the track curved back around to gain the ridge of the mountain, and I followed that by the boundary wire to the summit.

The presence of the hill was out of all proportion to its height. It was lonely, quiet, untrodden, aloof. By the Ordnance Survey pillar, around which spread the light new green of the bilberry, the view – particularly to south and east, for to the north The Berwyn was boiling with cloud – was long and luxuriant in detail and texture. The summit was a singular, up-tilted place, crags rimming the hill to the south. Just down there to the west I could see the chimneys of the topmost terrace of Llanrhaeadr, perhaps as little as four miles away. In these moments at the hilltop of Gyrn Moelfre, some force of attraction, powerful and undeniable, was operating upon me. Though I would have liked to linger, I had started late and it was already well after eight, rain in the wind and the car miles away. In the valley beneath to the north a small building, a Bronze Age tumulus marked on the map distinct in the valley just beyond it, drew my eye whenever I looked that way. I plunged down the steep hillside and through good and tended land towards it.

It was a church – very small, very simple, completely unadorned, its fabric mid-Victorian and its foundation palpably much older. It was open. I went in and looked around. Diamond-paned windows with gentle tints of blue and green let in a soft light. Hanging oil-lamps had been converted to electricity. In the parish register, open in the vestry, what caught my eye were the packed attendances for *plygain* down the years.[6] In these marches of northern Montgomery, something of the old Wales seemed to endure. I remembered that my Welsh tutor in Bangor, Dr Enid Pierce Roberts, was from this region – '*Darn o Gymru Biwritanaidd y ganrif ddiwethaf ydoedd hi*'[7]. 'She was a sliver of the old puritan Wales of the last century' is how that translates, but I shouldn't use the past tense, because Enid is still alive and active, living in Bangor, devout and churchgoing though well into her nineties now – a spry, sharp, amusing, kindly woman who gave me the clearest sense of an interlinked physical and cultural landscape that has now all but disappeared from Wales, and for some trace of which I was still searching. For these old churches, '*Hen longau ydynt y tu ôl i'r llifddorau/Yn llercian yn y llaid a'r llacs*' 'they are old ships behind the floodgates/Lurking in the silt and the mud.'[8] Yet by how much do I prefer their quiet intimations of a lost connection between land and spirit to the vigorous and overweening rants of Professor Richard Dawkins[9] (for more information on which, as he himself might say, go to www.richarddawkins.net). In front of the pulpit, a single-barred fire had been perched across a pew corner. The great Welsh Bible was open at John 21:18:

> When thou wast young, thou girdedst thyself, and
> walkedst whither thou wouldest; but when thou shalt

be old, thou shalt stretch forth thy hands, and another shall gird thee, and carry thee whither thou wouldest not.

I went outside and sat on the hallowed ground within an ancient circular enclosure beneath a dozen yews maybe a thousand years old. In the wrought iron of the gate into the churchyard, enigmatically, there were figures of birds and a sun-disc that could have come from the great Celtic treasure hoards of La Tène or Gundestrup, could have illustrated the *Táin bó Cúailnge*:[10]

> With the passage of time, and with the influx of new ideas and techniques, the preoccupation with solar phenomena must have lessened, and the sun bark, with its swan terminals, and the entire solar symbolism of the early period degenerated into a set of artistic motifs in which the various distinctive elements of the sun cultus become blurred and confused.[11]

A sweet scent of honeysuckle filled the air. Surrounded by this ancient earth, this quiet, secret churchyard dedicated to Cadwaladr, the last High King of the Britons, who died of the plague in 664 – Cadwaladr the Wise, whose name meant 'battle-shunner', whose saying ran, 'the best crooked thing is the crooked handle of a plough' – my brain was suffused with a sense of the magical. It felt to be a right, an epiphanic place, long-settled, little changed. As I sat there in the twilit churchyard, a farmer who'd been separating out sheep in an adjoining field to treat against blowfly puttered along the road on a quad bike. His dog leaped down from the carrier and they came into the churchyard. With shadows lengthening, deepening under the yews, the fragrance of honeysuckle and hay-making all around us, we shared the remnants of my flask and talked: of his family moving here a hundred years ago after his grandfather's sacking and eviction from his tied cottage on the Nannau estate by Dolgellau for taking a pheasant – there was his grandfather's grave, he gestured, and there his parents, and by them his, in time. I told him about Ermanno Olmi's sombre masterpiece of Italian cinema, *The Tree of the Wooden Clogs*. We spoke of dogs and their characters, and farmers I'd worked for whom we both knew, of marts we'd attended and of sheep-country and its long traditions. A quarter-moon was stalking through the clouds as we parted – he for his home close by, me to the long miles by the bridleway over the hill in the faded light, the firing of the engine, the pointing of the old Citroën down a dark road. I had lit upon the 'dear, particular place' near to which I wanted to live, and only the task of house-hunting now remained.

In the event it proved straightforward. I went back to Llanrhaeadr, found a house for sale that I could afford, with a tiny forecourt garden and a profusion of tumbling white fragrant roses, on the corner of the prettiest, swift-screamed square leading down to the churchyard, and arranged to view it. The estate agent was a statuesque, attractive blonde woman in her forties, distinctly friendly in a tight-bodiced, short-skirted black suit, who spent three hours showing me around what was quite a small cottage whilst giving me the whole history of every village house and household. The previous owner had died and some of the furniture was also for sale. At one point in an upstairs room the estate agent called to me, as I gazed out of a window into the square below, to help her demonstrate the action of a sofa-bed. I glanced around; caught her eye as, bent over the sofa, she peered at me over her shoulder; noted with due and distant appreciation the exotic line in black lace underwear on display and hurriedly returned to my study of the square with a polite assurance over my shoulder – and a slight concern over possible ambiguities – that I was sure I'd manage to get it open if the need arose. I had the feeling more strongly than ever that I was going to like the place, so I made my offer, it was accepted, and within a very short space of time I was moving in. Will was my first visitor. He drove over from Llanberis in his old red diesel van, poked his nose into every nook of the house, and alleyway of the village, sat on the bench outside with a mug of coffee in his hand, looked me in the eye and with a knowing smirk delivered his considered and I suppose approving opinion: 'Good place to grow old, this, Dad.'

Within the first couple of days, something happened that I had never experienced before. Welcome cards from the people of the village started arriving through my letter box. By the dozen. Invitations to dinner were extended, including one from the estate agent, though I was soon informed – Llanberis not being the only place to turn on an axis of gossip – that some of her soirées were supposedly of the car-keys-in-the-bowl-and-choose-your-partner-for-the-drive-home variety, which was not a ritual I'd ever found enticing. When I sat on my bench, passers-by engaged in conversation. One delicious near-neighbour in her eighties, Claire, who must in her youth have been of staggering physical charm, and who still exemplified Donne's lines on the Lady Danvers, 'No spring, nor summer beauty hath such grace,/As I have seen in one autumnal face'[12], walked past each morning and afternoon with her little grey Bedlington terrier called Harvey Smith, and insisted on my attendance for the small-Scotch-at-six observances, to which order I submitted gladly, and found the 'small Scotch' wholly inadequate to describe the quantities on offer. Whenever I went in to the village store on the corner of Waterfall Street, run by Glenda, the doctor's widow ('Oh, don't have those, sweetheart – I got fresh in the back. Those are just for the visitors and you're local now, isn't it…'), and stocking everything from fresh coriander, Jameson's and firelighters to Roquefort and good ground coffee, I'd be given the first degree, directly by Glenda or more hesitantly and circuitously by her sons Ian and Mark. Cross the road to the butcher's, and Roger Evans would do the same in Welsh, the speaking of which here was a shibboleth. Head into the main square to buy a paper and there was Ian again, setting the same questions in a different way whilst keeping up a ruminative disquisition on the actual and likely weather. My old Citroën parked on the forecourt of the house came in for its fair share of attention too, most of it friendly from the older men of the village, once from a wuffler on the side of a tractor, that left it with an intricate and quite becoming yellow tattoo against the black, as the farmers crowded down from the hills on a Saturday morning to stock up at Glenda's, gossip for an hour and slip heavy boxes of produce into their tractor cabs, before setting off back to Cwm Blowty, Cwm Maen Gwynedd or Llangadwaladr.

Very soon it became apparent that the social life of the incomers to the village was fixed in orbit around two characters. Mrs Frances Denby had bought Plas yn Llan, the village's most imposing and central house, from Sheila Fleming, whose husband Charlie had died and was buried in the little cemetery at the crossroads on the road out to Llanfyllin, where I would catch a glimpse of Sheila's flaming hair from time to time as she laid flowers and tended to his grave. She had moved just outside the village, and at Plas yn Llan, Frances now held court. Astute and generous, behind the hesitancy of a stammer, she held strong opinions that politically were diametrically opposed to mine. Perfectly aware of this division, she was unfailingly courteous, hospitable and generous towards me. She had been a beauty on the King's Road in the 1960s, as far as I could understand had moved to Llanrhaeadr on the death of Mr Denby, and had shared a house surrounded by a vast, elaborate and imaginative garden in surroundings of which even Vita Sackville-West would have been envious above the village with a retired General of great distinction. He had been allowed by the MCC, of which he was an honorary member, the unique privilege of having made a facsimile of the Lord's Cricket Ground Father Time weathervane, which now adorned the rear outbuildings of Plas yn Llan. Frances, of whom I became very fond, was a disarming mixture of the charmingly congenial and the not-to-be-trifled-with. A slip of the tongue could result in months of political exile – which was a deprivation, because Frances's salons were pleasant occasions and her cooking was excellent. That I wrote regularly at the time for the *Daily Telegraph* earned me points towards her favour; that I was often to be seen emerging from Ian's paper shop carrying a copy of the *Guardian*, and that I was a man of a certain age who lived alone and was frequently visited by assorted women friends (who for all the sharp-eyed village knew may well have been, in the current phrase, 'friends with benefits' – mostly in fact they weren't), were matters that raised doubts. 'So what are you then?' fluted one apparently very proper member of the village circle of ladies-who-lunch, when she had called around at my house for coffee one morning, 'a connoisseur of cunt? There's all sorts of specula-tion going on, you know. Still, at least you don't appear to be queer – that wouldn't be much use to us, would it now?' I left the response at a wry shake of the head, and recorded a new and exotic addition to the long list of things-I've-been-called.

This exchange, with its bawdy undercurrent, was one that I came to see as by no means surprising in this village. The previous resident of my house, I was told, had been in large measure ostracized because of her complaints and disapproval of all that went on during the Young Farmers' Dance that took place on the last Friday night of every month – a ritual that was as good-natured as it was lively and debauched. The young people from surrounding farms and villages flocked in, paired off to fifties and sixties rock 'n' roll music in the village hall, and meandered down into the graveyard to fuck on whatever tomb or patch of grass was unoccupied. I walked through once in ignorance soon after my arrival, and from every quarter came gasps and groans, giggles and sighs, pale arses fluttering in the moonlight. The village elders smiled benignly on a custom that in some form or other had clearly existed for generations and was not going to be brought to a halt by the prudery and – so it was said – lesbian tendencies of some spoilsport incomer.[13]

Frances's opposite pole and her close confidante was the

broadcaster and writer Mavis Nicholson, with whom I had many friends in common. Mavis is a short, dark-haired, voluble South-Walian woman, long resident in Highgate before she and her husband – who had been sports editor on the *Observer*, had written an excellent book, the best on its subject, about the Tour de France, and who had died of cancer two years before I arrived in the village – retired to their cottage at Aber Rhaeadr. He was buried in the chapel graveyard opposite Jacob's Ribs on the road out to Llanfyllin, close to the grave of Christopher Wordsworth, another *Observer* writer and one to whom I owed a debt of gratitude for a fond and appreciative review he gave to my first book of essays.[14] Mavis very quickly became the focus of my social life, and I a frequent adjunct of hers. She edited the local newspaper, the *Chronicle* – standards on which put many national titles to shame (and many of the contributors to which were in fact staffers or retirees from the national broadsheets) – from an office opposite my house, and she was prime mover in the cinema club, which ran every Friday night from September to April in the school theatre in Llanfyllin. She had had her own television series, *Mavis on Four*, in which she interviewed significant cultural figures: James Baldwin, Margot Fonteyn, Lauren Bacall, Kingsley Amis, Maya Angelou had all received the Mavis treatment, the latter whilst she and Mavis were sharing a lover. I came in for it once in front of about 300 people attending the *Guardian* Hay Festival. At the graveyard hour of ten o'clock on a Thursday morning, Mavis's opening gambit, unanticipated and as far as I know unrehearsed, ran thus: 'Jim, you're on record as saying that LSD should form an essential part of any writer's education. Would you care to explain?'

I loved her for tricks like that. She probed, even in every-day conversation, with the concentrated interest and calm subtlety of a surgeon wielding the lancet. I've never met a finer or more astute interviewer. And of course, all that she un-earthed in our regular dates for lunch or dinner would very soon selectively have been transmitted around the village – the difference between Llanberis and Llanrhaeadr being that in the latter the gossip seemed predicated on human curiosity and was both reasonably accurate and devoid of malice. Glenda very quickly spotted the connection between Mavis and myself, and in her best husky stage whisper as Mavis called in to the busy shop to buy milk for the *Chronicle* office one lunchtime, put the question, with a teasing, drawling stress on the crucial word: 'So, Mavis, 'ave you fucked him yet?'

The bawdy and the sexual gossip aside, the one common factor linking Glenda, Frances and Mavis – the three head women of the village, or so it seemed to me – apart from their very feminine shared curiosity, was the exceptional kindness all three possessed and regularly exercised. If these three were the most prominent points in the village's human landscape, the physical fabric of the place rapidly became an entrance-ment to me. It started with my house. When a county archaeologist visited to be shown the location of the three stone circles and the stone row above the waterfall, he seemed even more fascinated by the structure of the house – its ancient oak frame, the cobbled cellar. 'Without a doubt medieval,' he explained, 'the stone cladding's much later – look, there are traces here of the original wattle-and-daub.' Whatever the origin and date of the house, its atmosphere delighted me. The old boarded floors swayed in all directions, the roughly-

worked beams – whole tree trunks, their wood iron-hard –
divided space into uneven and intriguing shapes, and gave an
organic feel to the house, as if its structure had scarcely ceased
growing. It was vociferous too – summer and winter, day and
night coaxed differing voices from its timbers, the rains of
autumn sent a small torrent down a channel that cut across
one corner of the cellar, down into which you climbed through
a trapdoor in the kitchen. Big windows gathered the sun. My
bedroom was in the loft, oak-beamed, tent-like. When I looked
out of the skylight, the ancient rooftops of the village billowed
towards the churchyard like waves. I've never much held with
the notion of 'property' rather than home, and have certainly
never subscribed to the sentiment of 'falling in love' with a
house. But living in this one suited me, calmed me. Looking
out of its windows was like looking down into a film set. And
it was called 'Manchester House' (all Welsh villages seemed
to name their shops – my house had once been the ironmon-
ger's – after the great centres of commerce. Llanrhaeadr
had its Liverpool and Birmingham Houses too): 'Across what
distances in time do the elective affinities and correspondences
connect?'[15]

In the event, there had proved not to be much relief from
work-time interruption, and there was further distraction in
the landscape round about. The walking was a continual
temptation to be out-of-doors. At any break in mental concentration I could make the usual excuses to myself, leave the
house and take the slant path up the hanger above the churchyard, that was springy with larch litter, loud each evening
with calls of young ravens. It led to a sunken, westering lane
that rounded the hill, its dense green corridor offering gated

glimpses of the wide strath of Tanat below. Two or three times a day, rain or shine, I came this way. The extraordinary abundance of the hedges on either side thrilled me. Elsewhere throughout Britain they may have been devastated, but in this soft country around Dyffryn Tanat the hedges were inviolate, the old country crafts of laying them still practised, the land's fabric so much richer in consequence. There was such beauty and variety burgeoning out around bank and woven frame. In the space of a hundred yards along the lane I could list holly, oak, hawthorn, hazel, field maple, beech, willow and alder. The elders cupped their paired leaves skywards, and from the warp of the laid hedges' lateral branches, a weft of shoots strove towards the azure, interwoven with the woodbines – honeysuckle and traveller's joy – and draped with thorns, the imperial purple of the dog rose lording it over vigorous pink demotics of the bramble. White trumpets of bindweed relieved the predominant green palette, blackthorn branches were bobbled in their season with misted dark sloes, ripe blackberries burst on my tongue, in the under-hedge late campion was stellar and the bryony, cranesbill and rest-harrow gleamed fitfully. All this in my first months in the village. Overarching foliage of oak and sycamore carried first hints of the sere. A buzzard's pinions brushed my shoulder as it glided low over the gate I was leaning on, to land in the field beyond with an assertive hop, and feast on grubs and worms. Lightning had ripped the top from an old Scots pine which marked the farther point of my daily walk, its bark crazed and sweet with dribbles of resin. Wire and gorse had kept the saplings seeded all around safe from grazing kine, and a warm autumn wind was soughing through the broom. This place in which I'd arrived was a temporal heaven.

Behind the village the foothills rose up steeply to The Berwyn ridge – lonely, spacious, a bulwark blanking off distances to the eye, reminding that this, down the centuries, had been harsh barrier for the lovely hill-country of Wales. I'd known The Berwyn for as long, almost, as I'd been coming to the outdoors. There was for me always a kind of magic about its name. In part it was to do with my bookishness as a child. The library of my grammar school was a safe and quiet haven, from which there were glimpses of the Derbyshire hills. And it had an outdoor section, with a few mountain books that I devoured time and again, avidly: Charles Evans's *On Climbing*, Colin Kirkus's *Let's Go Climbing!* Both of them recounted outdoor odysseys that started on The Berwyn. The latter had an idiosyncratic Bartholomew's one-inch-to-the-mile map of The Berwyn high tops, contour-shaded in fawns and umbers and russets at strangely irregular intervals, its summits white in unconscious cartographic homage to the meaning of the name (Ifor Williams, in *Enwau Lleoedd* – the bible to anyone interested in Welsh nomenclature – explains *Berwyn* as deriving from *bargwyn* – white-headed – 'barr' having the same meaning as 'pen', the more usual Welsh word for head). I was transfixed by this map, at the age of twelve knew its every name and hill and detail, their position and their meaning by heart. So inevitably I had made my way to The Berwyn very early in my own outdoor journey, and had periodically been doing so ever since. '*Anial chwith y Berwyn*' – the forlorn wilderness of The Berwyn – is how the Welsh essayist Tecwyn Lloyd, from Corwen to the north, described this moorland rampart between the river valleys of Tanat and Ceiriog to the south, and Dyfrdwy to the north. These are Housman's 'blue remembered hills' that swell to the west of the Shropshire of his poems. Now my home, this was my 'land of lost content'.[16] And now that I was based south of The Berwyn, I could explore it from that direction – much the most interesting of approaches – rather than those from east and north that I'd previously used. All of it was good country for the lover of spaciousness, crossed by old trackways – Ffordd Saeson, Ffordd Gam Elin, the Maids' Path along the Nant Rhydwilym – and chorused by curlew and buzzard. With its immemorial passes and stone circles and mountain-top burial cairns, its stories of medieval military operation and brutality, of continual movement across the borders of time and land, The Berwyn felt as redolent, enduring and resistant as anywhere in Wales: 'Whenever a shift in our spiritual life occurs and fragments such as these surface, we believe we can remember.'[17]

One clear evening following a day of rain shortly after I had arrived, I walked up the Maids' Path. There was a kind of peace, a clarity and a glow upon the place. Wafts of a light wind sent showers of drops down through the heavy leaf cover of the sycamores, warning of their descent in a pattering rush. In the little gorge beneath, the waterfalls jetted their burden into tormented pools, the sides of which were mossy and ferned, brilliant and jewelled in the close view. Beyond the last fields above Swch-cae-rhiw, climbing all the time, the old way curved around a bluff and pointed due west, into the heart of the moor, and I followed it along with the consciousness on me of those who had trodden this way – all those who, for whatever reasons, had found themselves crossing The Berwyn down the long centuries before ours. This would have been the way by which impoverished daughters from the farming and quarrying communities of the Welsh heartlands made their way into service or agricultural employment in the English shires. I found myself involuntarily scanning the track ahead to see if by some trick of time one would come tripping barefoot down the turf, belongings slung in a shawl on her back. Heading in the other direction were the agricultural workers and countrymen seeking more lucrative and less seasonal employment in the slate quarries of Gwynedd or the coal mines of Flint. It thrilled me, the way this new home landscape was coming alive, resonating in my imagination.

From time to time the *Telegraph* would send me away to write travel essays on foreign places for its Saturday supplement (this before travel-writing for newspapers became the mere compiling of breathless-lexis lists and website addresses: 'The Twenty-five Happening Places for Transvestites to Hole Up at Hallowe'en', 'The Forty-nine Best Spanish Inquisition-themed Boutique Hotels', 'Sixty Must-see Beaches East of Scunthorpe' and so on). In my first winter in Llanrhaeadr, just before Christmas I went out to Montreal, and crossing the mountain above the city, stopping by woods on a snowy evening, a bitter and unimpeded wind down from the Arctic creaking through the birch trees, suddenly I was overcome by longing for my new home place. What fixed in my mind, disjunctively, in the cold Canadian twilight, was what I saw each morning when I looked out to view the world from the skylight in my loft bedroom. Across that roofscape to which the warping of timbers over centuries had imparted the sense of wave-motion, beyond the old and moss-grown church tower that stands foursquare to all weathers, rising steeply

above the banks of the swift-flowing, alder-shaded river, there
was the hill the hoving-into-view of which, as I journeyed up
the long valley after each absence, told me that I was home. I
loved the sight of this hill. It is barely a thousand feet high, and
the summits that rise to the north are almost three times that
elevation. I would think that very few reach its summit from
one year's end to the next. It doesn't attract attention somehow. It is a low, bracken-clad hill, its southerly slope shaggy
with small outcrops of rock, and all around it there are other
heights shapelier and grander. Yet I came to be charmed and
enamoured and contented with this hill. Its name in translation is 'high place of three fountains', and its presiding quality
is that of a repository of light. With a low, bright sun on
evenings before the equinox I saw it aflame. On winter mornings it rose above valley mist and frost as a shimmering
presence, its bracken a sodden, heavy terracotta against the
sky's wan blue. Sometimes it seemed to stretch itself, elongate,
become a dragon-like form emerging from wooded ground
behind, and above it a crescent moon sailed into evening brilliance and solitary ravens made for home. All these pictures
were vividly in my mind that twilight on a hill top of Quebec.
Perhaps this is how you know your own right place – by the
longing it evokes when you are far away. At some deeper level
than mere residence, this was the effect Llanrhaeadr had upon
me. It was not that it had become my home. It *was* my home.
I would walk down in the night often into the churchyard, sit
on a projecting stone at the base of the tower, watch the moon
in all its phases traversing the sky, and enter a state of feeling
that was transcendent:

If, when there is quiet, the spirit has continuously and uninterruptedly a sense of great joy as if intoxicated or freshly bathed, it is a sign that the light-principle is harmonious in the whole body; then the Golden Flower begins to bud. When, furthermore, all openings are quiet, and the silver moon stands in the middle of heaven, and one has the feeling that this great earth is a world of light and brightness, that is a sign that the body of the heart opens itself to clarity.[18]

This was the condition to which dwelling in Llanrhaeadr had brought me, and at this point, I believe significantly, I entered a vital dimension of approach to – a making-ready-for – the loving relationship that was entirely to change my life. I look back on this now with a sort of incredulity at the good fortune that befell me. I was happy to live alone with my cat, friends around me, my son visiting from time to time. After too many catastrophic and demeaning encounters I'd given up on the notion of happiness being predicated on a harmonious man–woman relationship – perhaps especially difficult to a writer, for whom preoccupation and detachment are natural states of being. My work was fulfilling and plentiful. I had enough, and of everything else I had had enough. And then Jacquetta came back into my life.

8

Communion

As I begin this chapter, in a solitary house of the high Pyrenees where I now live, on sudden impulse I walk over to the dresser, take a bottle of *Rimmel 247 opal* nail varnish from a dwindling stash in one of the drawers, and to the fascination of the cats (Serafina now having a portly young friend, Isabella, of very amiable disposition), who temporarily abandon their study of finches in a nearby cherry tree and watch from the sill of an open window, I paint my toenails in this shade, which Jacquetta, whose ritual this was, always referred to as 'fairy wings'. The ritual sets me thinking of the encounter in London after a twenty-seven year desolating separation between François-René de Chateaubriand and his lost love, the Suffolk parson's daughter Charlotte Ives. Lady Sutton at the time she sought him out again, married to an admiral and with two teenage sons, their encounter is passionately and sorrowfully described in Chateaubriand's auto-biographical prose masterpiece *Mémoires d'outre-tombe*, completed in 1841 – one of the crucial texts of European late-romanticism as well as a fascinating historical perspective on the Napoleonic and post-Napoleonic period in France and the French colonies. I first read this story of Chateaubriand and Charlotte Ives in an odd volume of the two-book Pleiade edition that I picked up from a backstreet junk shop in Saint Malo, to which town rumour had led me in the hope of chance encounter, within a year of Jacquetta's disappearance. Instead of her, I came upon this profound contemplation of memory and loss.

What connection there is between the circumstantial and the predictive, Freud can dispute and others postulate. For me, this Chateaubriand story implanted itself as suggestion, as a 'what if?' of remarkable persistence and longevity. As further testimony to the subliminal power of the story – and a further shock to me when I came across it here very shortly before Jacquetta and I were reunited – it's one on which Sebald, in a close translocation from Chateaubriand, ruminates in his dark journeyings through Suffolk described in *The Rings of Saturn*:

> the fact is that writing is the only way in which I am able to cope with the memories which overwhelm me so frequently and so unexpectedly. If they remained locked away, they would become heavier and heavier as time went on, so that in the end I would succumb under their mounting weight. Memories lie slumbering within us for months and years, quietly proliferating, until they are woken by some trifle and in some strange way blind us to life. How often has this caused me to feel that my memories, and the labours expended in writing them down are all part of the same humiliating and, at bottom, contemptible business! And yet,

what would we be without memory? We would not be capable of ordering even the simplest thoughts, the most sensitive heart would lose the ability to show affection, our existence would be a mere never-ending chain of meaningless moments, and there would not be the faintest trace of a past. How wretched this life of ours is! – so full of false conceits, so futile, that it is little more than the shadow of the chimeras unloosed by memory.[19]

This train of thought as I pursue it jolts me into a recurrent sense of the joy and good fortune there has been in my life by contrast with the lives of so many. But all this is to leap well ahead of myself, and I must come back to the autumn of 2002, seven years before the time at which I now write in this distant, necessary and self-imposed exile.

I had just returned from Spain, where I had been with Ed Douglas, one of my closest friends, and as intelligent and decent a man as I know. We had had a week of experiences and adventures in the hills behind Alicante. In a secretive small valley of the Serra de la Carrasca we were guided by a Spanish friend, José, to a rock face, pocked with depressions, roofed with overhangs, a cave at its farther end. We made out designs, framed within the forms of the rock. 'Macroschematic art – it dates from about 5,000 BC and the birth of farming,' José explained. We concentrated – on an energy of upward-aspiring line, on an assurance, a haunting expressiveness, seed and growth like sparks from a furnace, the affecting madonna-inclination of a woman's head towards husband and child in a family group. In these swirling, scattering compositions were contained, ready for germination, all the myths of mankind: there were gods here, underworlds, regenerations, quests. There was a complex magic at work, Proserpine and Rhea and Dis thrown further from us into an older conjunction. On another day we went to the Cabo de la Nao by Xàbia. From behind luxury coastal mansions in the colonial style, razor-wired and swimming-pooled, a slight path contoured the coast above plunging, high cliffs. Beneath us the face sheered down vertically for 400 feet to the sea. Looping down its features was a bizarre series of rotting palm-strand ropes that crumbled to dust at the touch, rusting wires, old electrical flex, bamboo ladders, flaking iron spikes, globules of quickset concrete dabbed and shaped on slanting gangways. It was one of the strangest things I've ever seen in the outdoors, makeshift, flimsy, decayed. We descended to a wood-and-bamboo-framed ledge lashed to the cliff twenty feet above a sea that sucked and heaved at undercuts beneath. In places the rock was little better than compacted mud. Those desiccated, slender bamboo rungs lashed to their poles with rusted wire snapped here and there like brittle bones beneath my weight. My every sense was alert and battle-joyful; the old addictions to risk still running strong, I found myself cackling with good humour. This access route, José told us, was made by the poorest of the poor, by fishermen who couldn't afford to build or buy even the smallest of boats, and hence came down and cast their lines night-long at the foot of these cliffs, climbed them again in the dawn, before walking the ten miles back to market in Xàbia to sell their catch.

Though somehow, these ways of theirs are too extreme to be explained so simply away.

We descended also into the gorge of hell – the *Barranc de l'Infern* – by a winding trail that fretted and veered into its depths. Gradually the rock walls narrowed, occluding even the high Spanish sun. We passed ruins of hunters' huts. Light filtered down, giving a pale blue cast to the shade that the pale grey of the gorge walls seemed to be sucking in. Every stone we stepped upon clacked into a sharp reiteration of echoes, our breath amplified, lizards scampered into crevices impossibly tiny, etching their greens and browns into the grey. Across the rocks now, from one to another we moved in quiet elation.

The depths of the gorge were vastly impressive. We slipped from rock vat to rock vat where the flood waters are boiled, bolts here and there, chains, frayed lengths of knotted rope down awkward short slabs, or stretched across traverses high over pots. Into some we abseiled, and had to climb the scoured and polished element out again. Above me on one thirty-foot wall with a severe move for the top, Ed slapped for the rim, his groping hand dipping into a pool, sluicing water down the slab. I cursed him playfully, moved tentatively up, boots angling on buffed, small edges, absorbed in the nature and element of rock, ever-conscious of the absent, sculpting one of water that had formed this place and expressed itself in vortices, stilled whorls whose shaping spirit, brutal and capricious in its dynamic power, had for the brief space around our time of passage given temporary place to soft and quiet air. Fig trees that would never fruit lodged in inaccessible niches high above. Flood debris was jammed into cracks far beyond our reach. In pale imitation of the water itself, its ghost-absence inviting us to dance, we raced through.

The gorge opened. On pebbled shores we rested and ate

and laughed. A wind riffled past, stirring the leaves. Innocent grotesqueries of limestone were exposed to view. A bluff above the dry bed of the river had the texture of decayed wood. We left by a Moorish constructed way. Interlocking cobbles were laid across slick stone, a road for pack animals formed thus across a featureless slab. Riprap! I thought of Gary Snyder's poem of the same name, with its insistence on 'the body of the mind/in space and time', its espousal of solidity of things. That night I dreamed of a tutelary spirit, in my notebook in the morning described her thus: 'On an almond terrace centuries ago, Al Medrahi watches lightning flicker under a crescent moon, dreams of healing herbs, heart's-ease, rocks and solid things. Subtle, she is with us in space and time.'

You could think of her name in Welsh as meaning 'she might'. The dream of her was of piercing clarity. Her back was to me, the hair hennaed. When she turned to smile at me over her shoulder, her face was Jacquetta's, exactly as I had seen it in that acid trip nearly three decades before. Two evenings later I stood at front-of-house in the Llangollen International Pavilion, preparing for a gig I was sharing with a story-teller friend, Fiona Collins, when a slight, red-haired woman in blue dungarees over a yellow top bought a ticket from the kiosk behind me, walked down the aisle towards the auditorium, and as she did so, cast a backward glance over her shoulder and the face that smiled at me was that of the woman in the dream.

If this sounds uncanny, let me assure you that it is less so than it seems. By my bed in the hotel room Ed and I had shared in Spain was a copy of *The Rings of Saturn* with its retelling of that long-pondered story of Charlotte Ives. The dream was 'of the chimeras unloosed by memory'. Jac's appearance at the reading too was the simple result of a chance sighting in her local post office twenty miles away of a poster for the event. A calm appraisal of the circumstances would wholly endorse Freud's rational view of the supposedly uncanny. That it did not, either to me or to Jacquetta, feel that way was simply a matter of subjective emotion – of hyper-investment, if you wish to use the jargon. There were things in which we both *wanted* to believe. Yet even in recollection, none of this consideration robs the moment of any of its force. And there is another element here that is wholly mysterious. It is the nature of love itself, the way in which the sense of the other sometimes manages to sidestep our defences and colonize the heart. In those first instants of seeing the red-haired woman in the blue dungarees walking away from me, even before she turned her head and smiled, my breath was suspended, and I knew that she was the woman who would, from that moment on, be central in my life; who had always been central in my subconscious life. The subliminal recognition preceded the actual, the instinctual had been more alert than the visual.

Shaken to the core, I had to put all this aside and perform. When she came up to me in the interval, waiting at the periphery of my vision and centre of my consciousness whilst others occupied my time, and then introducing herself with the wan, quizzical 'You won't remember me', I could scarcely speak, was transfixed by an incredulous happiness. We arranged to meet afterwards, by the fire in the Sun Inn out along the road to Y Waun. I had trouble getting away, ended up running to the pub. I can hardly remember a thing from the babble of words that passed between us, can only recall that I could not take my eyes from her, that we could not let go of each other's hands. Certainly information was transmitted between us – that I now lived in a place that was one of her favourite haunts; that every Beltane for years she had made her own pilgrimage to Pistyll Rhaeadr; matter about the ineffectual manner in which both of us had gone about trying to find the other down the years; her having found out the address and passed the house in Dinorwig where I lived with Will, but fearful that I was with another or would not remember her or wish to know her had not dared to call; and much else besides.

I find myself hesitant and conflicted in recounting the events of the next two-and-a-half years. All human testimony is in some measure unreliable – my own no less so than that of the next person. We all present versions of our experiences to each other, that are quite as stylized as those of the macroschematic art on the Spanish cliff face. The actual becomes subservient to the story, which has its own purposes to fulfil. I cannot entirely subvert this equation, the craft of writing being insistent on degrees of its application – selection, characterization, the colours of rhetoric, structure, pacing, chiasmus, sub-text, the exemplary dimension. And yet, unless I am to hold as closely as possible to the actual, to the order and manner in which things took place, my grief is not exorcized but enshrined. Even as I write this, the somatic illness that has all but crippled me these last two years and been read by the medical profession as terminal cancer clamps my chest so that every breath comes panting and laboured and my head spins in anoxic blankness. This is a book that I have to write, and at which task it seems every cell of my body protests. My fingers are numb on the keyboard, medical supposition being that the diagnosed carcinoma my body has created is causing pressure on the neural pathways. If I could tell you a story, if I could give you an idyll – would not you and I both prefer that option? But it is not an option: '…if way to the better there be, it exacts a full look at the worst.'[20]

The easy formula is to write that from the moment of re-encounter we were never apart, and in our thoughts I believe this was the case on both sides. The immediate physical reality was other. We went back from Llangollen that night to our separate homes, but the planes of our lives had shifted and over the next several months would position themselves to enmesh. I climbed up the narrow stair to my loft in something of a sad perplexity alongside the continuing joy. What for years I had most wanted was converging now on a calm and contented existence forged in its absence after years of turmoil, which would be entirely disrupted by that which had been so long desired. Jacquetta phoned, after the requisite two days that denote no inappropriate keenness. I remembered then, and with ambivalence, the fretful waiting that attachment to another can often induce, the issues of abandonment that shadow the surrender to love. She arranged to drive over to Llanrhaeadr from her house among the moors near Cerrigy-drudion in a few days' time. On the appointed evening she was very late – there had been difficulty around a borrowed car that delayed her leaving the house, the mist across the moor was dense – and the pub where I'd planned we would eat had stopped serving food. So we drank Guinness there, went home, and I have a curiously literal-minded memory of making a quick, late supper of prawns in a yoghurt-based sauce with fresh red chillies and fresh coriander, tamarind and garlic naan.

In the way of women, meanwhile, she wandered around and made a thorough mental inventory of house, contents and order in which kept, as well as cleanliness of bathroom, scrupulousness of housework, tidiness of bed, signs of the presence of other women. I remember asking her jokily if she had run her finger along the tops of doors and reveals to check for dust. She was amused and aghast at the crammed volume of food in cupboards, refrigerator and freezer – my neurotic hangover from a childhood where sparseness and scarcity held sway over sufficiency. The stove was lit. She leaned back against me in her old confiding way. I played 'Ripple' and she glanced around to meet my eyes with a quick, pleased look of acknowledgement. She told me how exhausted and depressed she was – when she described herself as 'spent' the intonation was that of the heaviest sigh – and something of the present conditions of her life. She asked if I had really loved her all those years. I took up her last three words and gave them back as response. She left as a grey early November dawn was seeping into the fabric of the blinds, the two of us having talked all night, as decades before we had often done.

She lived twenty-eight miles away over a high, wintry moor – Milltir Gerrig the road's called, 'the stony miles', and much of it is at over 1500 feet above sea level, frequently blocked, often fog-bound and icy, with huge drops to the side, not a road for reliable travel between the end of October and the onset of March. The Berwyn – the white barrier – is aptly named. For much of the time through these months it is snow-bound, impassable, the ways around immensely long. We saw

each other fairly frequently during this winter, correspond-
ed, had long telephone conversations late into the night, the
battery of my remote phone up in the loft often running out in
the course of them. Over Christmas she was away on a dutiful
and extended tour of relations and I had Will to stay, his
mother calling in too for a couple of nights, which was difficult
and bizarre for all three of us, and left Will and myself op-
pressed by criticism, as untoward as from that source it felt
inadmissible.

Both Jacquetta and myself led busy and industrious
lives. Her stained-glass and fused-glass work, with its refined
draughtsmanship, luminous simplicity and exquisite, playful
detail was in demand and she had time-consuming commissions to fulfil. Apart from my monthly work commitments,
I had trips away – in particular a long one to Bolivia in
February. There were protests in La Paz when I arrived. Along
the Prado what seemed like a revolution was going on. Crowds
were gathered, placards were being waved about, lengthy
handwritten demand-posters brandished aloft. Rockets and
fireworks exploded against the downtown skyscrapers, chants
and shouts filled the streets. My alarm turned to bemused
interest as I saw the police smiling on benignly, engaging in
conversation, flicking a lighter at the fuse of a proffered fire-
work. There was, beyond all the animation of protest, a
curious tranquility about it all, an on-looking wry phlegma-
tism. 'Teachers protesting for pay,' a young man told me, 'and
the nurses, you know – they're on hunger strike; but in four or
five days they'll have lost enough weight, think how pretty
they now look, start feeling hungry and they'll sign a bit of
paper that gives them a fraction of what they demand. It's the

Americanos, amigo – they stamp out the coca, give the government money, the government promise this and that and the money goes who knows where but not to us. Then the farmers have no coca to sell, and here in this country, where we live so high, the coca is a medicine, it helps us work. Why does America not deal with her own problems, and stop making them for us?'

Campesino roadblocks kept me in Potosi for days on end, through which I had to escape eventually concealed among indigenous Aymara travellers on a night bus heading south – the opposite direction to the one in which I needed to go. I visited silver-miners in deep tunnels of the Cerro Rico – vital, laughing, superstitious men who would, from the conditions of their work, all be dead by the time they were forty. Jacquetta had wanted to come with me, 'to carry your bags', she'd pleaded, but it was not possible in the short time available to arrange it, and I was anyway not convinced that it would be a good thing. Instead, as a poor substitute, I wrote to her. I find one of the letters here in the Pyrenees in a drawer of my desk and smile at its formality, its maintained distance, the years of her absence having left their mark, trust slow in the re-establishment. It was posted from the Isla del Sol, birthplace of the Inca culture, on Lake Titicaca:

the lake is astonishingly beautiful, sapphire-blue, its shores terraced and wooded, its islands as those of the Aegean must have been a century ago. The village of Challapampa where I'm staying tonight straddles an isthmus near the north end of the island. Little friendly pigs root along the sandy shore, gorgeous Indian children in vibrantly-coloured clothing squalling and playing among them. A band strikes up by the school on the opposite side of the isthmus, and from there, rowed by one of the villagers, I take a small boat that bucks and battles alarmingly – I've no life jacket and I've told you how pathetic I am in the water – through the waves of this inland sea to round a promontory and land me in the rocky cove of Bahia Sabacera. By goat-tracks that lead through sweet-scented herbs and savagely-thorned shrubs (my arms are lacerated now – I look like a self-harmer – think I'll apply for a job as lyric-writer for the Manics!) I climb up to the ridge of the island. The views all around in the clear air of altitude to distant mountains and coasts, or of golden capes against slate-grey clouds, are breath-stilling in their loveliness. I descend the other side. Here, above a white-sand beach, is the *Palacio del Inca* – a labyrinth of thick, dry-stone walls and tiny doorways that is inscrutable, ancient, solid and unexplained. If you were here you'd be making a den and planning to sleep out – not much wood for a fire, though, the nights are below zero, and who knows what moves here in the hours of darkness? A little way above and to the south, beyond a great flat rock that you might mistake for a picnic table before the darker purpose of human sacrifice creeps into your mind, a bluff of tawny rock outcrops from the backbone of the island, its form that of a crouching puma. This is Titi Khar'ka – the rock of the puma – from which the lake takes its name. I trace the natural features in it by which the Inca creation legend is delineated: the face of the puma; the four long and pronounced niches, those on the right known as the Refuge of the Sun, those on the left the Refuge of the Moon. Here, according to Inca myth, during the times of flood and darkness the sun made its first appearance; and thereafter came Manco Kapac and his sister-wife Mama Ocllo, son and daughter of the puma-god, and they were the incestuous progenitors of the Inca empire.

'In the granular rock-pavement leading away from the bluff are ironstone intrusions like footprints – those of the sun, as he walked away after his birth here. They look just like that feet-on-a-beach panel of yours you said you were taking down to sell at Druidstone. Even in the crystal light of an Andean afternoon, there is a distinct eeriness about this remote and little-visited place – as if the rocks not only carried stories, but memories also; as if its extraordinary beauty had to be tempered and haunted with a measure of human sadness, or even tragedy. It reminds me of that essay by Camus called 'Helen's Exile' – he's such a fine essayist (if you want to borrow the book, it's in a shelf on the right as you go into my workroom): 'if the Greeks experienced despair, it was always through beauty and its oppressive quality. Tragedy, in this golden sadness, reaches its highest point.'[21]

Whatever the reason, I hurried away from it by the little, lonely tracks that led down towards the settlement of Challabamba, an inquisitive cow leaning over the wall of its small field to greet me as I arrived, and felt glad to be back there among domesticity and cultivation and the more customary and amiable strangenesses of Bolivia again.

Reading through this letter at a seven-year distance, something about its restraint, its detachment, the sombre preoccupations given that this comes from a man who is also joyful at being reunited with his lost love, suggest to me at another level a subliminal awareness of something of what was to come. Even at this stage, a part of me was uneasy, fretting at any straightforward progress into assured futurity. I think I already knew that for us there was no for ever, knew by instinct how ill Jac already was, and that love between us would again, differently, tragically, lead to loss.

At Epiphany, before I'd set out for Bolivia, I'd gone for a long, circular walk in the Shropshire hill country – close and easy of access to Llanrhaeadr, and that winter the lodestone place that was drawing me to re-explore. It's the landscape of Mary Webb's novels – the fashionable fiction writer of the 1920s, her bleak and tortured tales of women victims in cruel emotional landscapes tuning in somehow to the zeitgeist. The feminist publisher Virago gave her a second run in the 1980s, but her austere settings, passive heroines and lack of explicit sex and shopping failed to stir much interest then among a more cosmopolitan readership. Bruce Chatwin plagiarized her (as well as Hardy and D. H. Lawrence) extensively in his novel *On the Black Hill*, but since none of his reviewers had read her, none of them noticed. I'd come to her over forty years before because the second-hand bookseller at the bottom of John Dalton Street in Manchester, with whom I was friendly and who was kind towards me in my teens, suggested I should; because you couldn't pick up a volume of Hardy for threepence; and because there is, in her communicated sense of place and its effect on peoples' lives, an economical literary skill that I can still reread with pleasure. From Chirbury, through Priest Weston by way of Whittery Bridge across the Camlad gorge – the names in this part of Shropshire, in their mingling of the Celtic and the Saxon, are an unending source of puzzlement and delight – I drove to park on the broad heath saddle between Corndon and Stapeley Hills, then climbed the snow-covered flank of the former. It has an Ordnance Survey pillar and Bronze Age cairn – there are five of these in total around the perimeter of the plateau, the north-easternmost an extraordinary triple-chambered construction into which I clambered to shelter from a sharp-toothed bitter assassin of an east wind. Along the horizon to the west as I sipped tea from my flask were the ridges of Pumlumon, Cader Idris, Aran and Berwyn, rising from haze into crystal air. I plunged down the craggy slope of Corndon, through White Grit to Squilver Farm and through the mining country where lead was extracted for the shot used in the Napoleonic and Crimean wars, over the ridge to Nipstone Rock on the Stiperstones, capped and crested along its most dramatic section by shattered tors of quartzite, their faces black-crannied, blocks and shards lying everywhere about like innumerable white jagged tombstones among the cowberry and the heather. Even the popular ridgeway is a hard and stumbling track to follow; the weekend strollers limped slowly along it and sought relief from their labour by scrambling up steep rock to the high point of the Devil's

Chair. Here's how Mary Webb describes it in *The Golden Arrow*:

> a mass of quartzite, blackened and hardened by unaccountable ages. The scattered rocks, the rugged holly-brakes on the lower slopes were like small carved lions beside the marble steps of a stupendous throne. Nothing ever altered its look. Dawn quickened over it in pearl and emerald; summer sent the armies of heather to its very foot; snow rested there as doves nest in cliffs. It remained inviolable, taciturn, evil. It glowered darkly on the dawn; it came through the snow like jagged bones through flesh; before its hardness even the venturesome cranberries were discouraged. For miles around in the plains, the valleys, the mountain dwellings it was feared. It drew the thunder, people said. Storms broke round it suddenly out of a clear sky; it seemed almost as if it created storm. No one cared to cross the range near it after dark – when the black grouse laughed sardonically and the cry of a passing curlew shivered like broken glass.

The uneasy mood of the place finds expression in Shropshire's own version of the European folktale motif of The Wild Hunt – led in its incarnation here by an eleventh-century Mercian thane who has transmuted into Wild Edric. With his scaly-tailed demon band, to view which is to die, he shrieks, howls, swarms and swoops over the Stiperstones to signify impending war. Not wishing to encounter this despairing vision, distraught at Blair's and Bush's clear current intentions towards Iraq, with the sun westering and making all the miniature globes of ice embroidered into the heather glint like pearls, I slipped by icy paths down into Mytton Dingle, jogged along footpaths through spinneys of holly, and oak from which the trailing mistletoe hung down, into the old lead-mining region again and over to Shelve. The Hope Valley, into which I descended, was deeply shadowed, and the Bronze Age circle of the Hoarstones barely discernible against the dark hill. Through boggy conifer plantations that squeeze wealth for investors out of soured ground, I gained the bridle-way along Stapeley Hill. Frost-diamonds feathered the quiffs of blond grass and caught at the afterlight. The day was fading fast, the snowy track a glimmer. Corndon Hill's great bulk ahead, I raced along in gathering night, hill-shapes and the creak of my footsteps across the snow for company, skated across frozen flashes, and came to the dip in the hill called Mitchell's Fold. In it is a stone circle dating perhaps as far back as 2000 BC. I stood there in the night, leaning against a restraining upright, looking up at the stars. To the south, silvery, rose the thinnest sickle moon, cradling Venus, and after this arduous day of passage through the dark moods of landscape it filled me with joy. When I returned home, Jacquetta phoned and I spilled all this out to her in what had become our habitual night-time conversation. At the other end of the phone I heard her warm pensive chuckle before she signed off with a whispered phrase as my head was dipping towards the pillow: 'There's my man!'

This, I think, was the point at which our connection was truly re-established, through a mutual sense of the symbolic journey and its concluding vision. She intuited what I was

communicating elliptically in describing all this, and it gave
her peace. I was very wary – of women in general, and even
of Jacquetta. Bitter experience in the years of long separation
had taken its toll, and her mysterious disappearance had been
a lingering hurt. But beyond Epiphany, mistrust was giving place to a growing sense of harmony. As the snows of
February melted from the high barrier between us, her visits
to my house became more frequent. On my birthday at the end
of March I came back from having dinner with Mavis at the
West Arms in Llanarmon Dyffryn Ceiriog to find Jacquetta's
car parked by the house, to which for the last couple of months
she had had a key. Inside all was silence. From the bottom of
the winding loft stair I heard her giggling softly to herself. I
climbed the stair. The room was lit by candles, two glasses and
a bottle of chilled champagne on the bedside table. She threw
back the covers and lay there naked, looking at me, with a red
ribbon tied into a bow and braided into the dark hair between
her thighs.

'Happy Birthday! I'm your present, and it's about time for
this. Come here, and give me some weight.'

And so I undressed and slipped in beside her.

'I'm getting very fond of you, you know,' I growled at her
defensively.

'Oh, you *man*! Why don't you just say what you mean,
which is that you're falling in love with me again. Because I
can tell, and I am with you. So it's all right.'

She didn't leave in the dawn. The morning sun streamed
down through the skylight on to her hair. I lay next to her as
she slept, looked at her in a state of wonderment, and the
barriers I had set up between us over the last few months

evaporated. Increasingly now, we were together, and if for whatever reason we had to spend time apart, the phone calls took up more and more of the night, or even the briefest meetings were planned. Once I had been down to Radnor Forest – despite conifer plantation and the Euro-grant-aided incursions of farming across its lower slopes, still one of the finest moorland areas south of the Scottish Border. There were golden eagles here as late as the 1940s. The last wildcats (proper *Felix Sylvestris*, not feral domestic cats) in Wales were shot here by 'sportsmen' in the early 1900s. All the insignificant small harbingers were telling of spring. The little celandines were open in shafts of sunlight along the banks of the stream, wood anemones gave off their foxy scent. Bright yellowy-green flower-cups of the wood spurge were vivid against their older, dark foliage. I bent to snuff in the sharp, sweet hyacinth scent of the year's first bluebells. Long-tailed tits flitted about restlessly, stripping dry moss from the walls to line hidden and intricately woven nests. By a plantation of larch, pale delicacy of the young sprays opened out along all their graceful, drooping branches. Sheep bickered across the moor beyond and called to their lambs on smooth sward around isolated trees of rowan and birch. Lonely thorns and wind-seeded spruce broke up a monotony of heather, sun glistened on the new growth of bilberry, a raven called distantly. I walked the rim of Harley Dingle. Two ravens flew out noisily from their nest on Great Creigiau and mobbed a hen harrier that continued to ghost unperturbed down the valley. Fox scats and the grey pellets of short-eared owls, tiny bones of voles and mice obvious within them, were scattered across the turf. In the valley beneath, peach tones of bracken slopes contrasted with umber of the heather. A cold wind sprang up. Metal signs warned against straying from the path, for most of Harley Dingle is occupied by a munitions testing range – commercial, not MoD – and the signs advised that live shells may be lying around. Gimcrack buildings, targets and brutal roads scarred the ground, untouched now by the sun. I descended into the valley of the shadow of death, wondering where the rounds tested here ended up, whether any of them had been responsible for those dreadful injuries to Iraqi innocents that had dominated the news for weeks, and whether any of them had been exported to enable the Iraqis to defend their land, commerce knowing no side but profit. I thought of George Bernard Shaw's visit to Radnorshire: 'One day... as he stood gazing at the surrounding hills, so accessible and yet so solitary, with arms outstretched he suddenly exclaimed: "No man ought to be in the government of this land who does not spend three months every year in such country as this."' I wondered what effect this landscape might have on Tony Blair, and with a sense of nausea at how he and every other politician would justify the continuance of a weapons-testing range in one of the loveliest places in our lost land.

Beyond a plank bridge set high above the stream in the dingle, a path branched along the margins of a wood and led back to Newgate Lane in New Radnor. A woman – the first person I'd seen walking all day – and a friendly dog came along it and exchanged greetings. The blackthorn was in blossom, recalling William Cobbett's peerless description:

> It is a remarkable fact that there is always, that is every
> year of our lives, a spell of cold and angry weather just

at the time this hardy little tree is in bloom. The country people call it the *Black Thorn winter* and thus it has been called, I dare say, by all the inhabitants of this island, from generation to generation, for a thousand years.[22]

I wondered what straightforward, radical old Cobbett, the 'wandering and single-handed champion for those on whom corruption feeds', would have made of our times, of their 'spin', duplicity, ulterior motives? All these depressive thoughts put me in need of my woman. I phoned her, we arranged to meet at a pub near her house, and from there went on to the Romany Bridge across the Afon Alwen. It was close to dusk as we walked down through an oakwood where the bladed leaves of the bluebells were already rising among the leaf litter and the moss. A shot badger lay across the path, the air pungent with its decay. We slithered down a steep shaly crag to a shingle bank by this prettiest of little rivers, which flows down from Mynydd Hiraethog – the moors of longing.

'I often come here,' she told me, 'to sleep out or just to be somewhere quiet. Once I fell right down the way we've just come and broke my coccyx…'

'What did you do..?'

'I just rolled a couple of spliffs to ease the pain, then crawled back up again.'

I remember us talking of the disturbing savagery of images of war we had both been seeing; I remember a little owl flying down to a branch within a foot of where we sat, so near we might have touched it. I remember the strength I could feel in her large hands. The moon rose and the stream flowed on. It became cold, frost sparkling in the moonlight. We held very close to each other, drank wine and broke bread in what for both of us seemed to signify an act of communion. We had entered a world of ritual, of symbols to which we were both equally and unspokenly attuned. Eventually, it being too cold to stay any longer, we climbed the bank again, drove back to where she'd left her car, said our farewells and departed for our separate homes. This shared experience gave the pattern to what brought us most delight throughout the coming two years – to be together, in an intensely experienced way, among the quiet places of the hills and coasts. It seems so simple, but this is what we came to live for, and what we sought at every opportunity. The first night we spent under the stars happened towards the end of the same week, and this time we slept out through the bitter April cold, sharing a sleeping bag, in the dunes north of Harlech where we listened to the waves, watched the stars wheel above us all night, our bodies so gently intertwined, so perfectly fitted together, that I could not distinguish between us, felt as though we had merged into a single being. And so, in a way, we had.

9

Idyll

One sunny May morning in Llanrhaeadr I was drinking my breakfast coffee on the bench at the front of the house, aware that the constant smile on my face was the widest I'd ever worn, when my neighbour Brian, a poet – his birthday the same as mine, he nineteen years older to the day – stopped on his way over to Glenda's shop, and I asked him whether every spring was like this one as we journey through life, always more perfect than the last?

'Every one more glorious,' he replied, 'an added brilliance with every year that passes.'

As he walked away a pang of sadness throbbed behind the sense of present happiness. I was due that day to drive up to the hospice in Lancaster where my dear friend Annette Mortlock lay dying. I had been visiting her for the last year – in a Preston hospital when she'd first been diagnosed with cancer; in the Lyth Valley in the South Lakes when, post-operatively and with the disease apparently in remission, she'd been allowed home; and now in the hospice where she lay with her belly swollen with ascites, unable to keep down food, nearing the end, with her daughters and husband and friends around her. As I drove up to Lancaster later that morning, through hissing squalls of hail on the motorway, arcing rainbows, bright spasms of sunlight, I thought with a sense of indignation of the clumsiness and arrogance of the medical treatment and changing diagnoses visited upon her, its contrast to the gentle assiduities of her nursing care through the same time, and her calm, wry acceptance of both. I thought too of the gifts Annette had bestowed through the decades of our knowing each other: of friendship, love, happiness, knowledge, an attentive reverence for what Simone Weil so beautifully terms 'the plenitude of being'. The most perfect clematis I've ever seen was in full, cascading bloom outside the French windows of her little ward in the hospice. She joked with me about the quality of her hotels having improved of late – the Preston hospital had been very dour and lacking, didn't even allow flowers, the nurses being too busy to put them in vases. I'd taken her white tulips, so pure; sat holding her hand, following the dancing of a still-clear mind, and it was a benediction. 'I've spent my whole life in a bubble of happiness,' she told me, reassuring, not wanting others to be anguished by her going, 'and I'm still in there, safe. No need to worry about me. I'm all right...'

She asked me about Jacquetta, of my connection with whom she had known years before, by my reunion with whom she was thrilled, making a laughing-solemn point of giving us her blessing though she knew she would not see us together, holding out even in her last days grace for futurity. Annette taught me as much – and in a woman's way, not dogmatically, but by example, by the kindly ellipses of commentary, and by her joy in things – as anyone I ever knew. When we first met I was working as an outdoor pursuits instructor at the City of Oxford Education Committee's outdoor centre in Glasbury-on-Wye in the mid-1960s. I was little more than a schoolchild myself at the time, and yet was trusted to adventure in the outdoors with groups of schoolchildren only a few years younger than myself, trusted to enthuse them, challenge them, and bring them safely back. In truth, I was the one who was being educated, and Annette, busy as she then was with her own young family, the new daughters arriving by the year, played a crucial part in this. She would attend to what I was doing, enquire around values, add in her stock of wise enjoyment and scientifically-detailed but awed and excited appreciation of the natural world that, as a biologist, was her domain. I might see, for example, a delicate fern glistening with spray on the Silurian rocks by the secret waterfall high in the recesses of the Bach Howey gorge whilst traversing through with a group from the centre, come back and describe it to her – in which process her attentive, eager questioning would alert me to what I should be seeing, was a lesson in itself – and then the fern book would be laid out among the children's colouring books on the kitchen table and avidly, excitedly, she'd scan through, enthusiastically offer possibilities, whoop with pleasure when the right one presented itself. And my store of knowledge would be augmented, my enthusiasm kindled, as happens in contact with the best teachers. The conversations we had in her last months, in the hospital, in her brief respite at home, in the hospice, had that same quality of animated absorption in the greater world of outside and expressed also her great gift for friendship. In a piece in celebration of Annette after her passing, I wrote the following:

> I love the way that women are, their difference, the subtleties of their approach, the way they move through the world, the things you learn from them in the quality of their absorption in the natural environment – in which, somehow, they seem at a lesser remove, more nearly a part. I see the men out on the fells, hurrying, hurrying, pressing through, acquisitive, eyes intent on goal and summit and the completion of lists, itineraries, records. And I think of my own lover, whom I've known joyfully and lifelong, and the times we have spent outside my house in the moonlight, in the dawn, sitting on the bench, hearing the birdsong inviting the day, watching the slow pearling of the sky. I think of her responses, whose art is all colour and vibrancy and light, as simple and heartfelt as the swell of love itself; of her quick glance up at the first sailing sickle moon of May when we glimpsed it from the stone circle of the fairy cow, her beautiful face shining with rapture. And under this bright moon that translates all to longing, in the spring that is birth-essence of the world, I know the otherness of the essential feminine and am enthralled, become again captivated by all the knowledge that Annette has imparted over the long years of our friendship. How few the men who've given me any sense of this, and how special; how slow and sensuous in their loving response to

the world, how gentle. Bill Condry is the only one who seems truly to inhabit here.[23] I think of his hands uxorious among the mountain vegetation, the January saxifrage, discreet in their explorations; moments of vision flood in, of him and his wife Penny in their garden, the regard between them focused on nurtured bloom, he watching, attending, as the love flowed through her. Women's rapture in creation – their capacity to lose themselves in the natural world in ways that our men's minds disallow, from which we are kept apart – it is so beautiful a thing.

All this is summary – is certainly to try to define something Annette communicated and embodied through the long years of our friendship, but it is also a musing on what Jacquetta was now bringing to my life, an acknowledgement of the transformational grammars of love, to which strange sickness I had clearly and gladly now fallen prey. Another extract, again from early May, little more than a month from when Jacquetta had first come to my bed in Llanrhaeadr, tells me how indissociable love and landscape had become:

Today... I drove up to the cataract that falls from my home hills, where I'd last stood at Beltane with my lover and been absorbed through her into the flow and the pulse of the world. Solitary on a May evening now, I walked up into the valley of the little Afon Disgynfa above, the bushed oak and the alder along the stream like green flame, boulders relief-mapped in quartz, coloured by lichen, forested with moss in a way so subtle and understated as to render more stridently offensive the dark, alien and regimented conifers with which men had patched the opposite hill-slopes, their spirit defaulting to rule and cash return. On a rock-bluff a raven had left the scapula of a lamb, paper-light, picked clean. Beyond, stone row led through masking rushes into stone circle like some rigid and barely-comprehending celebration of birth-canal and womb. Here on the moor of the graves are two other stone circles – one to which few go; another unmarked and unknown, to which no one ventures unless they stumble across it by accident, and then, troubled by its atmosphere, they hasten away. I climbed the hill above, black-braided and unopened buds of cotton grass waving across its flank, came down by way of Llyn Lluncaws, the cheese-shaped lake whose surface was mauve tonight, and stippled with the leaves of bogbean and circles of small, rising trout. There was a glimmer all along the twilit green track. By the time I reached the valley, the full moon, freed from cloud, was sailing across the sky, silvering the springtime world, the stream singing and flashing in its goddess-light. And I felt so glad, privileged and grateful for the friendship of good women, for their love, and the knowledge they bring.

In all this flow of feeling the central event had been the evening with Jacquetta at Ffynnon Fair, the cliff well at Pen Llŷn, when after a day of torrential rain the clouds had cleared from the west and the world had gleamed. The offshore island,

Ynys Enlli, seemed to float in a sea of light, behind it a west-ering sun. The sound between us and the island, the roaring tide race of which at times could be terrifying, glimmered with a satin sheen of slack water. The soft swell licked lazily up low, black cliffs that we had traversed to gain the well. A seal swam up to inspect us, a raven and a chough flew close by:

'There are our witnesses,' she said.

'Witnesses for what?' I asked, characteristically obtuse where Jac's mysterious thought processes were concerned.

'For our marriage,' she grinned, 'look – I made this for you.'

She held out her hand and in the palm was a plain, untarnished silver ring. I looked at it, mystified, and in my hopeless, bookish way, at which she so perpetually teased, by which at times she could be quite exasperated – 'Just *look*,' she would say, 'don't always live out of a book!' – came out with a quotation from my favourite chapter of Stevenson – 'As if to be more like a pedlar, I wear a silver ring' – and felt pleased and curious and puzzled as she slipped the ring on to my finger, which it fitted perfectly and where it remains to this day.

'This is a place that's naturally holy, here are our spiritual familiars for witnesses...'

At this point I swear that the seal bobbing up and down in the waves ten feet away gave me a broad wink of one of those dark and deep-set eyes.

'... and here we can make our vows to each other and then we'll be married and you'll be my husband and the ring will keep the witches away. You can find one for me too. It will appear when it's ready. Now think of what you're going to promise me, and tell me, then I will you, and that will be our wedding, properly pagan and always to be honoured – break it and your heart's dead!'

At that she kissed me fiercely, threw her head back and looked wildly into my eyes. We were silent and pensive together, and when we were ready, we spoke from our hearts to each other, and the seal listened and the raven and chough cried in acknowledgement, and we slipped naked together into the cold waves where she supported me for the water was deep and I'm a poor swimmer, and we emerged dripping on to the rocks by the well and she spread clothes across their roughness and anxiously, passionately, drew me down and took me inside her.

'... and now it's consummated, you see, so we're properly married, and if we stay faithful and true to one another always we'll become an angel together when we're dead, and a perfect union of man and woman, which is what an angel is.'

We huddled into our clothes as the evening grew chill.

'Well, husband,' she explained, 'this is the only proper marriage for us, you know. Civil contracts are meaningless, worse than nothing because always on one side or the other there's blackmail or force or some other bad thing. In church it might be all right, if you believe, but this is our church. Here...'

She looked around and talked on in her wild, laughing way, her red hair dark with the salt.

'Once before I was married, you know. To Gypsy Jed. His family lived in a caravan down a lane on the other side of the golf course above Kendal and my mother told me I wasn't to go there. We were both seven or maybe eight. What you had to do to marry if you were a gypsy was both piss in the same pot, so we did that, and then we were married. But I could divorce him, you see, because it was never consummated. We started out as the virgin and the gypsy and we stayed that way.'

'How did you divorce him?'

'I pissed in the same pot we'd used by myself, and took it out in the garden on a night with no moon and poured it over the monkshood. Then the bond is broken. Which ours can never be now...'

I have a card – one of my most treasured possessions – that she sent me during this week – 'Dear Husband, Blessings on our Beltane union, from your loving wife Jacquetta'. On the front of it is one of her own paintings, perhaps seven inches square, beautifully executed, delicately coloured. It's a nude self-portrait, her face turned in profile, the scale reduced. She is sitting legs akimbo in a vivid mother-of-pearl shell, its nacreous sheen picking up on the red of her hair. The pose captures perfectly her slender strength and elegance, the perfection of her breasts, the expression of rapture that was never far from her features. In each hand, the colour exactly and miraculously achieved, she holds bluebells large in relative terms as small trees. It's a dream-picture from fairyland, and that is where her presence and conversation and startling fancies continually took me. Back in Llanrhaeadr after our wedding, late at night, we sat on the bench and drank champagne and felt the spirits flit along the silent streets.

'You are,' she told me, in her serious and considered rather than playful and imaginative tone, 'exactly what you want yourself to be, and you must always be mindful of that and be the best that you can be.'

Throughout this spring Will was away on extended

climbing trips to the Czech Republic and Baja California, from which places I'd get occasional laconic emails and postcards:

> This is the tower we climbed yesterday – a fairly horrendous splitter off-width on its front face first climbed by a party of five in 1956! The towns, Teplice and Adripasske, are beautiful, as are most of the Czech and Polish women. About forty of them – students – have turned up at our campsite. Unfortunately I have huge scabs on my fists and ankles [from the crack-climbing]. They have challenged us to a football match this evening, which should be interesting. See you end of May-ish. Love, Will.

Jacquetta and I too seemed perpetually on the move – retreating into our work for short, intense sessions and then sallying forth in the fine spring weather with each other again. Often she would drive over the moor in the early evening having finished work for the day, and bound barefoot into my house – from April to October on principle she never wore shoes – embrace and kiss and nuzzle at me like some exuberant and mischievous puppy and roust me out from my study to drive the few miles down-valley to the Horseshoe Inn at Llanyblodwel. This ancient, crooked, primitive little pub by the Tanat river became an intensely pleasant habit for us that spring. There was an ash tree overhanging the water where the two of us could sit in the curve of a branch, beneath an ever-densening canopy of feathery leaves that were opening from dark buds and caught the late sunlight as it slanted down-valley. Sometimes Dennis, the landlord, would pass by, rod in hand ready to cast a fly into the dark eddies upstream, and would look on us fondly in our riparian perch and give us an evening greeting. I'd be sent off to buy Guinness – my shoes had been confiscated by now and I had to trek barefoot and gingerly across the gravel of the car park – whilst Jac installed herself in the tree, and I would come back and watch the river flow with her, and rafts of water crowfoot gently undulate in the current and the trout dart from under the bank. The white limestone rocks on the river bed had taken on a jade tinge and sometimes Jac would point at one and ask me to lift it out for her, its luminous colour fading as it slipped from water to air.

Sometimes she would phone me in the afternoon and tell me to pick her up at a certain time from the end of her lane and we would drive west on to the Lleyn Peninsula. One night we found a perfect little balconied hollow, sheltered and unseen, in the sandy cliffs above Porth Neigwl – Hells Mouth its English name – and lay there through the night, making love to the sound and gentle rhythm of the waves, watching the moon sail across the sky, feeling the soft rain on our skin, waking to the bay empty and sunlit below and the white surf curling in. In the daylight, in this 'good morrow to our waking soules' there was something resplendent above us as our eyes faltered open. We registered it, turned to each other in affirmation, and back, wordless, to the brightness again. It was no more than the grass of the overhanging dune transmuted by some alchemy of the rising sun to a silvering against the azure. Yet it was visionary, breath-stilling. Later that same morning, walking the beach at Porth Oer, rippled sand under the small waves caught her attention. I glanced at her beautiful face. It was all radiance and joy, 'For love, all love of other sights controls.'[24] The quality of her attention was teaching me to see. Donne's line is astute. There is an extraordinary intensity of seeing in the shared experience of love. The world then offers up its beauties to you beatifically. Towards the end of his life the philosopher Bertrand Russell wrote, in the prologue to his autobiography, that:

> I have sought love, first, because it brings ecstasy – ecstasy so great that I would often have sacrificed all the rest of life for a few hours of this joy. I have sought it next, because it relieves loneliness – that terrible loneliness in which one shivering consciousness looks over the rim of the world into the cold unfathomable lifeless abyss. I have sought it, finally, because in the union of love I have seen, in a mystic miniature, the prefiguring vision of the heaven that saints and poets have imagined. This is what I have sought, and though it might seem too good for human life, this is what – at last – I have found.[25]

We each have our own versions of this experience, some disappointed, some hurt, others heartfelt, positive and hopeful. Russell is surely referring elliptically here to those same transformative grammars of love to which Donne alludes. By them, we come to fresh ways of seeing. The energy of love is that of clear-sightedness, perception, joy, all imperfection filtered out by the desire absolutely to share. Through its agency, the world is enhanced, and by its lasting and growing is affirmed.

Perhaps the adrenalin passages in the 'Reach Out Your

Hand' chapter offer a reductive explanation for this. But this seems to me only a small part of a picture complete anyhow without it. Of course lovers run on adrenalin – the excitement of meeting, the extremity of joy, the fear of non-mutuality or loss, the extraordinary rapture of becoming one loving flesh – and hence you can at one level reasonably conclude that lovers are tripping. All that heightened awareness, all the exquisite sensation, the joy – put it down to naturally occurring bodily chemicals. Jacquetta and I certainly knew that the means, whether acid or adrenalin-experiences, that we had formerly used to reach this state were unnecessary, no more than a shortcut to a place at which we now continually arrived without them. Thomas Merton's most authoritative biographer, in the 'Kanchenjunga' chapter of *The Seven Mountains of Thomas Merton*, conveys the point:

> Talking about the use of drugs and their capacity to induce mystical or such-like experiences, Merton said that he never really felt the need to use LSD. A cup of coffee after the usual period of prayer and meditation... was often enough to turn him on.[26]

For Jacquetta and myself, the simple *being* among scenes of natural beauty had come to be both prayer and meditation – and if the little spirit stove made the kettle-lid clack away and the steam rise like fragrance from a censer, a shared cup of coffee in the outdoors for us was sacrament enough. What we experienced in this blessed period is perfectly defined by Stevenson in his 'A Night among the Pines' chapter from *Travels with a Donkey*: '...we have escaped out of the Bastille of civilisation, and are become, for the time being, a mere kindly animal and a sheep of Nature's flock.'[27] Both Jac and I had a natural capacity present even in childhood to still ourselves dreamingly in the outdoors and be at one, be in harmony, and responsive to the bright particularity of things – the blue flame of a bluebell wood, the curl of rosetted lichen on a sunlit rock. I suppose, sadly, that it is not so for everyone, and even those, like Wordsworth, who did once thrill to 'the visionary gleam... the glory and the dream', can forego it, allow the societally desired and egotistically desirable to displace it, covet carriages and cars and kudos, and lose sight.

> Ah, as the heart grows older
> It will come to such sights colder
> By and by, nor spare a sigh
> Though worlds of wanwood leafmeal lie[28]

It need not, though. Hopkins's Goldengrove may be 'unleaving', but as Jac and I were finding, spring can come again thereafter, of the world and of the heart, and due process continues of the seasons and all their signs and beauties. For this reason, together, we craved continually to be outdoors and witnessing:

Night is a dead and monotonous period under a roof; but in the open world it passes lightly, with its stars and dews and perfumes, and the hours are marked by changes in the face of Nature. What seems a kind of temporal death to people choked between walls and curtains, is only a light and living slumber to [those] who sleep afield. All night long [they] can hear Nature breathing deeply and freely; even as she takes her rest, she turns and smiles; and there is one stirring hour unknown to those who dwell in houses, when a wakeful influence goes abroad over the sleeping hemisphere... Cattle awake on the meadows; sheep break their fast on dewy hillsides, and change to a new lair among the ferns; and houseless men, who have lain down with the fowls, open their dim eyes and behold the beauty of the night.[29]

Or of the dawn, at any of the outdoor places Jacquetta and I would choose to rest. To see a world informed by light. Illuminated. As you may see a mountain, illuminated, the gold ridge against the grey cloud: '...there seem to be certain constants which all cultures have found beautiful: among them – certain flowers, trees, forms of rock, birds, animals, the moon, running water'.[30] Each of them, in each moment of witness, is individuated, gleaming still in memory. In these first months with Jacquetta I listed once these significant moments of beauty – odd male tic that it is to do so – as they had occurred in my life: the snipe that once nestled in my palm at Soar y Mynydd; the ginger fox by the women's well at Pen Llŷn; an arctic wolf strolling unconcerned through camp on the Kent Peninsula in the High Arctic; the shimmer on the sea from the cliff-top path at Druidstone Haven; the raven with the intense violet aura that communicated with me at closest distance for minutes; the rafts of water crowfoot undulating on the clear water of the Afon Tanat; an avocet stalking down gravel banks of a stream through Tapovan, the high meadow above the source of the Ganges from which rises the perfect ice-spire of Shivling; the seal's benign curiosity and the chough's pealing call in witness as Jacquetta and I exchanged vows.

'Everything that lives is holy', wrote Blake. What my mind spins on in recollection of this time is that through our sense of the numinous quality in creation our consciousness became more attuned to natural beauty, and our gladness was thus continually amplified. The principle, the lesson, still holds. All else but this bright particularity, and the loving attentiveness, the reverent consideration for the whole world we inhabit that it elicits from us, is surely nugatory, fading, unfulfilled?

This renewing was Jacquetta's gift to me, from her essential gladness of spirit. On the first of our many honeymoons I had picked her up from the end of the lake at Bala and we drove together down to Druidstone Haven in Pembrokeshire. In the grounds of a charming, old-fashioned hotel there she had told me of a round, stone-built croquet pavilion converted into an eco-cottage right on the cliff top with windows looking out panoramically on to St Brides Bay, Ramsey Island, and the South Bishop lighthouse on its remote rock. I'd felt how tired she was, urged her to a break. 'Get the Roundhouse and I'll take a week off,' she'd agreed. I'd phoned. There was a cancellation. She hadn't believed I would have been able to book it for a year or more, and was overjoyed. On our way down through drenching, fitful showers she opened the sunroof of the Citroën, reclined her seat, gazed up laughing at the grey sky and picked out every shred of blue to bring to my attention: 'Enough of it now to make a sailor a pair of trousers...' There was a log fire and a deep zinc tub with water heated by solar panels that began to gurgle as the sun rose. The hotel bar sold Guinness, the bed was soft and huge, at night the beam of the lighthouse stretched like elastic across the water and rebounded again. She told me she was in heaven, concentrated continually on the changing light upon the sea. 'The shimmer,' she would mouth to herself quietly, 'the shimmer,' and I would tease back at her with it, point out where every new shaft of sunlight seeded on the water. But in truth the shimmer was now everywhere, and everything we saw was infused with the new intensity of its light.

If I were to attempt to describe every one of the experiences we shared in the natural world during this spring season, it would become like an illuminated psalter, each account a hymn to some new aspect of natural beauty, and to her beauty as it reflected there. The ease and the joy were a continual rapture. We came to a state of such mutual ease that there was seldom need for words. Her hand was in mine, and the world was perfect. Will came back from the Czech Republic and in the brief time before he went out to America met Jac in Llanrhaeadr. I watched in delighted, silent astonishment as he – always so reticent and wary where women were concerned – opened to her, was confiding, close, affectionate. 'Your dad loves you, you know,' she told him. He laughed, put his arm around her and hugged her. 'I know that,' he said, 'and he loves you too – anyone can see that, so you two take care of each other whilst I'm away.'

Spring passed into summer. One Saturday afternoon early in July Jac arrived at Manchester House, the day was fine, and we thought to head down to what for me had long been one of the habitual places – one about which I'd told Jac and to which I'd often gravitated, where I'd slept out over the years on innumerable occasions. It's in Radnorshire, my favourite among the old Welsh counties, the quietest of them, sweetest of memories, secluded somehow, with soft green and rounded hills and wide horizons unlike those of any other part of the country. Here, in the crook of the Wye where it flows down from Builth then veers around easterly to pass Hay and head out of the high country for Hereford, is an insignificant group of hills looking across to the Black Mountains southerly and the Brecon Beacons to the west. These little hills are called The Begwns. Among them is a pool above the farm of Gogia created nearly fifty years ago to regularize its water supply. It has yet to appear on any Ordnance Survey maps, but it now looks entirely natural. Surrounded by a copse of Scots pine, the trees nearest to its margin are dead, their roots drowned. We drove the sixty or so miles there, stopped at an odd and old-fashioned pub of crannies and mirrors by the cattle mart in Builth for Jac's Guinness, and then by Hundred House and the hill road from Rhulen and through Painscastle up on to the high, open common of The Begwns. I found the tortuous green track along which you arrive at the pool and we lurched across its dips and gullies to park hidden from view among the drowned pines. The stump of a grey willow in the water itself was putting forth strong shoots, with leaves silver-felted on their undersides that gleamed in late sunlight. Bulrushes at the shallow end of the lake blended into a collage of green and copper and tawny and chocolate, round their bases the stems of reeds slipped on crystal capillary rings. It was absolutely still, not a breath of wind to stir the surface of the water. I put up the little green tent we'd taken to using on recent damp excursions, even though the weather was clear and calm, and unrolled a sleeping bag inside it. Jac had grown to like this tent – its colour, its small-scale elegance and the shelter and privacy it afforded – and it was an old favourite of mine. We sat quietly outside it for a time and watched moorhens busy around and a pair of tufted ducks glide and dive, lost to view at times in the low sun's dappling reflection. Swifts skimmed the water, leaving little spreading ripples as they drank in flight, then soaring and hawking in screeching pursuit of insects. As they tore past the willow stump, a tiny goldcrest alighted there and wheezed its native protest. I gathered sticks, of which there were always plenty in this place, cut a square in the turf, made a hearth around it with stones, lit a fire and, when the bed of charcoal was glowing, set on it the wooden-handled frying pan I'd used for these occasions since Will was tiny. We ate, opened a bottle of wine, tended the fire so that the flames crackled and leaped and the resinous wood spat and sent the sparks whirling high. A nightjar was churring away, its pale form just visible, from a tree by the boundary wall of the farmland beyond the end of the pool. Jac lit a candle, placed it against one of the drowned trunks, and its flame rose unwavering there, the bark texture beautiful in its illumination. We talked late into the night. She told me of her happiness, of how for years she had felt that to be allowed to live until just this month – July 2003 – had been her continual prayer, her bargain with fate. Now it was here, she confided her fear – that she would be kept to the bargain, when she had finally found a reason to want to carry on living. I wrapped my arms around her in reassurance. The embers of the fire still glowed outside the tent as we subsided into sleep.

In the bright morning she slept late. I scraped the charcoal together, blew it into life and piled more twigs on until the flames leaped once more, fried eggs, cut and buttered bread, laced it with her favourite HP sauce, made coffee, roused her gently. She rolled on her front, butter and egg yolk running down her chin as she ate, and we spent the morning and most of the afternoon simply looking at the close textures of landscape.

In the shrine alongside me as I write this is a small fused-glass panel she made to express the pool, the round hill, the latticing of weed in the water and the pouring bright holiness of its light. We left this sanctified place with regret and drove home slowly, her hand in mine, scarcely a word spoken between us. In Llanrhaeadr I cooked while she showered and changed. She came downstairs in a short, pale-grey skirt of denim-like material that showed off her tanned, slim legs to perfection, and a turquoise top. I looked at her and thought I had never seen her more beautiful – the elegance of her figure, the glow on her face. She teased me when I refused to let her help with dinner. As twilight came she sat at the table and rolled up her sundowner, poured a glass of wine, set out through the door for our churchyard moon-watching seat at the base of the old square tower.

From the door as I followed her out, I saw her skip on to the low wall around the forecourt, glass and joint held out. The round rock on to which she'd bounded rolled away, she landed on her side on the stones that remained with a crunching thud. I ran to her. The red wine had spattered across her skirt, her face was contorted in agony. Somehow we got her back in the house and on to the sofa. Two of her left ribs were shattered, their splintered ends visible beneath the skin of her back. In that shocking instant, the brief and carefree season of unfettered joy we had shared came to its abrupt and unforeseeable end.

BOOK FOUR

Life, dismantled

10

Carity

Though Jacquetta to me was the best of women, she was certainly the worst of patients. She had no truck with invalidity for herself, every sympathy and concern where it was demanded by others – a compassionate quality of which many took ceaseless and selfish advantage. I picked her up, carried her into the house concerned that any movement might worsen her injury, and laid her down on the big white sofa, propping her up with cushions into the most comfortable position.

'Let me take you into casualty,' I pleaded.

'No you fucking don't,' she snapped, pain giving rare liberty to temper and sharp language. 'Do you know what they'd do? They'll X-ray me to find out what I already know, then tell me to go home and take an aspirin – they don't even bother strapping ribs up any more in case it causes pleurisy and pneumonia. And for that we'd have driven sixty miles there and back. What I need...' the colour and animation were back in her face, and the impudent grin she'd always wear when she'd decided that the best fun to be had was to twist me around her little finger '…is a fucking big brandy!'

There was none in the house. I ran across to Glenda's and bought a large bottle of Martell, fresh ginger and lemons.

'What're you doing?' Jac asked as I busied around back in the kitchen.

'Fixing you a drink, sweetheart – won't be long.'

Into a glass half full of brandy I grated the ginger, added a squeeze of lemon juice and a teaspoon of honey and topped it all up with boiled water.

'Try this – special recipe of my grandfather's!'

She rolled her eyes at me and sipped, and as it cooled she gulped it down, sticking her finger in to pluck out the ginger and chew on that too.

'Good! Worth a tumble for a tumbler of that.'

I made her another: 'One for each rib…'

After she'd finished that one she stood up, walked stiffly over to the table, filled the wine glasses I'd brought back in and left there, and turned to me:

'Come on – give me your arm…'

We walked slowly back down into the churchyard and sat on our usual stone at the base of the tower. I'd brought a fleece and put it around her shoulders – around this indomitable, uncomplaining woman who was still shivering with the shock of her fall.

'I'm going to have to put this skirt in to soak when we get back – red wine's such a bugger to get out.'

'I've already got all the information on what you have to do – it's in *Jacquetta's Book of Household Tips*, next entry after "how to get candle-wax out of a carpet."'[1]

'So you *have* been writing them all down.'

'No – they're in my head, being preserved through the oral tradition…' This vein of amiable bickering had been going on between us for weeks. She was convinced that a man had no idea how to run a house, and I was gently playing up to this not-entirely-false notion whilst teasing her into a role of domestic science teacher, dispenser of traditional female knowledge, and all-round wise woman who was descended, she gravely informed me on several occasions – the implication being that I'd better watch out – from the Pendle Witches.[2] So in all of this I pretended to be her scribe: '…and you've already told me how to get port stains out of my pinafore as you insist on calling it, and the principle's bound to be the same. So give me your skirt and I'll put it to soak. In cold water, of course…'

'No – this stone's too cold to sit on just in my knickers; and anyway, someone might see.'

That set her off giggling, which in its turn made her gasp with pain.

'Oh-oh – laughing's out for a while…'

Sex wasn't. I was astonished when she initiated love-making that night. The principle of making up for lost time apparently still obtained whatever the circumstances.

'Won't it hurt?' I asked.

'Just be gentle, and try to keep your weight off me. We'll have to do it like this – I won't be able to support myself on top. And once we're into it, I won't feel the pain, will I? Sex as anaesthesia…'

In the morning I was dispatched to scour the local gardens and hedgerows for comfrey.

'Knit-bone,' Jac lectured, never one to pass up the opportunity for a quick exposition of herbal lore, 'that's what I need.'

The lore was clearly extant in Llanrhaeadr. Frances produced a pot of comfrey ointment and Claire told me to help myself from a dense growth along one side of the drive at the back of her house: 'And tell Jacquetta to come in and use the swing seat in my back garden any time she wants – she can let herself in by the side gate. It's not locked. You can come too, if you want a private spot for some outdoor canoodling.'

She flashed me a sly smile that intimated both personal acquaintance with the need for privacy and village interest in all things romantic. I went off to Oswestry to buy arnica 'for the bruising', and painkillers, leaving Jac installed on the sofa with more of the brandy concoction and a pot of comfrey leaves stewing on the stove. I was away for perhaps two hours. It was the longest time we were to be apart for the next two months. I had never in my life been together in so prolonged and intense a way with another human being, and though at times it was difficult, being by nature solitary, I think with anyone other than Jacquetta it would have been impossible for me. She simply took it in her stride and adapted to each new day and situation as it arrived.

The difficulties began almost immediately. Jac's accident happened on a Sunday. On the following Tuesday I had an eye operation in St Asaph, sixty miles to the north of Llanrhaeadr.

'I'm coming with you,' she pronounced.

'You should stay here and rest.'

'I'm coming with you, so that's that – and I'll drive.'

We reached a compromise – that she would come, with the seat reclined and pillows under the seat belt to stop further damage to her ribs, but that maybe driving a big car with heavy steering was not a good idea. In the hospital, to the amusement of the nurses, every five minutes she hobbled along the corridor to the treatment room where I'd been taken, to check on my progress. On the way back to Llanrhaeadr she picked up things from her house for the weeks ahead, including a kiln for her glass work that we installed in my kitchen, and she settled in with a good grace to a period of convalescence. My ruse initially was to keep her quiet by continuing the medicinal brandies and laying in a stock of videos for her to watch from the sofa. The brandy treatment proved acceptable, a bottle a day and Guinness at night keeping her relaxed and taking the edge off the pain. In parallel she kept assiduously to a regime of dosing herself with comfrey tea – unpleasant-looking, vile-smelling, thick and green. But the first video proved a disaster. It was the Coen brothers' *O Brother, Where Art Thou?* She sat through it holding herself, rocking back and forth and making a peculiar stifled wheezing noise of suppressed laughter whilst belabouring me for deliberately and sadistically trying to give her hysterics. After that, comedy was edited out.

There were other problems. In the first week, I came into the house one morning and found her crouched on the floor weeping, helped her to the sofa, asking her when she'd calmed a little what had happened. She'd tried to do press-ups.

'I just wanted to keep fit,' she told me, between spasms of tears.

The pain must have been excruciating. Even sitting by her I could hear the broken ribs crunch as she shifted position. After this incident, I kept discreet watch, stayed close, helped as unobtrusively as I could, and she bore all the attention with wry humour and patience. She had a stained-glass summer school to teach in Deeside, at the country park centre in the grounds of Basingwerk Abbey. The weather was good and, typically, she'd planned to sleep out in the woods whilst she was running it. I persuaded her to let me drive her there and back each day, and took work to do myself, sitting under a tree in the sun whilst she supervized students nearby. Day by day we got through. In the evenings at Llanrhaeadr she'd sit on the bench outside the house in the late sun and I'd head off – barefoot, to scoldings from the villagers that I might step on glass, which were preferable to the scoldings from Jac if I showed signs of wanting to don footwear and hide the *fairy wings* toenail varnish she'd painstakingly applied – to the pub at the top of the village, The Plough,[3] and return with a pint of Guinness in each hand and fierce concentration divided between where I was treading and what I might be spilling.

Her broken ribs continued to cause her intense pain. She resigned herself to a restful routine of reading in the sun in hidden nests she made in the long grass between the tombs by the river at the bottom of the churchyard. Occasionally we headed down to the Horseshoe Inn at Llanyblodwel in the evenings, or took picnics to nearby riverbanks and easily accessible hillsides. I had readings to give in August – one to a course at the National Writers' Centre for Wales in Llanystumdwy, delivered in the room where Lloyd George had died. I love doing readings here. The acoustics are uncannily perfect – a whisper at one end of the long room transmitting with absolute clarity right down to the other: which is where Jacquetta sat, on a sofa with another red-haired minx, Helen

Burke – a sharp-witted and savagely irreverent performance-poet from York who'd been on several courses I'd run and was a good friend of mine. So the reading I gave had a comic-critical subtext, all acutely audible, by way of running commentary, and one that left the audience perplexed, kept careful watch over the minutes, and included loud whispered hints about the amount of drinking-time left in the village pub.

The second reading that August was at the Edinburgh Book Festival, held in large tents erected on the grass of Charlotte Square Gardens in the Old Town – a small park with tall trees and wrought-iron railings in the centre of an elegant Regency square. The events are always sold out, the audiences as keenly attentive and intelligent as you expect of Scotland – and for the trip Jacquetta had again painted my toenails and confiscated my shoes. The evening atmosphere in the Gardens that year was a mellow blend of wine, starlight and velvet air. We walked back barefoot to our hotel through the night streets of the city, had a midnight feast of sandwiches, Guinness and drams of Edradour sent up on room service, for we'd not eaten, descended to breakfast next morning and were joined by Rob Macfarlane, whose first book, *Mountains of the Mind*, I'd just reviewed. The conversation over scrambled eggs and smoked salmon and coffee flowed – two hours skipped by as we played ducks and drakes over the surface of a bizarre range of subjects. One of them – that matter has memory – came back strongly as Jacquetta and I made our dawdling return journey to Wales over the following few days.

We'd gone for a walk – a month on from her accident she was assertively more mobile – on the Berwickshire coast. I'd wanted to show her a place I'd visited and talked to her excitedly about over thirty years before when we'd first been together – the ruined promontory stronghold of Fast Castle on the coast above Coldingham. After leaving Edinburgh we'd slept out under the stars at the margin of a wood close to the path leading over the moor to it. In the morning we were discovered there by the farmer, Ian Russell, who merely raised his eyebrows on happening upon us cooking our breakfast on his land, remarked that he'd not seen anyone camping here before, sat drinking coffee with us and talking about the state of agriculture in Scotland and Europe, about communities and cooperatives, setaside, comedy on the Edinburgh Fringe and local history, before presenting us with a packet of home-made herb-flavoured sausages and heading off in his Land Rover to gather samples of the organic barley he grew. We wondered how many young farmers on whose land we'd been found 'trespassing' would have accorded us the same treatment, and ambled off under a bright morning sun along the coastal path to find this ruin that had exercised my imagination for more than three decades.

The curious thing was, that I had no visual memory of the place, could remember almost nothing about it apart from a vague sense of its defensibility – of the ridiculously narrow isthmus above a sea arch that connected the plug of dolerite on which it's set to the mainland, and the plunging cliffs all around. I'd gone there with a view to exploring the rock climbing potential of the latter with a particularly loud magazine editor one Hogmanay at the back end of the 1960s. It had been one of those louring East Coast winter days. We'd flogged for miles through heather and rain from a minor road that ran seaward of the main A1, taken a brief look at the castle and at the nearby coastal stack of The Souter, then headed north for Aberdeen. Climbers, I've long maintained, are of all groups of people among the least aware of their surroundings, and in those days I was one of them. To arrive there with Jacquetta, it was as though I'd never seen the place before. We climbed the shoulder of the hill above Dowlaw Farm, descended by paths through fragrant heather in bloom, and suddenly below us the most dramatic ruin. Scott's romantic description from *The Bride of Lammermoor* of the crumbling towers of Wolf's Crag, last possession of the ruined Master of Ravenswood, is based on Fast Castle and captures its atmosphere perfectly. What I retain from the novel (and the Donizetti opera, *Lucia di Lammermoor*, derived from it) is an overbearing sense that when love and fate are at odds, the former will not necessarily conquer and the forces of antagonism and unreason some-times tragically prevail – all this reflected and bodied forth in this elemental setting. What we encountered in the landscape – fanged remnants of masonry hanging at crazy angles over fearsome cliffs, thick chains to protect the crossing rusted through, a polished slab of rock to be climbed – beggars imag-ination. You could not conjure up a more rugged and exotic fastness than this.

So Jac and I made our way in, peered down from the promontory's end at cormorants hanging their wings out to dry on dragon-scale rocks two hundred feet below, watched the white spume of the tide surge rhythmically in through savage, dark slits in the reefs, with me hanging on to Jac's heels as she craned giddily over the drop, and when we'd had enough of all the excitement and drama, we made our way back, picking through baileys and wards and roofless rooms until we came to a hidden enclosure mattressed with soft, springing turf and bowered with thrift and daisies, and there we lay down and chattered dreamily about the theme of matter's memory. We'd read that Margaret Tudor, daughter of Henry VII of England, had stayed here in 1503, on her way to marry James IV of Scotland and by that alliance maintain the peace that ended so bloodily ten years later on Flodden Field. What must the thirteen-year-old princess have thought of these surroundings, would she have found them rough and terrifying? we wondered, as we lazed on silken grass the comfort and ease of which no marriage bed of hers could have surpassed. Tumbled top of a tower, pink-sandstone-revetted, sheltered us from a cool stream of air flowing from the north. The sun warmed our stretched and naked limbs. An occasional walker bustled past along the coastal path. When had children last played within this curtilage, or man and woman made love within the walls? we mused. What names had they borne? The sea's whispering them maybe, we laughed, as it sighed up to us repeatedly: 'Morag, Hamish, Morag, Hamish...' My own memory so apparently unreliable, why should not that of the rocks be as quirky and selective too? These shards of dolerite, these blocks of sandstone, have written into them the heat and glitter of the sun, the surge of waves from aeons past. In the crook of my arm my lover, a smile playing across her lips. A decayed incisor of masonry tilted perilously at the drop, impendent, its base cracked and shifting, its gravity askew, its tenure at the mercy of old mortar frail as memory. One winter soon, the north wind's blast would consign it to the sea, like old Caleb in *The Bride of Lammermoor* breaking chipped crockery on the flagged floor in vain pretence of solidity. We, in the joy of our brief present, in sunlit embrace slept and dreamed, unaware in our moment of recaptured glory of what fate had in store for us.

We drifted on southwards, crossed the border and towards evening, just upstream from a fine sandstone bridge at Ford in Northumberland came upon a bend in the River Till, that flows down from here to join the Tweed three miles from Norham Castle, subject of the most optimistically visionary of all Turner's works; his *Norham Castle, Sunrise*, painted between 1840 and 1845 and now hanging in the Tate – a shimmer of carmine, cyan, yellow and palest lilac in which all points of reference glow out from teasing proximities to definition, their promise as much that of our lives as of the dawn. It's a painting that realizes and defines the crucial aspects of his work: 'his devotion to observed reality, his exalting experience of light and colour… his desire to express something of significance about human destiny.'[4]

The river flowed and rippled between brakes of holly, stands of Scots pine and copses of birch and willow. White cow parsley flounced the far bank and the sinking sun glanced along the surface. Kingfishers – animated air-jewels – whirred constantly back and forth, perched on branches overhanging the water, darted after small fish. A sea trout leaped. We found a perfect place for the tent among the withies and built a fire on the shingle in front of it. Ian Russell's herb sausages were soon sputtering and crackling in the frying pan, their smell mouth-watering on the still evening air. We sat on a grassy edge to eat. Feet from us, the broad, whiskery muzzle of an otter forged its way downstream, heedless of our presence, wild and unconcerned. As day turned to night eddies caught at the reflection of flame, stretched it downstream, 'cork-screwed it like a wriggling worm'.[5] Among the willows, by the glowing embers, happily, in each other's arms we slept.

Back in Llanrhaeadr, with autumn coming on and the prospect once more approaching of that winter road over The Berwyn, there were some hard decisions to be faced. Jac had come to me exhausted, drained, depressed and filled with forebodings. She hinted often that, though we would never part, though she hoped it would turn out otherwise, our time together was likely to be short. Look away as we might, we know when the grave illnesses are taking hold, are growing inside us – the crab nips before it wrenches and tears. Our marriage and time together was joyful and restorative, continually playful, supportive and mutually delighting. In its brief season she had been relieved of difficulties she'd been facing; but her injury and the constant pain of it took their toll. Also, my house was not ideal for her work, for which she had a passion as well as a remarkable gift, and the constant care she needed came at unbegrudged cost to my own time for writing. To add to all this, she was in considerable debt and I was under heavy pressure to deliver on book contracts that there was little chance of fulfilling in our present situation. One night she had discovered an old bathtub lying on the cobbles of my medieval cellar. The house only had a shower, and women in my experience like to luxuriate in their baths, eyes drowsy, toes beckoning for attention, summoning the glass of wine, the soaping of the back, the massage of shoulders and neck. This cellar-tub was not plumbed in, so she set me to work whittling a cork plug for it from the top of an old jar. We ran a hose-pipe from the hot tap in the kitchen down through the trap door, set night lights in niches all around the rough stone walls, and when it was full we climbed in together. In these flickering and macabre vaulted surroundings, we talked seriously of what was to be done. I had no material assets, my small reserves were dwindling fast, friends of friends had expressed interest in buying my house. The future could take care of itself. For me to sell, release equity and rent somewhere on her side of the moors meant I could settle Jac's financial liabilities and also give her the things she had long been denied, go with her to places she had not seen, about which she often talked enquiringly – I wouldn't say my Bolivian trip early in the year had become a point of rancour, but it was certainly now the occasion for pointed reminders and to me a source of regret.

Sitting there in the candlelight, the water becoming cool, Jac frothing away at it nervously with her fingers, she pondered that we might buy a static caravan – caravans and teepees and all things with the sense of the vagrant and the temporary about them appealed to her – put it by the little stream that ran close to her rented house among the moors near Cerrigydrudion, and live in that. It seemed a straightforward choice, and even in retrospect, though it deprived her of the place of escape and refuge that my house had become, pitched her back into many of the stresses of her former life, and left me destitute and homeless after her death, I am not sure it was entirely the wrong one.

To help her recovery and give her sunshine and rest before the rigours of a Welsh winter, I booked us a beachside apartment for three weeks in the little port of Mastihari opposite Kalymnos, that she remembered from having visited during her time in Bodrum. The balconies of the apartment looked out on to Aegean sunsets:

> The Mediterranean sun has something tragic about it, quite different from the tragedy of fogs. Certain evenings at the base of the seaside mountains, night falls over the flawless curve of a little bay, and there rises from the silent waters a sense of anguished fulfillment.[6]

In the endless heat we lazed through the days, read much, took languorous siestas, ate at a taverna on the sand, adopted a flea-bitten, exuberant small dog with an undershot jaw that Jacquetta immediately started scheming to transport back to Britain, drank too much wine and metaxa on the balcony each evening with the moon that sailed low across the sky in front of us waxing and then waning. We rationed ourselves to a book of *The Odyssey* read aloud every night, her favourites from among which she would often have me repeat – Calypso, the death of the suitors, Circe:

> Come then, put away your sword in its sheath, and let us
> two go up into my bed so that, lying together
> in the bed of love, we may then have faith and trust
> in each other.[7]

She shopped among the little bazaars, bought small gifts of local jewellery, spent an hour discussing with a shopkeeper the intricacies of a round, hand-tatted tablecloth and then a few seconds persuading me to buy it. In one boutique I watched from the corner of my eye as she prised from its rack a cream silk skirt gathered at the hips and flounced like a gypsy's or a flamenco dancer's, which she held up against herself, admired the reflection in the shop window, checked the price tag and put back with an expression of resignation. Knowing better than to interfere at that moment, as she slept after lunch I slipped from her side, pulled the door quietly to behind me and went back to buy, was harangued when she woke to find it by the bedside; and was then drawn down into her arms as she came back naked to the bed having tried it on. So the days passed by, the stillness of them a stretched moment of tranquility and connection that was, and then as suddenly was not. As I age, I am no longer quite sure about the nature of time.

We returned to a cold, wet autumn under The Berwyn, rain drenching down. Each day the air was heavy and still, mist rendering the seasonal glory of the trees into a shimmering suggestion behind the veil, a muted depth of coloration stripped of brilliance but given instead texture and mystery. All the usual sights along our daily walks were obscured, dimmed, unavailable. The negotiations over the sale of the house were concluded and the legal process set in motion.

One day in October I drove up to Chester Services on the M56, met Joe Brown and Morty Smith there – the three of us black-suited and broad-shouldered like elderly mafiosi, Joe the white-haired godfather of our clan – in the car park. I'd known both of them since my early teens, had even seen Joe – the greatest climber across all disciplines of the sport that Britain has ever produced – and his friends from the Rock & Ice Club setting off to go climbing on Saturdays from his home on Dickinson Road when I was four or five and my grandfather, with his big brown shopping bag, had taken me with him to Longsight Market: scruffy, wiry men with ropes draped around their shoulders and nailed boots sparking along the pavements. When I was a young Manchester climber myself, Joe was kind, funny, encouraging. I remember showing my father a photograph in a guidebook of Joe on a rock climb, 'Suicide Wall' in Cwm Idwal, taken whilst he was making a film for the BBC in 1956, and my father, to whom my climbing was anathema – perhaps for the same reasons that I didn't really want Will to start thirty or more years on – snapping at me, 'You'll never be able to do that – you've only got one eye' – and tossing the book aside. Just after my father's death I was climbing on the same cliff as Joe, whom I knew well by this time. I was on a difficult recent route of his in the rain, he on an easier and more sheltered adjacent one. My feet slipped off the small, greasy holds and I took a huge fall, ninety feet from the hardest section, my second stopping me on the rope just short of the ground. Joe immediately abseiled down to check if I was unhurt, put his arm around my shoulders and with a wide grin told me, 'It's all right, lad – it 'appens to the best of us.' His instinctively generous fathering, who himself had never known a father, is a memory I treasure. When I came to make a four-part series for HTV on the Welsh mountains in the 1990s, Joe, who was sixty by then, and I were filmed for it on 'Suicide Wall', and I intercut the sequence with the old BBC film footage of him on the climb nearly forty years before. They are so disparate and resonant, the means that, in Larkin's phrase, 'link us to our losses'. Memory, friendship, community, good fellowship – the way things roost in your heart...

The three of us drove on in convoy to the funeral in Manchester of Audrey Whillans, widow of the mountaineer Don Whillans whose biography I had been commissioned to write.[8] Afterwards I went on to Carnforth, where I bought the 26-foot Pemberton caravan in russet and cream for which Jac had measured up a place by the stream and then located one of the right size in *North West Auto Trader*. So this would be our home. I arranged for it to be delivered down to Wales and installed within the next fortnight, the vendor breezily dismissing my dire warnings about the difficulty of the task. All the cosy familiarities and comforts of Manchester House went into boxes from which, in some cases, they would not emerge for three years. Space was made in a barn for my furniture and belongings. In hired vans and incessant rain, with Will's help before he set off for a job working through the winter on a huge and dangerous dock-building project on the coast north of Mumbai, they were moved there.

Jac and I began saying our goodbyes to the people of the village – to Frances and Mavis and Glenda, and to dear, gracious, elegant Claire, who was now suffering from sudden-onset motor-neurone disease. We went down to the Horseshoe Inn at Llanyblodwel to say goodbye to Dennis and Jess, the landlord and landlady, who had become good friends. As we walked across to the pub door Jess came out and collapsed in tears into my arms. Days before, Dennis had been taken into hospital in Shrewsbury for a biopsy on an enlarged prostate gland. The necessary nick had become infected. Two days after the procedure, in the night he'd suffered massive septic shock, cardiac arrest, and had stopped breathing. Jess had rung for an ambulance and tried mouth-to-mouth resuscitation to no avail. Nor could the paramedics revive him. We had last seen him within the fortnight, and as a strong, humorous, healthy man walking along the riverbank 'to a place/Where stone is dark under froth,/And the down-turn of his wrist/When the flies drop in the stream'.[9]

On the day before the sale of the house was completed, when I went out into the square a pall of gloom hung over the village, people huddling in groups on the rain-swept streets. The son of an old lady of whom we were fond – she would often stop and talk to us as we sat on the bench, tell us time and again of watching and reporting the flights of German bombers passing overhead during the war aiming for the docks at Liverpool – had been found dead that morning in the annexe to her house where he slept. His Jack Russell terrier was by his side, the two of them killed by fumes from a faulty gas-heater before he could set off back to his work and family in Aberystwyth after looking after his mother for the weekend. If I were a Suetonius, I might at this point give you an account of reading the entrails. The auguries were not positive: the swifts had long screamed away south from the little square; the summer was gone; in so many instances around us the fragility of life was being asserted; the weather was cold and relentlessly drear as a Welsh autumn in the hills can be:

> No warmth, no cheerfulness, no healthful ease,
> No comfortable feel in any member –
> No shade, no shine, no butterflies, no bees,
> No fruits, no flow'rs, no leaves, no birds,
>   November![10]

On our final night together in Llanrhaeadr we walked down to The Plough (shoes by this time had been returned as concession to the seasons, though the toenails were still painted) for pints of Guinness by the log fire, came back, stoked up the little stove and sat by it in the now all-but-empty house, talked late into the night, slept for the last time in the attic with the old wood frame and beams, and rain pelting on the skylight, woke to a grey dawn. After a few hours of thrusting last things into a Transit van parked outside, in the afternoon and already-fading light we locked the house behind us, left the keys for the new owner with Glenda in the shop, and drove away from Dyffryn Tanat, our brief paradise-place, into the desolation of the moors:

> And they are gone – ay, ages long ago
> These lovers fled away into the storm.[11]

‖

Caravan

It was the twelfth of March, 2004 – Jacquetta's fifty-sixth birthday. This was not a fact many knew. She looked twenty years younger, and whenever possible made a point of lying fastidiously about her age. I'm sure she would have fibbed to me too had I not known her since her teens. Her figure was slim as a girl's, hair without trace of grey and skin without blemish. When I found a small crêpey patch once on the inside of her elbow and was both touched and fascinated by it, she drew her arm away in indignation and quickly changed into a long-sleeved top. For her birthday we had taken a room at the Ty Newydd Hotel in Aberdaron, westernmost village of the Lleyn Peninsula. In the night a fierce storm surged the towering waves into the bay, tore off their crests and lashed the spray against our window. She opened it wide and leaned out naked into the blast, her hair streaming, foam like soft white roses blown in and settling on the bed, the expression on her face exultant, animated. 'Come here, come behind me,' she ordered, her body glistening with rain, gasps of her pleasure and release harmonizing to the rush of wind and wave until cold and sensation became too intense to bear and we collapsed on to the bed in fits of laughter. The couple from Esher in the next room, on whose conversation about property prices and seafood platters we'd eavesdropped over dinner, hammered their complaints upon the wall. Come the morning, mercury columns of rain swayed and drifted in across the sea as we slipped down from the coastal path, out of the gale and into tiny Porth Iago, most secretive of bays in Lleyn. Refracted light caught at our footsteps, blanched into sand wet from a retreating tide. We crossed to the farther wall of rock, rested there in the calm below the storm, the wind sighing and roaring above like a beast frustrated of its prey, then crept into fractal mimicry of a sheltering crevice-cove. On its miniature dry strand, in still air, we huddled in our waterproofs, lit our meths stove, filled the kettle, waited for splutter of spout, clack of lid, made good, strong coffee, passed the mug between us, hot sweet liquid on our lips, watched quietly, looked around.

A flight of six cormorants struggled in awkwardly from the north, stiff-winged, veering this way and that, craning their necks to find leads through air that was buffeting and solid as water. A solitary raven in virtuoso display tumbled and soared nearby, watchful, as though a basilisk glare from the sea-hags might turn him to dropping stone. One of them peered towards him, wings labouring, and then, losing ground in the ragged formation, looked away and flapped on. Two choughs fluttered and screamed. An oystercatcher scurried and piped. The peregrine of Pen y Cil swept past imperiously, and the sun emerging from under cloud turned a kestrel's wings to fire. We sat in a silence of shared joy, sipping our coffee, the mug going from hand to hand: '...the place of Angels and the Gate of Heaven.'[12]

The light had come and we looked for it in the waves as they drew themselves up, unrolling sheets of milky ultramarine, their careering crests balanced tenuously into slant sunbeams so that they became lapis lazuli infused and set with gold brilliance, intensity, cascading prisms. Here one swirled sand across the palette, streaking itself ochre; the tempest-gust caught at another and gave us sudden, flung diamonds. The rain ceased. I watched this lovely, slender woman cross the strand, saw the wind spin the red-gold of her hair into a net to catch the sun. She picked up a great rope of seaweed and, strong shoulders bending to the task, sketched all across the empty canvas of the beach, like a child dancing in the wind, playful and skittish as the raven above her. Then she crossed to the other, needled wall of the cove. Pre-Cambrian. The first stilling out of the magma. Again that fractal sense. I struggled with scale. Aiguilles? The Cuillin? All miniature here, but somehow the same. The overall cast sombre, until you look closely: 'The World is a mirror of infinite beauty, yet no man sees it.'[13]

A washed-out purple that the powdery grey of limpets and barnacles shows off to perfection; creased and pillowy crags frilled with salt crystals where the spray reaches; greens and blues, seamed quartz crosses like spirit-kisses in the grain of the cliff. The waves surge continually, the light is a gold suffusion of air, my loved one dancing and I very still, without property here, heart wide open.

If we see things as they are, then we do not have to interpret or analyze them further; we do not need to

try to understand things by imposing spiritual experience or philosophical ideas upon them.[14]

This old, far-off region of Pen Llŷn is of the margins: of
land, of the country of Wales, home of those the Saxons termed
the *Weallas* – the foreigners. Westerly, westernmost, west – it is
a mood, a feeling, a need, a cultural and historical entity as
well as all this exquisite physical fabric. I have felt the complex
atmosphere in so many places of the West: on Beara out in
West Cork; by the shores of dark Loch Hourn, looking across
to Ladhar Bheinn on Knoydart; in the silky *machair* along the
seaward side of sacred Iona. Rooted in the actuality of these
landscapes is the locating and the embodiment of a concept
complementary to what we understand as East. And as meaningful and valuable – this affective mood-concept, this stilling
before landscape, this meditative and quietistic response – as
what many from western societies find the East offers in spiritual, philosophical and cultural terms.[15] A sense of historical
irony enthralls me here: that the relict and exigent cultures that
lighted upon these stony coasts flickered here and there into
glories, into visions of holy life, into mythopoeic achievement
– Columba, Patrick, the *Book of Kells* – which tantalized and
occasionally informed the real barbarism and malevolence
that had swept them there so many centuries before.
Augustine of Canterbury – ambitious politician rather than
devout priest – ordained the massacre of monks at Bangor-is-
y-Coed, yet fifteen centuries on the quasi-monks and nuns are
still fleeing here, to the place where survivors fled then. To
Pendraw Llyn. The dominant and displacing cultures themselves dead or in decay, these rocks and coves and wild

sanctuaries have transformed and located into places of pilgrimage, means of expiation and escape, refutations of the
values of material possession, national supremacy and martial
power that once marginalized them:

> In cities that
> have outgrown their promise people
> are becoming pilgrims
> again, if not to this place,
> then to the recreation of it
> in their own spirits.[16]

A tenet of Celtic Christianity – the branch religion Augustine was concerned to eliminate[17] – is that to follow sunwise,
westwards, is to take some steps towards the wisdom the
access to which is through a loss or abnegation of power; is to
apprehend the metaphor implicit both in the sun's slantwise
celebration and enlargement of the natural world (think how
small the hills become at high-summer noon, how they rear in
the evening light), and in the greater beauty at its setting than
at its zenith. Reflective fragments of history and culture still
attach to these furthermost places of an old land: Scotland and
the Western Isles, the West of Ireland, Cornwall, Wales. I
wonder at the values to be found by those who come seeking
them? More dangerously, do those who search also at times
import superficiality, self-esteeming inattentiveness, and hence
traduce? The structures, contexts and perceived necessities of
our 'western' society, its insistence on straight thinking and
dismissal of the crooked path of the sage, have marginalized
the unsupported *living* in these places more than ever before.

Physical and mental skills of survival have been lost. 'Wild' is no more than notional now in most people's experience, an abstract and travestied visitor-attraction abjured by that dangerous body the Health & Safety Executive, and imperfectly understood, as a recent glut of books with the word flashily incorporated into their titles more than amply demonstrates. Here and there throughout the margins too, the barbarism has leapfrogged through into occupation, and the affective glory of the land is lost: wind turbines, oil terminals, tourist *facilities*.

Yet where landscape has imagistic power, where it is a threshold elementally stated – as here, at Porth Iago on this ragged, thrust-out fist of Pen Llŷn – that shadow-life of historical presence haunts most potently. There is a potential for spiritual regeneration here, a resonance between shades of history and the elemental place that quickens the imagination, makes us better able to see, and seeing is the all.[18] 'Is all knowing *mastery*, and not rather *attention*, the natural prayer of the soul,' is the subtle way the philosopher Gillian Rose makes the point.[19] I watch the walkers on the coastal paths of the West, and catch at the sense emanating from them of something unstated, unconscious, drawing them there, aspiring in true pilgrim fashion after Grace. If the land inspires in us the capacity to love, then love has entered our souls, and we are connected in The One. And connected too in the loveliest places with the echo of moments in locations where humane values have flourished, and may flourish still, as they do not flourish throughout much of our soft-totalitarian state, with its subservience to capital, its desperate need to control and restrict and own and possess, its posturing inauthenticities, its addiction to empty and gratuitous sensation, its rabid underbelly, its abject squeaking fear of difference: 'It is a region of Light and Peace, did not men disquiet it. It is the Paradise... more to man since he is fallen than it was before.'[20]

So I make an effort to give definition to the idea that West, like East, is not only place but also distinctive and therapeutic state of mind – a letting-go, a coming-to-terms with the wilderness within, a celebration of the beauty of wild nature, without which spaciousness and annihilating glory our lives are the more savage. Our society's multi-dimensional failure is in the turning to security, the reliance on currency you can grasp and hoard. That gilded wave-crest, those flung diamonds, the squeal and scattering flight of mating choughs – inexpressible riches! – what vault would hold them, and what could they buy? Prolongation of the time Jacquetta and I had, and the ways she so wisely insisted it be spent? This moment, she knew, is all the life we have, and it is for the living.

The storm having passed, we climbed out of our fractal, sheltering cove, carried on around over Mynydd Anelog, and arrived at sunset atop the last headland of Braich y Pwll, a seaward mountain the heather slopes of which keen down into the tide race, and from whence we looked across to Ynys Enlli, where the surviving Bangor monks found refuge – Bardsey, with its lighthouse flashing across in the gathering shades. In looking forward to that view, I thought of the last time I left Enlli's harbour, gazing back from the stern of a small boat and seeing a woman on the promontory above holding her yoga position, rigid, angular against the sun, self-consciously, proprietorially, somehow engendering irritation in her assertion of spiritual superiority, her colonizing, her pose, her desire to be noticed. There is a materialism of the spirit, a possibility of avarice there too. Saint Dunawd, Abbot of Bangor-below-the-wood, has a well named for him in the corner of a field on the *taith y pererin* – the pilgrims' way – as it toils up from Black Rock towards its eventual goal of Enlli. It is cattle-mired and broken now, unregarded, trampled, its water fouled. You can no longer drink there, the old stone basin where the spring's pure issue collected now a receptacle of filth, drained by a blue plastic pipe. What blasphemy is this, reiterated across our planet? What index to our irreverence? What abuse of the source?

> ''Tis hard to find a well nowadays',
> says Bridget filling the bowl again.
> 'They're hidden in rushes and grass,
> choked by green scum and ferns,
> but, despite the neglect,
> they've lost none of their true mettle.
> Seek out your own well, my dear,
> For the age of want is near:
> There will have to be a going back to sources.'[21]

From the path along the cliff top above Porth Iago as Jacquetta and I left, I looked back down, and in the sand, etched there, her message – an open heart, and beyond it the white tide, turning. We returned late that night to the caravan in the moors of Hiraethog, which means longing for a home place.

I was working on the account of —— given above. It was an arduous task. Often I could not get on for hours and days at a time, and not infrequently I unravelled what I had done, continually tormented by scruples that were taking tighter and tighter hold and steadily paralyzing me. These scruples concerned not only the subject of my narrative, which I felt I could not do justice to, no matter what approach I tried, but also the entire questionable business of writing.[22]

The caravan had been winched carefully sideways on skids to a position between a fine old sycamore and two graceful and well-grown young larches. Getting it there had taken all day and large tips to the men who delivered it. Behind it was the stream and beyond that a dense row of gnarled blackthorn sheltering it from west winds. It had bedroom, bathroom and kitchen, many cupboards for storage and a large living space. We set to work connecting water, drainage, electricity and a phone line, anchored it against the likelihood of gales, painted the interior in a light glowing terracotta, fitted bookshelves and a thick-pile soft-green carpet, installed an efficient little multi-fuel stove that could warm the whole caravan in minutes with a flue that became blued by the heat. It sat on a bevelled slate slab, the side panel of a box tomb that Jacquetta had found among nettles stacked against the wall of a deconsecrated churchyard and had me carry to the car. We hung bird-feeders for peanuts, fat-balls and niger seed in the larch tree by the bedroom window.

By the time the Llanrhaeadr house was sold, it was a comfortable place in which to live and a base for our activities. And so, almost immediately, we set off on our travels. 'Another honeymoon!' Jac had insisted, in January. We flew to

Vancouver – one of the great scenic cities of the world, down every downtown street a glimpse of the Pacific, snow-capped peaks ringing the horizon – where we stayed at the Wedgewood Hotel in Robson Square, our room looking out on to the waterfall in the centre. An old, clackety, hard-benched trolley with a garrulous, singing driver took us on a sightseeing tour, through jiggly, up-and-down streets of Gastown with its hissingly eccentric steam clock into Stanley Park and up to Prospect Point, where the view is of the Lions Gate Suspension Bridge – Vancouver's unpublicized but equally spectacular version of the Golden Gate – and mountains beyond. In Chinatown we idled into the exquisitely harmonized, high-white-walled, Ming-style Dr Sun Yat-Sen Classical Chinese Garden, where contorted limestone, jade ponds, carved screens and pebbled courtyards are built within a relatively small space into a marvel of texture and mood. We had become tourists, and Jac loved it. A zippy bathtub of a ferry took us across False Creek to Granville Island, the city's major tourist attraction. We indulged in bouts of gourmet excess: authentic French at Le Gavroche; cold savour of all manner of sub-aqueous creatures that bloop and pinch and crawl in the Blue Water Café; burgers in a down-home Canadian diner as we waited for the white-gold ring from a Chinatown jewellers to be sized, which Jac had finally decided upon to betoken our marriage.

After a couple of days we boarded a floatplane out to Victoria on Vancouver Island. It veered over the wooded Gulf Islands and ploughed noisily down after an hour into the shelter of Victoria Harbour. We treated ourselves to more luxury at the ivy-clad, chateau-style Empress Hotel. It dominates the harbour, views from the turret sitting room of our suite were ethereally of Mount Olympus to the south, its summit snows tinged pink by sunset. We took a 'Couples Treatment' at the Empress Spa, were rubbed and massaged and anointed and finally left fragrantly to enjoy crisp wine and crispier health food by an armchaired fireside, Jac feeling more at ease physically than at any time since her accident. After we'd recovered from all this pampering, the Empress High Tea ritual beckoned – a procession of pastry, teapot, trimmed sandwich, even lacy-pinafored maids, all presented in a dream of cupola, stained glass and marbled halls with the small harbour waves whispering outside. There was a wry Canadian humour at work, affectionate but sidelong somehow, which Jac loved and teased away at: 'OK guys,' it seemed to say, 'maybe it never was thus, but let's just add in a few modern touches, give it the best, have us a good time and pretend.'

That neat sense of detachment that's always been Canada's defence against its brash southerly neighbour put us in the mood to trawl through the brew-pubs and music venues of the city, where good old boys, 'bald heads forgetful of their sins', strummed melodically through rock 'n' roll standards of thirty or forty years before as diners munched their salad-and-wholesome-tuna-burgers and a crescent moon rocked low like a boat above the lamplit waves.

I'd lured Jac here on the promise that she'd get to see the Pacific, so on a day of drenching January rain we drove out to Port Renfrew, south-westernmost settlement on Vancouver Island, and peered across the San Juan River at wooded slopes opposite traversed by the first section of the West Coast Trail – reputedly one of the World's great walks, unpunctuated by civilisation and unspoilt. We watched skeins of mist threading old-growth forest, but the path's only open from May to October so we turned for home and by the Jordan River made our way down to a grey pebble beach stippled with white quartz and heard the hiss of waves sluicing in from the Pacific, rolling past Cape Flattery into the Strait of Juan de Fuca. All the way along this great inlet you're looking out towards Japan across the greatest of oceans, unfathomable as love itself. I unscrewed a thermos, filled the cup and handed her coffee as we snuggled close, gathering mementoes from among little rocks by our feet, the vastness in front of us palpable. Later, in a hot tub under a gazebo at an opulent, isolated log cabin in the woods of the Sooke Hills to which we'd moved – with all the verdancy of the rainforest, the hanging mosses, glimpsed shy deer, the ferns and festooning spleenworts and the lovely, filtering green light, heady British Columbian wine at our elbows and a roaring waterfall in the gorge beneath – there was another brief heaven, from which we climbed out of steaming water to run naked along frosty decking, slip under goose-down and sink into dreams feathery and fresh as new worlds bring.

From Vancouver Jac flew back to Britain whilst I headed north into the Yukon and then east to northern Saskatchewan to write travel essays for the newspapers on mushing and wolf watching, on neither of which assignments could I take her because of the continuing discomfort from her ribs. By the end of January I was home with her in Wales, and the snows came. For one period of over a week the track to the caravan was drifted over to a depth of five or six feet. We were absolutely alone in the silent, white world, the caravan cosy amid a frozen landscape. The birds – goldfinches, a young female great spotted woodpecker, reed buntings like handsome over-sized sparrows – flocked to the feeders and we sat in bed in the mornings for hours over pots of coffee and toast to watch their feasting and squabbling. A fox walked up and sat outside the caravan door, waiting for scraps, Serafina observing it from the top step with green intensity in her eyes and a low rumbling growl. The thaw came. I launched the Citroën at the steep track and we slithered out to Chester one night to hear the Scottish singer Dick Gaughan picking out centuries-old laments on an electric guitar. By the end of March Jac felt we needed another holiday, 'sunshine assured this time!' she insisted. We agreed on La Gomera. But first of all she needed to make a quick family visit to London. I put her on the train for Euston at Chester station one lunchtime, was waiting on the platform two days later for her return.

She stepped down from the carriage, I ran towards her, she turned to me and slumped into my arms, her face ashen, her expression one of agony. She had fallen in the night at the flat where she was staying, had cracked a lumbar vertebra. These falls – and they were frequent, though usually not so dire in their effect – were the result of the man she had been with for several years during the time we were out of contact punch-ing her with full force on the side of her head in the course of what she described as 'a trivial argument'. She was concussed for days by the blow, her proprioceptive faculties permanently damaged, the cervical vertebrae out of alignment. When I massaged her, which was often because much of the time she was in pain, the extent of the damage was palpable. The injuries from her falls were a direct result of that assault fifteen years before; its effect on her life had been catastrophic.

Offers to drive her back via hospital were summarily dismissed. We returned home to the caravan. I suggested we cancel the holiday. She looked at me and shook her head, a rueful smile on her lips. We were due to fly in four days' time. For most of it she rested in bed. Will, who was heading back from India, phoned, talked for an hour about his Indian fellow-workers on the dock project, the lack of concern for their welfare or provision for them or their families in the many serious accidents he witnessed. I had never heard him sound so grave, so affected by the inequalities and injustices of the world. He promised to visit in April. Jac and I flew to Tenerife and from there made the two-hour ferry crossing to La Gomera, relieved to have fled the wintry dreich of the moors. In a hired Skoda from San Sebastián de la Gomera – Columbus's last port-of-call before setting sail for the New World – we veered and faltered and crept around along hairpin mountain and forest roads in dense mist and past fantastical huge rock pinnacles before threading down through tunnels along the walls of a vast *barranco* into the oddest resort, Valle Gran Rey on the western, Atlantic coast of the island. The sun sank into the sea and as gaggly a collection of frantic drummers and wistful strummers, frazzle-haired, kaftan-wearing and beaded, as I'd set eyes on since the sixties, emerged from whatever retro-quarters they inhabited. An extempore Celtic band composed of fiddle, bodhran, didgeri-doo, guitar and serpent struck up a ragged ersatz version of a Clare jig, and a woman in red twirled and shimmied away with hieratic self-consciousness to a different beat. Partners of the players puffed on large joints, and attempted in desultory fashion to palm inept and grubby sketches of local landscapes and strings of plastic beads off on to newly-arrived tourists for large amounts of Euros. Touts pushed German flyers behind windscreen wipers, advertising ascent to the third level of consciousness in exchange for a mere sixteen hundred Euros at a local ashram. A cold evening breeze sent a bristle of Teutonic willies that had been parading and posturing all across a neighbouring black-sand beach shrinking into the cover of their clothes, and we looked on in complete bemusement. The garden nature of the landscape of the hinterland, especially around the island's highest peak of Alto de Garajonay, was better. Finches flitted through blossomed latticework of the jacarandas; mimosa, hibiscus and bellflowers were blooming; dandelions tall as small trees beguiled us along the short, level distance to Garajonay's summit from the nearest road-access. Here, at Las Puertas de Orahan, an archaeological dig was in progress, the ground within the walled enclosure excavated and marked out with a grid of measuring strings, public exclusion enforced by iron pickets strung with orange plastic tape. A sign explained to us the symbolic significance of the site for ancient Gomerans: 'They held sacred the areas where nature was magnificent. The Gomeran symbolic scenery is full of theatricality and transcendence… Those people who reach the top will immediately realize their irremediable human condition.'

Above our apartment among the stepped and cobbled alleys of La Calera a jagged arête soared, and from the jumble of houses a walled and corbelled path emerged to zigzag up its lower, steeper section. We saw walkers straggling down it occasionally, took out the spy-glass and studied their progress, which was often concealed from us. We traced the path's crazed meanderings on the map, found that the ridge was called Riscos de la Merica, and that it rose two-and-a-half thousand feet from sea level in the space of a mile. Two things particularly enticed. Quite low down, the path disappeared from view, having led into a rugged rock basin rimmed with red cliffs and crests. How, we wondered, did it find a way out? And in the late afternoon the ridge became an exact line of demarcation between light and shade – a jagged mountain Yin–Yang symbol. I've always been drawn to the typology of landscape, and that subject was manifestly dear to Gomerans ancient and modern. After several days in contemplation of the phenomenon, Jacquetta, supine on the terrace in the sun one idle afternoon, unable herself to move much, and having picked up on the fascination, prompted me to leave the cave and explore. 'Wave to me and I'll watch,' she promised, with a languid flutter of a sunning hand. I unscrewed the trekking poles, filled a water bottle, and followed alleys that mounted in a hopeful direction, eventually resolving into a single path by the side of a dried-up stream bed from the end of which a walled and cobbled ginnel broached the lowest slopes of the ridge. What immediately struck me was the obvious age of the path. It must have existed for centuries, would have been crucial before all the blastings and tunnellings higher up the gorge. And it was strangely beautiful in itself, working with the terrain, as robustly yet sympathetically constructed as a Le Corbusier dwelling. Also, the plant life across this seemingly barren hillside was spectacularly lovely. Sweet-scented thyme and delicate mats of Argyranthemums spread across the rocks, and every available crevice billeted a militia of sturdy, balsam-exuding, starburst-leaved Euphorbia. As it climbed higher, the old donkey trail slipped out across ledges from the cliff-stopped basin, crept behind a guard of ruddy pinnacles and gave out on to the convex gable of La Merica, the western isles of El Hierro and La Palma appearing above the haze behind.

Down there, the construction sites for new tourist complexes buzzed and clanked and thrummed, and at the beach the strummers and drummers were beginning to congregate for their evening ritual. Up here along the old way, only the dart of a lizard or slither of a stone marked the sun's descent, the day's change into night. All that effort, and I found myself reciting what I could remember of a passage from Lama Anagarika Govinda's *The Way of the White Clouds*:

The machine-made time of modern man has not made him the master but the slave of time; the more he tries to 'save' time, the less he possesses it. It is like trying to catch a river in a bucket. It is the flow, the continuity of its movement, that makes the river; and it is the same with time. Only he who accepts it in its fullness, in its eternal and life-giving rhythm, in which its continuity consists, can master it and make it his own. By accepting time in this way, by not resisting its flow, it loses its power over us and we are carried by it as though on the crest of a wave, without being submerged and without losing sight of our essential timelessness.[23]

I looked across at the islands where lights were coming on in the gloaming, looked down the ridge, with its flanks divided between deep shadow and bright bathing light. Far below and tiny, I saw my woman waving and hastened down after a while from the hill, tripping as I rounded one corner and was blinded by the light. I sprawled headlong, felt the dull clunk of impact between my brow and an edge of rock, sat on a step and saw bright crimson drops blotch the ground, soaked a cloth in water and bound it around my temples, carried on down. A hawk, smaller and brighter than a kestrel, paraded past garish and threatening, controlling the air. Two white birds – doves, perhaps its prey – fled into the rocks. On the terrace, Jacquetta bathed the wound, taping its edges closed. The sun stretched like melted plastic to the horizon, the tom-tom beat from the shore pressing it down. Most nights an awkward, disparate couple at the restaurant where we ate observed us fixedly, never talking to each other, the woman striking, heavy of body, often drunk. Something about these uncommunicative encounters stuck in my mind, as though there were a significance here that would only later be revealed. In the daytime I'd drive Jac to beaches, rub her softly with sun cream and she would lie goldening on the black sand, casting an amused eye on the naked Germans who thronged past, propping herself up sometimes to sketch models worthy of Lucian Freud whilst I read.

We came back to the moors with spring promising in the bubbling crescendos of returning curlews, and to the death one morning of Jac's cat Charlie. He and his sister had been her favourites, but the sister had died as a kitten, exsan-guinated beyond recovery by the fleas with which she'd been infested when Jac had found them abandoned in a box in a wood. She repeated the story on many occasions, unwittingly, brooding in her distant way on its symbolism. Charlie lay in his basket by the stove in the caravan, ready for burial, and that morning Will called around, sat in the caravan on cushions by the stove to talk of the confusion of feelings from his time in India, the impact of that beautiful, hard and terrible country on him. I saw him reach out to stroke Charlie as he talked, saw the puzzlement and then the recoil from the little animal's stiffening corpse. He left to pick up a friend, Pete Robbins, and drive up to Orkney on a climbing trip as I dug a grave for Charlie. I had never experienced Will so bewildered at the world – not even in the frequent crises of his childhood. I heard him out, could not disagree, and my attempts at ameliorative gloss sounded hollow even to me.

Jac still incapacitated from her falls, clearly ill, and exhausted from the continual pain, I would sometimes leave her sleeping and explore the landscape around the caravan. One dreary afternoon as I set off, the startling geometries of sunlight, suddenly cloud-freed, lit up a green rowan like a lamp against the slate-grey sky, and wheatears drove like blown petals across the shadowy green of the slopes. Sedgy leads through heather interlocked as I made my way up on to a broad moorland crest. The land around us was the eastern sector of the Migneint. 'Black and barren' is how George Borrow characterized this vast swathe of wild country when he passed through in 1854, before noting that 'one must not be over-delicate on the moors'. This region is no respecter of dry feet, its name deriving from 'mignen', which means a morass, and parts of it are just that. I kept an eye open for the occasional bright-green and waist-deep-pool-concealing patch of sphagnum moss and pieced my heather-avoiding way on to the whale's back, the red grouse chirring away, a couple of ravens passing overhead with a call that sounded like a deep and sonorous 'Hello!' To the south, slopes of deep heather descended to remote and unvisited Llyn Hesgyn. Down there in a barn by the side of their house, the wife of an artist-friend, Clyde Holmes, had hanged herself a few years before. All around the southern and western horizons, suggestions of peaks among the clouds, glimmers and flashes of lakes the locations of which I sought to identify, the names of which I strove to remember and the associated stories to recount to myself as I ambled along. The moorland vegetation was rain-beaded and glittering as the sun itself seemed to dart in and out of wreathing mist. Behind me across unvisited Cwm Penanner was Foel Goch, at the summit of which Augustus John attended the wedding of Abram Wood, King of the Gypsies, and danced to the gypsy fiddlers' and harpists' tunes. The hill-gable I was on undulated along at about the two-thousand-foot contour. There were slithery, black gulfs into which I had to leap, and grotesque, isolated, heather-capped peat-hags looming out of the mist, and old cairns of white quartz rather phantasmal in the greyness against the dark cast of the land. I saw no footprint as I toiled along in enveloping cloud to the summit cairns and scatter of splintery stones, the shelter-encircled, moss-grown Ordnance Survey pillar at the summit of Carnedd y Filiast. A gap cleared in the mist. Distant flash of water to the south was Llyn Tegid. Scanning around, not twenty yards away a brown hare loped, came to a halt, reared up on its hind legs, fixed its soft gaze in my direction.

Llyn Tegid, 'Bala Lake', takes its name from Tegid Foel, 'Bald Tegid', husband of Ceridwen, enchantress, who distilled in her cauldron insightful knowledge and deadly poison: a collocation as humanly poignant and apt as Philoctetes of the stinking wound and invincible bow in Sophocles' play of the same name. Ceridwen set the boy Gwion to stir the brew for a year until the time it could be given to her hideous son Afagddu – 'utter darkness' – but as the year drew to its end three boiling drops splashed on to Gwion's finger, and to cool it he sucked them, thus receiving the inspiration she had prepared for her own son. The cauldron split, spilling the poison that remained and alerting Ceridwen to what had happened. His chance gift detected, to escape Gwion changed into a hare and Ceridwen into a *filiast*, as in the hill's name – a greyhound bitch; and the chase and the shape-shifting, the stranger births and poetry itself all began. These old stories are still happening, are all around us. They give us keys and clues to understanding our planet and place upon it, give us warnings. I believe in them, as I do not believe or have faith in politicians, profit, commentators and other such perfidies. I continued on my way. The boundary stones lead from Carnedd y Filiast north-west to the rim of Cwm y Gylchedd and a steep, knee-jarring descent to the *corlannau*, the sheep-pens, at the head of that place. Its atmosphere unsettled and disturbed me, as though bad things had happened here and were still happening. Each boundary stone is of slate, set into a cairn of white quartz, and bearing the letters CD on one side – County of Denbigh – and TI on the other – Tir Ifan, about which experts on land tenure in medieval Wales have written much. This was land belonging to the Order of the Knights of St John of Jerusalem, who established a hospice here in 1189 to help travellers across these barren wastelands.

They left. The region became a haven for robbers and

bandits. I quit the map-drawn line, headed out compassless into the mist to drink from Ffynnon y Waen, the well of the moor; and then by the feel of contour alone eased blindly around on to the spur of Foel Goch, dropping down out of the cloud in the course of its gentle descent to see diffused sunlight catching at the moor grasses on Foel Frech beyond Bwlch Blaen y Cwm, and transforming all to a russet glow, that faded slowly around me as I toiled over Copa Ceiliog and strikingly-cairned Garn Prys to stumble down in the last glimmerings, the afterglow, to the ancient cairn circle by Bryn Ffynnon. On the descent into Cwm Penannner, slew of a twittering bat against my face and the owls' screams from the trees.

This place had never felt like home.

12

Catastrophe

The old-fashioned, red and fragrant climbing rose given to Jacquetta by her mother she had planted at the back of the house in the garden of which we'd sited our caravan. Though it was the wrong time of year, she asked me to transplant it, to a place against the barn wall opposite the caravan door. I carefully uprooted it, pruned away dead and brittle stems, dug a hole, filled it with water and then good compost from the bottom of the heap and horse manure, spreading the roots, back-filling the hole, top dressing with bone meal, arranging the long branches fan-like across the wall and fastening them securely there. For a couple of months afterwards it had seemed dead, no sign of shoot or leaf. At the first anniversary of our wedding, we went away for a week in May to the Roundhouse at Druidstone again. The weather was kind. High banks along the lanes were white with scurvy grass and tinted with violets. We walked around Wooltack Point, holding to the rim of fantastically folded and arched cliffs above Mouse's Haven. A fast tide was running into St Brides Bay through Jack

Sound, a stiff north-westerly plucking glitter from the wave-crests. I peered down and saw the black cross/white cross flicker of a manx shearwater careening with urgent grace along the wave-troughs, inches from the water. The water eddied and boiled around Pitting Gales Point and its reefs. Clouds of gulls rose from the great stack of the Mew Stone by Skomer Island and trailed a small fishing boat as it took the tide through the sound. Puffins rafted up in the lee of the island. A seal slipped out of one of the caves in the cove beneath us, trod water and looked around inquisitively. When we returned to the caravan after our time away a green flush was spreading up the rose from its roots, and along every thorned stem were tiny red spots that would become leaf, bud, flower. A female redstart was carrying twigs, moss and hanks of shed fleece to a crevice in the wall, her mate dancing on air around her, flicking incessantly the rust brilliance of his tail feathers.

Will came to see us, told of his exploits in Orkney. On the huge and crumbling vertical cliffs of St John's Head on Hoy, which rise 1200 feet out of the sea where Hoy Sound runs out from Scapa Flow into the Pentland Firth, he and Pete Robbins had made a free ascent of the 'Longhope Route',[24] originally climbed over thirty years before with very extensive use of aid. It was the kind of achievement, accomplished in a rigorously ethical style all-too-rare in the ego-fixated and fantasist-ridden world of climbing,[25] that was rapidly establishing his reputation as the best young adventure climber in the country.[26] He and Pete had gone on to attempt another old aid-climb, the south-east arête of the Old Man of Hoy. The rock on the Old Man is blocky and treacherously fissile. On the first

long, difficult pitch Will pulled on a large flake, it came away,
Pete held him on the rope after twenty feet. The flake struck
Will's head as it crashed down, gashed his forehead and
knocked him unconscious. He pulled off his beanie to show a
stitched wound on his forehead, gurned to show the tooth
he'd chipped. He didn't want to go back to a doctor to have
the stitches removed, asked Jac to do it instead. She sterilized
scissors and tweezers, neatly snipped and pulled out the black
thread, bathed the scar and put a dressing on it. He told us
he had a dental appointment in the coming week to cap the
tooth. Treatment session over, we sat on the bench outside
the caravan, talked over his troubled response to India again,
talked too about the expedition in which he was involved in
the summer to the great unclimbed rock walls by Cape
Farewell, at the southern tip of Greenland and on the same
latitude as Hoy. He seemed amused more than anything else
by his tumble on the Old Man, quite unworried that it would
affect his going on the trip. In his usual understated and dismissive way he related some of his recent climbing. One of the
routes he'd done between his return from India and setting out
for Orkney went under the name of 'Bobok'. It took an overhanging line through disintegrating rock on a cliff on the Lleyn
Peninsula. Unrepeated for years, it had acquired a ferocious
reputation after its first ascent by a wild-eyed former para-
trooper called Ray Kay. Some of the most notable names in the
sport had fallen off or retreated from it. Will asked me if I had
a copy of the Dostoyevsky story from which its name derives.
We spent an hour searching through boxes in the barn before
it emerged. He pocketed it, had a last cup of coffee, ruminated
a little longer on the climbs he was now doing, and left me

with his concluding comment: 'It's not good to be frightened all the time, is it Dad?'

After he'd gone, I thought a lot about his last question, worried too about the morbidly funny and macabre Dostoyevsky tale with its graveyard setting that he'd taken away with him – one of the darkest even this master of the sombre and the bleak ever wrote:

I glanced cautiously at the dead faces, fearing my own impressionability. There were mild expressions and also unpleasant ones. The smiles were generally not very nice, and some were very much the reverse. I don't like them; they make you dream.[27]

I remembered back to an essay I'd written on underlying motivation in one of the climbing journals when I'd been Will's age, wondered to myself if my own thinking had moved on beyond its young and visceral perceptions from a time when I was absorbed by the sport and ambivalent about the effect it had on me, or whether it stood as valid response to his concern:

I am not referring to the mountain environment here, or to the quiet pleasures of days in the hills; not referring to the huge range of interest encompassed in this scene; not referring to the sheer bodily and sensual pleasure of movement on rock, although all these things impinge upon the central experience [which is] the intense, neurotic urge to seek out the limits of subjective possibility on rock, the desire to push oneself to the extremes of endurance, adhesion, physical and mental control... there is an element of the mystical about climbing, but the climbers are lost not in God but in themselves. This is valid enough at a certain stage in life, but it is a lesson that should not be allowed to harden into a habit. In a sense it represents a shaking off of the last egocentricities of childhood, and a coming-to-terms at last with the external world. The act revokes its own motivation. Commitment to a series of extreme moves on rock is a tenuous expression of belief in one's personal omnipotence; by its very nature it is an illusion, and one bolstered so often by the mean little tricks and dishonesties of the climbing world as to lose the integrity upon which its validity must rest. No one is omnipotent, and on rock we all strive to be so. The ego and the will are the driving forces in climbing, the philosophy behind it is one of despair. Consider us and what we are: we are not well-balanced individuals, as long as we climb, because we have committed ourselves to a pure sphere of self-assertion and will. We turn from a world of which we cannot be the centre, to an experience so intense that we cannot but see ourselves at the centre of it. Every new trip up Sisyphus' Hill hardens the ego a little by providing us with the proof that we can do it. Ego and will do not lead to happiness... these sudden explosions of the assertive will are a pathway to restraint, and not freedom, of response. They are lessons to be learned, not ones always to be lived by, and their repetitions become not only absurd, for this element was present in their nature from the beginning, but also negative and destructive, a denial of the potentialities of life. Obsessive climbing is a reprisal against nature for making self so small within it. The toying with death... that represents so strong a part of the attraction of climbing adds yet another facet to the basic negativity of the sport. Each new death is a reiteration of the question, 'Is it worth it?', from the answering of which we always shy away. At Lawrie Holliwell's funeral every face was haunted by the realization of a death that could as easily have been theirs.[28] Is it worth it? Yes, for those who are weak, aimless, discontent, strong and directionless, unresolved or in despair. For all who fit these categories the activity is eminently worthwhile in that it brings them close to ridding themselves of an existence that could so easily become a burden, and by the proximity of that negation increases the attractiveness of life... I have learned things from climbing: that the seemingly impossible can be achieved by precise, coordinated movement, by direction of energy and conservation and timed application of resources. That things are easier than they seem to be; that falling off is not the thing to do until every last possible scrap of resource has failed you; that a sufficiency of commitment will usually see you through; that a real and authentic desire is the only worthwhile spring to action. But these are lessons to be applied now to the creative act of living, in conjunction with the more warm, full and human values of love, feeling, knowledge, compassion. They are no longer ones to be squandered in the negative sphere of rock. We pass from one lesson to another armed with a new strength of knowledge, and should be glad that it is so.[29]

Green June came to the moors. The redstarts hatched their clutch of eggs, reared their brood, the parents dipping in and out of the nest-crevice behind the rose constantly, beaks racked with insects and flies. For a few days the speckled brown babies with their red tails whirred around, and then, with their parents, departed for the south. One morning, as Jac and I lay in bed in the caravan with our coffee, beyond the window we saw a nymph hovering vertically, its wings gilded in a shaft of sunlight. Jac pointed, smiling: 'Look! A fairy...'

In that instant a great tit swooped across. A snap of its beak and the nymph was gone. I turned to Jac and the tears were springing from her eyes.

Will found a dentist and had a temporary crown put on his tooth. At long last I had started in earnest on the Whillans biography, Jacquetta shutting me in the caravan until I'd completed the 2,000-words-per-day quota I'd set myself, bringing me provisions from time to time, busying herself about glass commissions in her workshop. We bought her a new car, the one she had having been trashed by borrowers, and she eased herself back into mobility and a social round. Then word came from Llanberis that Will was in hospital. The capped tooth had become infected, and the infection developed into Ludwig's angina. He was found by a friend and near-neighbour who was a nurse, rushed in to Ysbyty Gwynedd, had an emergency tracheotomy, massive doses of antibiotics, then the tracheotomy reversed – again under general anaesthetic – after a week.

He was discharged, carried on readying himself for the expedition, assured me that he was fit enough and that both his doctor and the team's doctor had cleared him to go. I grumbled away at him to take care, to rest, not to feel pressured into going if he didn't feel up to it. He grinned and ignored me, told me all his bags had been sent on ahead. I immersed myself in the writing I had to do, not entirely reassured, diverting myself from anxiety by concentrating on that. Jac and I lapsed into an easy pattern of her glass work and my writing in the days, turns taken at making dinner, evenings in the caravan or on the bench outside, her sundowner, music into the night, bed together, relaxed sweet mornings watching the birds.

One evening as we sat on the bench a cock blackbird sang from the gable of the barn – sang so sweetly, long and loud, self-delighting in his own elaborations or so it seemed, that we looked at each other and back at him in wonderment. The next morning I found him dead outside the caravan, without mark of injury upon him. 'He sang his heart out to us,' said Jac. We drove across The Berwyn to the garden centre she liked near Welshpool, bought a beautiful, dense, late-flowering cherry, planted it where he had fallen and buried him beneath.

Midsummer passed. We slept out near Mitchell's Fold – less frequent an occurrence these days through work and Jac's physical discomfort. I watched her as she sat in the firelight from the edge of a copse where I'd gone to collect wood. There was a pained quality to her expression now in repose, and the flames seemed to shadow where once they had illuminated her face. She summoned brightness now instead of emanating it continually, and our love-making had become pensive, languorous, intensely close, a fragile new neediness in it.

Will phoned from a raucous going-away party to say his goodbyes. I carried on with the Whillans book, wrestling with the task of deconstructing a myth that had wrought destruction in its subject's life, and seeking to present a human portrait in its place – not a project of which some in the mountaineering world were going to approve, bringing into question as it did male posturings, the insidious nature of celebrity and the damage done where it becomes a need in the individual. All the time there was a nagging anxiety about Will, who was so free of these traits and yet so troubled by their existence in others. A small incident from a climb we'd done together years before when he was fifteen kept coming to my mind. Will had wanted to do his first 6a pitch.[30] I'd led it, distinctly feeling my age on some of the contortionate and agile moves it demanded, had clipped the protection peg by the most difficult section and my hand had lingered there for a moment longer than Will, watching from below, thought legitimate.

'Dad,' he yelled up, 'you hung on that peg. You've got to unclip and do it again without, otherwise it's cheating...'

He was right, of course, and I had to accede, but that degree of rigour put him well at odds with the climate of the contemporary sport, and inevitably gave him a jaundiced view of human action and motivation.

Brain wrung-out and weary, I was twelve pages into the last chapter of the Whillans book at the end of July. Very late one night, as Jac and I lay in bed, close entwined and on the brink of sleep, the phone rang in the caravan. We ignored it. It stopped, then immediately started ringing again. Jac murmured that it must be important and I rolled out of bed to answer.

The person on the other end of the line was weeping, eventually blurted out his message. Will had been found dead in his house, hanging in his bedroom under the eaves. He had been there for days. Jac came up behind me, instincts charged, asked, and I repeated what I had been told. Her face gaped into an expression of horror and howling grief. She snatched Will's picture from our caravan shrine, threw herself into bed, and as I held and tried to comfort her, she screamed until she could no longer scream and, curled up foetal in my arms, subsided into racking sobs.

Five years have passed since that night. For almost a week now I have been sitting at my desk or pacing around this room a thousand miles away to the south, looking from the window down into the garden, scarcely sleeping at night, dragging myself from bed in the mornings exhausted, wondering how to continue with this narrative, unable to write down a single meaningful word. In my mind I circle endlessly around Will's decision:

> Suicide is... a solitary act, but paradoxically it deeply involves others. The person who takes their own life is making a powerful statement about life and about their relationships. In rejecting life, they are also rejecting those who were a part of it. Suicide is perceived as the only escape from an intolerable situation and, by implication, others are seen as unable to offer any solution which would make life worth living.[31]

What catches me out continually is the matter of understanding Will's choice – not that I don't, which might be easier, but that I can see all too clearly the factors that led him to make it, with many of which I have made personal accommodations by no means amounting to disagreement. The metaphysical despair is there, clearly outlined, in the two notebooks he left behind: 'You're given a cell,/it strips you of pride./To like it or hate it,/how do you decide?' The child in Will, however he might have grown in apparent confidence through his mastery of climbing, always seemed so terribly vulnerable. I remember an evening when he was fifteen, he had told me he was going to a school disco and would be back by midnight but had gone instead down to the local village of Deiniolen, met up with a couple of lads there, bought a bottle of vodka, decided to visit some girls they knew in a nearby village, so one of the lads, who was only fourteen, had borrowed his mother's car – she and his father, a policeman, were out for the night – and written it off at a roundabout. The three of them, unhurt, had run off through the fields and been picked up by the police, drunk and dishevelled, by the chip shop in the village. At midnight I was working, waiting for the phone call to pick him up. When it came I found myself speaking to the desk sergeant in Caernarfon. Would I collect my son from their custody? At the police station they told me all that had happened, that there would be no charges because technically Will had committed no offence, but that he'd had what they termed 'a right bollocking'. And that I was free to take him home and give him the same myself. There was no need. When they let me into the cell he was in floods of tears, abjectly frightened and sorry. I just hugged him, rubbed his head, told him how glad I was he wasn't dead and not to be such a daft bugger again; and to please tell me the truth about what he was doing in future. *The boy weeping in the cell…*

> Anguish is known to everyone since childhood, and
> everyone knows that it is often blank, undifferentiated.
> It rarely carries a clearly written label that also con-
> tains its motivation; when it does have one, it is often
> mendacious. One can believe or declare oneself to be
> anguished for one reason and be so due to something
> totally different; one can think that one is suffering at
> facing the future and instead be suffering because of
> one's past; one can think that one is suffering for
> others, out of pity, out of compassion, and instead be
> suffering for one's own reasons, more or less pro-
> found, more or less avowable and avowed, sometimes
> so deep that only the specialist, the analyst of souls,
> knows how to exhume them.[32]

Thus Primo Levi, written months before his own suicide.
That Will's was a considered decision is made clear by the
manner of it. He knelt into the noose, did not struggle to
escape it – rather saw it as the means of escape from a society
which itself was for him the noose, choking away all breath of
individuality. He had set off for Greenland – had driven his car
down to Heathrow with three friends, dropped them off at
Departures and told them he was going to park the car, texted
them from around the corner to tell them he wasn't coming,
threw his mobile out of the car somewhere on the journey
home, and stayed there without contact with the outside
world for at least four days – his computer provided the
evidence for this – before he chose to end his life. Nobody

knew he was there, or that he'd not gone to Greenland. His car was only noticed hidden away around the back of his house days after his death, which led to the same friend – a good woman, his girlfriend's sister – who'd found him when he was desperately ill with Ludwig's angina, to call the police, word having come back from Greenland by then that he'd not joined the expedition. I could look to find reason or ascribe blame – to my own inadequate parenting of him; to his mother's continual criticism of him as being 'awash in a sea of negativity'; to his horrified witness of world-shaming social conditions during his time in India; to the temporary loss of potency in his self-defining activity of climbing and the burden of expectation that awaited him in Greenland. All these were no doubt contributory, but my retained sense from those last meetings is of the anguish that Primo Levi defines – 'blank, undifferentiated' – a state in which the notion of motivation is somehow beside the point. Ultimately, all that I can say about my son's death is that he chose it, and I must respect that decision however much I might wish it other, however much I miss his living presence. A passage from Al Alvarez's dignified and humane book about suicide perhaps comes close to summing up Will's state of being in those last days of utter isolation:

>...mere intellectual recognition did no good and, anyway, my clear moments were few. My life felt so cluttered and obstructed that I could hardly breathe. I inhabited a closed, concentrated world, airless and without exits. I doubt if any of this was noticeable socially: I was simply tenser, more nervous than usual... But underneath I was going a bit mad. I had

entered the closed world of suicide and my life was being lived for me by forces I couldn't control.[33]

There was a funeral to be arranged. In the days after Will's death a phenomenon I had never previously encountered registered with me – that the bereaved must themselves at their lowest ebb become a means of support to many others who grieve. It seemed crucial therefore to make Will's funeral into a celebration of his life, and a carefully-orchestrated ritual that might bring some solace, some understanding. It was held at Bangor Crematorium – a traditional place of farewells to the dead of the climbing community – and the attendance was staggering. Hundreds were unable to enter the chapel and were left standing outside in the sun and the wind, the service relayed to them there by loudspeakers. Six of his friends – four male, two female – carried in his wicker coffin. There was music, Bob Dylan mostly, who was his favourite – 'Forever Young', 'Mr Tambourine Man', 'Shooting Star'; and there were poems read by his friends – Edward Thomas's 'The Bridge':

> All are behind, the kind
> And the unkind too, no more
> Tonight than a dream. The stream
> Runs softly, yet drowns the Past,
> The dark-lit stream has drowned the Future and
> the Past.[34]

and a lovely Welsh sonnet, *'Dychwelyd'* ('Returning') by the great poet of his Snowdonia place, T. H. Parry-Williams:

Ni all terfysgoedd daear byth gyffroi
Distawrwydd nef; ni sigla lleisau'r llawr
Rymuster y tangnefedd sydd yn toi
Diddim diarcholl yr ehangder mawr;
Ac ni all holl drybestod dyn a byd
Darfu'r tawelwch nac amharu dim
Ar dreigl a thro'r pellterau sydd o hyd
Yn gwneuthur gosteg a'u chwyrnellu chwim.
Ac am nad ydyw'n byw ar hyd y daith,
O gri ein geni hyd ein holaf gwyn,
Yn ddim ond crych dros dro neu gysgod craith
Ar lyfnder esmwyth y mudandod mwyn,
Ni wnawn, wrth ffoi am byth o'n ffwdan ffol,
Ond llithro i'r llonyddwch mawr yn ol.[35]

Not all the troubles of earth can disturb
The quiet of heaven, nor the voices down here shake
The overarching peace
Of empty seamless space;
Nor all the fuss of man and his world
Lay waste to the stillness, nor harm one jot
The faraway motion and swirl, that perpetually
Create new silence in their swift circling.
And all our life's journey,
From birth-cry to last sigh,
Is no more than spreading ripple or shadow of a scar
On the smoothness of that soft silence,
As we flee forever our daft pother,
To slip back into the vast tranquility.

His friends, Pete Robbins, Mark Katz and James MacHaffie gave their recollections, loving and funny and admiring. Mick Ward describes the scene:

The crematorium in Bangor was overflowing with people. Half of Llanberis was there and much of climbing's history. *Will was well loved.* If his death was sad, lonely and terrible, his sending-off was a sight such as I could never have envisaged. The collective emotion was massive. *He was well loved.* Jim's friends were there when he needed them. Ray Wood scurried around, unobtrusively fixing all the things a social gathering needs. Tony Shaw, whom Jim first met at Windgather forty years before, presided with authority and grace.

When Jim stood up to speak, he faltered. For moments he just stood there, looking thin and frail and lost. No words came out. Just as it seemed he was going to crumple, he began. What followed, his leave-taking of Will, was... something which I shall never again witness and could not bear to witness.

I had performed this task for so many of my friends over the years. To do it for my son was the hardest thing I ever did in my life:

Two things first of all: the exquisite portrait of Will in the order of service – which is the favourite one I have of him apart from one in which he's wearing a nappy, and I know he would have been mightily displeased had we used that – is by our dear friend Ray Wood, and has somehow slipped through unacknowledged. So I'm sorry for that, Ray, and thank you for the use of the photograph.

Secondly, Will was anything but conventional in his outlook on life – had he spotted any black ties here today one of his sly comments, one of his wry grins, would have been heading in its direction. So if any of you are wearing one, thank you for the respectful intention, which he would have appreciated, because he had the gentlest of hearts; but you can personalize that respect now by taking them off, shoving them in your pockets, and breathing more easily…

Will is my first-born son, and his presence in my life for the last twenty-four years has been something so precious it's beyond my capacity with words to express it. From the moment I first saw him, I thought him the most perfectly beautiful being I had ever set eyes upon. A sense of that remained with me throughout that phase of life when sleep is a memory and the sustenance of your sanity depends on substances that go under names like Milton and Sudocrem, Bonjela and Gripe Water. Us old people look at you younger people with a kind of fond, distant understanding of the changes that soon you'll be coming to. And the crucial word there is 'soon', and you would not believe how rapidly time passes…

It seems to me not as though it were yesterday but as though somehow it were happening now that I see Will in his papoose and his fleecy baby-gro in the snow on top of Clogwyn Mawr above Capel Curig at eight months old, waving his arms at the ravens; another second and he's sturdy, four years old, his mane of blond hair flying as he speeds though the bracken on Llanbedr Hill and leaps at me, clinging on like a koala bear, making me wade into the middle of the mawn pool there and then getting me to put him down waist-deep in the water so he can soak me with his splashing and his laughter; or we're cooking sausages quietly and harmlessly over an open fire on a beach and some countryside policeman comes up to us and starts brusquely to recite the book of rules, offences and misdemeanours; and when I rather more politely invite him to make particular use of the handle of the frying pan, and he's flounced off in a huff to get re-inforcements, Will appropriates the phrase, and stomps around in glee, kicking sand, chanting it to himself; and I have to instruct him in all the hypocrisies of appropriateness...

Will had already nearly been expelled from school at the age of eight – strange, the things in which a father takes pride. He'd flashed a V-sign at the head-master of Cricieth school one afternoon, and the phone calls and the vocabulary of moral outrage that poured forth upon him was Calvinistic-comical at its most extreme. What's disgusting about a child registering contempt for puffed-up authority? Will did that by instinct, and I aided and abetted him in it, and tried to bring his bewilderment around to laughter, and instructed him as best I could in the slippery arts of social self-preservation.

He was so mischievous, and so beautiful, and so innocent, and however thick a carapace he grew as the years passed, none of those qualities ever deserted him. He had to *learn* to be streetwise. Eventually I called in a private tutor, Martin Crook, to give him special tuition in the arts of wiliness, to teach him that 'Do what you will' is not quite the whole law, and needs the addition of that terse phrase, 'but don't get caught!'

Before that, there was the occasion when he made a hoax phone call to the Fire Brigade to report that a house down the road was on fire. He liked fire engines and things like that – first word he learned was 'digger'. The operator asked him for his number. He gave her our number. Within half an hour the local policeman arrived to give him a bollocking and leave me to explain again the means subversion must employ to escape detection.

The other time he was nearly expelled, from his secondary school, absolutely confirmed his instinctive and accurate view that society rests on a foundation of quivering and hypocritical bullshit. Will was born – necessarily I'd think in view of his parentage – with the most acute bullshit-detectors I've ever come across. On this second close shave with expulsion, some mate of his had been caught at school with the merest sliver of cannabis on him, and immediately blabbed that Will had given it him – which was probably true, because he was always very generous with anything he and I had. Naturally this aroused a shock-horror response with the powers-that-be, since enough blow to make a single spliff was obviously going to rot the brains of a generation, and, after Will had been suspended for three weeks, he and I were both summoned to appear before a special meeting of the Board of Governors called for the end of the spring term.

There was a long table, grave faces along either side. Will and I and the headmaster were seated at one end, the Chairman of the Board of Governors in all the gravity of his authority at the other. The headmaster opened the case for the prosecution – terrible, pernicious, social evil, serious view, necessity to stamp it out and make an example – and all the grave faces along either side nodded him along like toy dogs on the back shelf of a car, and it was clear that Will, who'd gone very pale, was on his way out, and I was calculating how I could afford private school fees.

At which point I looked up, and my eyes just for an instant met those of the Chairman of the Board of Governors and he, startled, dropped them to his notepad and began scribbling away furiously. Then it was his turn to speak. He rose to his feet; in measured speech agreed with all the headmaster had said, and began to talk of how, despite the gravity of the offence, to blight a young man's education for one slip was too harsh, and leniency was better than overreaction, and the poodles ranged along either side nodded him along, and suspension until the beginning of next term was suggested and they agreed and it was the headmaster's turn to go pale with anger and thwarted bloodlust; and with the illest grace and much rehearsal of his own words he was forced to accept. Will and I exchanged a surreptitious glance, I looked stern and kicked him under the table lest he should smile, and we walked through the playground and out of the gate, shaking with laughter. He asked me, 'What was all that about, Dad? I was going to be expelled, wasn't I?' And I said, 'Well, that guy at the far end of the table who spoke for you...' Will looked at me quizzically. 'In the sixties we all used to buy our dope from him. I think his conscience prompted him. He used to be a policeman...'

It's maybe as well that Will started climbing – God knows where all that subversive energy, all that innocent challenge of his would have gone otherwise. I never thrust climbing upon him, and in my heart, back then, I never really wanted him to start. Too many times I've been in this place or others like it for my friends. I think it began because he had a thing about Katie Haston. Whenever I mentioned her name – and you know fathers like to bait their sons a bit around these things – he'd go bright red and profess to hate her, and then he'd be off down the climbing wall at the Heights and I'd ask innocently, 'Was Katie there, Will?' and he'd glower at me and mutter rude things about 'stupid-old-bastards-what-do-they-know', and carry on doing pull-ups on the doorframes and it was obvious that he'd gone down with the bug. Or maybe two bugs...

So for about a year – and it was such a magical

year – because I wanted him to know how to be safe, we went out climbing together whenever we could. I was way past my sell-by date at this time, and as Will would rightly and frequently point out, an idle old bastard in whom motion was only ever discernible once caffeine levels were sufficiently high. This meant that, often as not, we finished routes in the dark, so it always felt like an adventure. We did a lot of the classic routes of Snowdonia together: 'White Slab' on a day when we were the only people on the crag and he was bubbling with excitement all the way back down with the setting sun streaming through the *bwlch*; 'Vector' after school one day, me hanging out of the cave and yelling at him to get back on the rock and do it properly, using his feet, when he'd just hurled himself at the groove coming out of the Ochre Slab and swung off. He used to believe that momentum was all the technique you needed. We finished the top crack in the pitch black.

His ability soon sailed way past the remnants of mine, and I was fortunate enough to get a shoulder injury that stopped my climbing, so I didn't hold him back. He became very, very good. I've seen many people climb over the decades who've impressed me. Will had the special gift, the rock-knowledge. The dancing god had visited him. He had such grace. But there was more to it than that. The grace was in his spirit, his attitudes were sound. Climbers are awful for bullshit. Will didn't bullshit, he just did the thing for the sharp, sweet thrill of it. He climbed with the best, and they respected him, and they liked him, because he was funny and warm and a bit mysterious. The humour of climbers can be quite savage. With Will, it was a kind of gentle, sidelong poking of fun that – for those who were listening – opened out perspectives. I think he was very wise. By the time he was about seventeen, he treated me, with great good humour and tolerance, as one might an errant adolescent.

He started travelling. He went off to America at eighteen, made many friends worldwide, did hard things in Yosemite, wandered all around Europe easing himself into scenes and enjoying the company and the climbs. He talked lyrically about the textures of rock, the atmospheres of place. More recently, I climbed with him a little again, but the gap between his ease and my age had grown vast, so I always felt what he never showed – that it was a condescension on his part.

Two occasions stick in my mind: he took me up some of my own routes from over thirty years ago in Pembroke a couple of years ago, drifting up them effortlessly, and when I came to follow, enthusing, helping me in every subtle way that he could. Generosity of spirit again…

Another time, we were driving to a Dylan concert in Manchester on an early summer day and it transpired he'd never been to Frodsham [a series of small and extremely steep sandstone outcrops in a wood above the village of that name, near Chester]. I was spared climbing because I had a suit on – he nicked

that from me as well as the Dylan records, has probably appeared at most of your weddings in it. Anyway,
we flogged up through the woods to Hoop-La Buttress
and there were a couple of sweet young lads from
Ellesmere Port with a mat beneath them bouldering
out the roof of 'Hoop-La' itself.[36] Will was in his jeans
and trainers and watched awhile, then the lads saw he
was itching to take a look, so they stepped aside. He
did each of the routes on that overhanging rock, one
after the other, with total ease and elastic elegance, and
the two lads looked at me with their mouths open, and
shaking heads and bemused smiles, and they all sat
down and smoked a roll-up and Will was friendly and
open with them, and you could see they felt they'd met
someone special.

Later on that night, outside the concert, we were
waiting for a friend to go for a Rusholme curry.[37] Will
was wiling away the time walking along one of those
swinging chains – his balance was amazing. A large
policewoman waddled across with intent. I interposed
myself, explained it was one of his recreations, and
harmless. Will stood on one leg on the gently swinging
chain, hands behind his back, looking with a kind of
mild interest elsewhere as this downbeat altercation
went on. She got into the regulations and all that, and
he carried on ignoring her, and at length, baffled, she
turned and grumbled away.

Will looked over his shoulder and down at me, his
grin was pure, impish, provocative delight, he did a
quick back-flip, stepped down, touched his finger to

his tongue and marked one up against authority. And I glowed with pride...

I cannot begin to do justice to Will in this short space. There cannot be a greater privilege in this life than to have someone like him as your child. I was asked three or so years ago if I'd choose a favourite piece from my own writing for an American anthology Pat Ament was editing. There was absolutely no difficulty in deciding. It was an essay about doing a climb on Anglesey with Will one winter's day when he was fifteen. In a brief foreword to it, I wrote, 'He is a supremely talented climber now, and a funny, lovely, endearing young man whose soundness of approach to the sport educates me as surely as the sport itself has educated him.'

Pat Ament ran into Will in Bishop, when he was out in California over that winter, and got him to write his response to the essay. I'll read part of it:

'Wow! this is a pretty scary place,' I thought as I left the vaguely solid ground I'd been belaying from and stepped around on to the huge white slab. I looked down at the void between my frozen feet and saw a piece of driftwood being tossed around in the frothy swell that crashed between boulders and the sides of the zawn. My body warmed a little, and the climbing became interesting and enjoyable.

'I was not finding it all that bad. It was quite peaceful really, listening to the wind whistle through the huge arch, watching the birds, with nature slowly taking its course. We were soon at the top, wrapped up

warm, and I scrambled down to the end of the promontory to see where we'd been. It was beautiful. A
patch of sun broke through the blanket of grey and lit
up the speckled walls. My dad came down to look
with me. I felt close to him. Those special moments
with special people in special places are what it's all
about. Isn't it?'

You, his friends gathered here today, were Will's
'special people'. And he, to me, was utterly so throughout his life. There is nothing with which I could ever
wish to reproach him, no decision of his I could ever
gainsay. Keep him safe and precious now in your
hearts. I want you to take a little time here, in silence,
to think of him, to think of his humour, the sly magic
of his presence, his modesty, his awareness, and to fix
that in your memories where it can live forever.'

My voice held out, just. I walked across to where his
mother sat, took her by the hand, led her to the dais and
we stood by our son's coffin in a silent space of memory.
Eventually 'Forever Young' came up again on the sound
system. Tony Shaw, who was managing the ceremony, pressed
the button for the coffin to slide from sight. The congregation
filed out, Jacquetta and I moved away into the garden and sat
quietly there, together, coming to terms.

I do not know where the dead go, have no resolved sense
or belief around that issue. I recall the extreme irritation
engendered in me by the flippancy of one rather arrogant and
vacuous young man's entry in Will's book of condolences:
'Have a good one, Will! Yo…!'

'What was he thinking of?' I asked his mother, 'does he not know that suicide's an expression of anguish, not an invitation to a party?'

'Oh, Justin knows that in the afterlife everyone's happy and having a good time. "Will'll be having a real groove," he told me.'

I walked off shaking my head at the heedless, cruel vacuity. It was a type of response that in the coming months I was to encounter time and again. So many people 'know' what goes on 'in the afterlife'. Elisabeth Kübler-Ross, 'one of the best-loved and most-respected authorities on death and dying' according to the blurb on one of her books, writes the following with supreme assurance:

> After death, you will also experience a review of your life. You will review it not in the first person, not as you experienced it in life. But you will review it from the perspective of how everyone else experienced you. You will feel all the consequences of your actions. You will know all the pain and more importantly all the love and kindness that others felt from you. This will not be a punitive experience but a learning one. You will see how far you have grown in your life and whether you have more lessons to learn. You will be asked how much did you love and how much service did you do for mankind.[38]

The only comments that I need make on the above are that it is based in assertion and not in knowledge – there is neither guarantee nor any human experience to support its Christo-

judicial catalogue of '*you will*'s – and that however sound its underlying ethical model might be, in effect its prescriptivism is dictatorially abusive of the vulnerability and desperate need of the newly-bereaved for a knowledge that in evidential – in tangible – terms simply does not exist. The false informants gather around death, and their name is legion.

Dazed, Jac and I tried to pick up the thread of work and set out on its therapeutic course again. That, and each other, were our tenuous lifelines. She told me she had the offer of some painting at a stained-glass studio in Chester and went off there on a couple of successive days. A week or so beyond Will's funeral I was behind the caravan one evening diverting more water from the stream there into a small fish pond at the bottom of the garden when I sensed a movement, looked up and saw Will glancing back as he walked away around the sycamore tree, smiling at me. A simple swing of rope and crossbar dangled from a branch of the tree. It was lashing about wildly, as though someone had just dropped off it. The day was windless. Jac was not long back from Chester and sitting quietly by the pond. I went over and asked her if she'd seen anything. Nothing. She gestured me to sit by her side on the granular boulder above the pond, told me the real purpose of her visits to Chester. A routine mammogram had shown up irregularities in her left breast. She'd rapidly been referred to the Countess of Chester Hospital, more investigations had confirmed the suspicion of cancer. She had not wanted, after Will's death, to further sadden me with this news. I asked her what her consultant had said. Her face streaming with tears she turned to me, we held each other, and she sobbed out that it was a rare and aggressive type of breast cancer, the chances of surviving which beyond five years were about 35 per cent. She was to start chemotherapy the following week.

The next fortnight was terrible beyond anything I had ever known. Grieving for Will was for the present an impossibility and caring for Jac had to become the priority. At one point she disappeared for a couple of days, phoned friends from a call box (she would never carry a mobile phone) to tell them that she could not bear to burden me further. I was only staying with her now because I felt sorry for her, she told them, and that the statistics showed a huge incidence of marital break-up after fatal diagnosis. They tried to reassure her. I was desperately worried, particularly because she had taken from the caravan Will's notebooks – to protect me, she later explained, and yet when I came to read the notebooks their effect was not devastating, was more one of comprehending and accepting a set of perceptions that he had carefully set out and thought through. Far from devastation, though they brought sadness, they also brought increase of respect and love.

Jac returned, and as best I could I reassured her that I was staying with her and would always stay with her as long as we lived and according to the promises we'd made at the well, not from sense of duty but because I passionately loved her. Once her condition had become widely known, we were daily besieged by kind-intentioned quackery, anecdotes and directivism, most of which she slipped gracefully. One well-meaning Tibetan Buddhist friend – a good man, essentially – sent a 'magic pill', to be consumed with due ritual, of dried Holy-Lama-shit. Chemotherapy began, and its effects became obvious. The Whillans book finished and delivered, I sought to distract her. In the fire-colours of autumn and the winds of the equinox we went to Much Wenlock, to stay at The Raven in this small, half-timbered, red-brick, lobelia-hung, narrow-streeted, alleywayed, book-and-tea-shopped town with the soft burr of the Marches on its streets. Jac dragged me around the town's pubs in search of Guinness, savoured every mouthful of unfussy perfection in the dinner we were served at our comfortable little hotel, and reminded me of the dawning astonishment and delight on the face of the general in *Babette's Feast* – her favourite film from the time of breaking her ribs, and one of the great cinematic hymns to life's riches. We visited – officially this time, for we'd several times climbed over the wall and sat among the ruins in the moonlight during our time in Llanrhaeadr – the monastic remains of St Milburga's Priory, vast in its groundplan, majestic in its remnant Early English and Norman architecture, peerless in the sweet, gardened intimacy of its surroundings. She pointed out to me, seeing them for the first time in daylight, carved panels ravishing in the simple beauty of their design that showed Christ walking on water alongside his Apostles' boat, and again holding one of them by the hand. Elsewhere she chanced on the innocence of a little carved angel above the entrance to the chapter house; in the elaborate false arcading on its south wall an extraordinary pagan design of sea-monsters; and a grotesque head in a north-door lintel. But at night in our hotel room she wept at the clumps of hair that came away as she brushed it before bed. Gillian Rose again:

I have lost most of my hair. Losing my long, heavy tresses of hair has been the motif of one of two recurrent nightmares as long as I can remember... Could it be the symbol of feminine power – hair to catch and petrify men? Or is it the longing for security – hair to hide in? Am I sworn to the Gorgon or to Artemis?[39]

We drove away next morning along Wenlock Edge, an unbroken reef of limestone like a roller stilled in mid-ocean, which stretches west for sixteen miles down to Craven Arms, looking out to the 'blue, remembered hills' of Wales, oak-woods the length of its north-western scarp richly coloured as old brocade, pheasants calling from the woods, mew of a buzzard cutting through the birdsong, and crossed the Long Mynd from Church Stretton to the Horseshoe Inn at Bridges. The little East Onny river trickled past in front of the pub, its clear pools starred with water crowfoot, and the long, low, white building bathed in afternoon sunlight. We walked to the stone circle at Mitchell's Fold with its marvellous associated eco-fable of the witch, the cow and the sieve,[40] and looked across at sunset to the ridges of Pumlumon, Cader Idris, Aran and Berwyn rising from violet shadow into crystal air along the horizon to the west, before descending a short mile to the Miners' Arms in Priest Weston. Entering from under a king-fisher-blue, post-sunset sky flamed with cloud, we met with a Harvest Home celebration, the place decorated with the good things of the earth – bread and fruit and cider and the crops of the land. Laconic, quiet men and glad women talked under the old beams of the seasonal things, and when the time came for Jac and myself to slip away, out of the window drifted the music of an old hymn – 'All is safely gathered in' – as a big bright moon sailed out from behind Corndon Hill, and the silvered landscape gleamed.

A few weeks later, on a raw afternoon we were driving back from Yorkshire where we'd been prospecting other forms of treatment for Jac and found ourselves within a few miles of the Chew Valley above Greenfield, a place important in my youth to which I'd not been since before Will was born. On impulse we headed there, threading down from the northern moors past signs each marked as of 'No Scrap Value', to a car park by a new reservoir, under the surface of which are greens on which I'd once camped, lit fires, played boyish games and talked long into nights that knew nothing of lives to come. We walked past a memorial forest where a priest was blessing the planting of a tree in the ashes of someone's beloved – a birch tree. At the edge of the old plantation called Chew Piece above, we sat on moss, our backs to a boulder, feet on a grit-stone slab into which was stilled an eddying wave pattern from aeons past. The sound of the stream drifted up, its water peat-brown, a dipper working the pools. The unexpected love-liness of the place stilled us. Suddenly we were at peace in the presences of the trees. There were beech, birch, rowan, sessile oak, Scots pine, an elegantly trailing larch gathered here, and the pink and umber hues and tints of the moor all around, the muted cast of landscape that expresses in greys, khakis, faint tinges of pale brown or washed-out yellow; and that cyclo-pean masonry of rock above, on which I and later my son used to climb. A dead tree twisted and writhed, one brittle branch pointing like a finger up-valley, two more enclosing empty, heart-shaped space. I picked up a fallen leaf from among the beech mast, and Jacquetta and I studied its remnant greens, so perfectly offset and balanced by purples, ochres, a flaring orange. On the moor rim, rocks balanced; the crags were seamed and riven; streams threaded down; through and through, the same fault-lines, pattern, design. Our fractal universe, faces and creatures in the rocks, what we perceive. In a beech tree two lovers had carved their initials; on a boulder too, bold lettering, the lichens softening, filling the incisions as tissue does a scar.

I held Jac's strong hand and watched the birch tree above us – 'Our Lady of the Woods', daintiest and hardiest of broad-leaved trees – found myself thinking of Vainamoinen in the Finnish epic *The Kalevala*, who loses his harp, and so makes a new one from the wood of a weeping birch that could find no joy in life, telling the tree as he cuts into its wood, 'Soon shalt thou with joy be weeping,/Shortly shalt thou sing for pleasure.' The western sky beyond the plantation was wild with sunset, a wind sweeping through, dark intersections of dead branches against the dancing leaves. Here in Chew Piece at autumn twilight, some healing power was at work. We sat quietly together, my arm around her, and found a degree of peace.

We went away to Tobago. One dawn in our hut above Castara Bay I woke to an empty bed, a note on the pillow: 'White Rabbits! White Rabbits! Good Morning! I love you. Am watching the light-show – fire-flies and lightning – and listening to the orchestra. Thunder's doing the bass. My body is wrapped in this velvet balm of the night and our love and saying thank you for the warmth and rest and comfort. Thank you. I love you.'

For the drear winter months we moved into a room in the house. At Epiphany, under a moon a day before the full, we drove down to Mitchell's Fold again. Well-wrapped against the cold we sat beneath ritual and enduring stone. It was exactly two years since this phase of our history had begun, here, with a moment of insight and mystical union under a gleaming crescent moon, and the telephone conversation that came after:

> *...immer*
>
> *Ins Ungebundene gehet eine Sehnsucht. Vieles aber ist*
> *Zu behalten.*[41]
>
> (...a longing always towards the Infinite. But much
>   is to be remembered.)

In January Jac went for three weeks to Yorkshire, staying with a sister whilst she tried different treatment. Whilst she was there I walked up Pendle Hill in the marches of the Rose Counties. Jac's mother's family came from Barley, sheltered from the west winds under the eastern flank of the hill. As a teenager, with friends, she had been up there as local tradition dictates on All Hallows Eve, and all across the summit plateau, flickering lights, strange attire, weird ceremonials, the atmosphere disturbing. In my sudden urge to go there I can see retrospectively the beginnings of the posthumous searching, the anticipation of compounding grief to come. It was a January day of sleet and winnowing rain, buffeting winds, sub-zero temperatures. I skulked out of the lash of the rain in the Pendle Inn, wiling away an hour over beer and a robust Lancashire delicacy of pie and mushy peas with gravy, before pulling on heavy waterproofs that exposed the barest minimum of skin to the weather and setting off for the hill. There were berries still braided along twigs of ancient hollies. Snow fretted the edge of Pendle's misty plateau, the vegetation was sparse, rocks and puddles patched across acid ground. The Bronze Age burial cairn at the summit was corbelled skilfully around the Ordnance Survey pillar, giving it additional presence in the gloom. I touched it fleetingly and retreated down the steepness of the lee slope, where the wind harried and hurled itself inches above my head as I sat in a calm hollow, heels dug into a snowdrift the surface of which was grey-grimed with industrial sully. A solitary runner, gargoyle-bent with yellow sleeves billowing, thrust down the way I'd come, and was gone. There were no views, just rain, hill and mist. I looked around at the intimate detail. In the rock of an inconspicuous niche, a small, rough cross had been carved. On the meagre grass at my feet, something gleamed. I reached down and picked up a new penny, its rim soured with peat, polished it and put it in my pocket to give later in superstition to Jac. After a while I went down by a slantwise path across the lee slope, with Pendle's dark dip rearing against the last western light. As I did so, above me suddenly the eternal-female symbol of the moon was hanging from the ridge, slightly occluded, like the pupil of a great yellow eye, its iris a cool green, a halo around it of Japanese ginger, looking down into all our histories.

The last months of Jac's life were long to live and are swift to tell. Inexorably the estimate of life expectancy had been reduced. Chemotherapy took its toll of her vitality. With the publication of the Whillans biography at the beginning of March I was involved in a round of interviews, readings and events, to all of which she insisted on coming and about which I was desperately conflicted – at one level not wanting to be apart from her for a moment more than was necessary and therefore glad; at another just wishing for her to rest. She had started her treatment with hope and optimism, wanting to live, willing to endure its discomforts and indignities with that goal in sight. By March, though her public cheerfulness was undiminished the prognosis was ever gloomier and her physical resources savagely depleted. I remember one night in Birmingham after a reading and book signing at the NEC when we had gone for a curry with a good friend, the Scottish writer and broadcaster Cameron McNeish. We'd walked from our hotel near the airport and crossed a road, having to hurry as a car sped up. On the far side she had burst into tears: 'I just can't *feel* my feet any more…'

From the hotel room's window that night we'd watched a seethe of rabbits chasing and playing across the lawns under the lights around the grounds. She smiled to see them there. We visited Mitchell's Fold on the way home, for the last time. Went to Aberdaron for her birthday again, the weather calm and clear, her vitality by now very low. We slept in the caravan at times, with the coming of fine weather. I remember her squatting on the bed in the sunlight with a red headscarf covering her baldness, the dark bush of hair between her thighs quite gone, looking so vulnerable, so fragile. When we made love now, there was a tenderness to it beyond all passion, an infinitely gentle experiencing of what was almost gone. She could scarcely eat, and then only the simplest food. On large white plates I would make designs of shape, texture and colour to tempt her, and she would nibble and rearrange and finally push aside. One April night I had to talk in the Rheged Centre near Penrith, and for the first time she decided to stay home. I drove back late at night, phoned her from a motorway services on the M6, and heard the utter weariness in her voice. She was longing to see the bluebells. We no longer spoke of anything beyond them. When I had talked of us going to live in the Pyrenees, and all the warmth and space and colour of a new landscape, she placed her hand in mine and looked at me, wordless, eyes brimming with tears. Surgery removed from her breast the minute and aggressive tumours the size of rice grains her form of cancer produced, and the lymph glands were cut out from her left armpit. She fretted in the Chester hospital, would not stay on the ward, when I visited each day insisted we spend the time in the canteen, told me that often she was locked out at night and had to ring to be let back in. After the surgery, every three or four days I would drive her back for lymphatic fluid to be drained. Her abdomen began to swell and she was in continual pain. There had been talk of radiotherapy after the chemotherapy, but it did not happen. Still she was restless, wanted to be moving.

'I'm here today, and I'll be here tomorrow, so where's the problem?' she would ask, in response to any concern I showed.

After one reading late in April near Leeds we stayed in Derbyshire, had dinner at the Ladybower Inn with friends – Jan and John Beatty, Tony and Sue Shaw – and next day went off at lunchtime in search of Guinness for her. We came across Jan and John's daughter Jodie, sitting on a grass verge near Abney with her horse Stanley, and stopped. I watched and listened, saw all the warmth and human interest that I so loved about Jac flowing out towards Jodie, and the way it was reciprocated – the lovely girl on the brink of womanhood, the beautiful woman approaching death, the quiet horse stooping to the long grass between them. On May Day she wrote to my dear friend Polly Biven, who had sent flowers after her operation:

This is a long-overdue note of thanks for the beautiful freesias, that have been wafting their scent before me for many mornings now when I awake, and through the day when, as now, I'm in this lovely space of our bedroom with the lambs bleating and curlews calling through the open windows. The light's like opals, promises one of those May evenings after a gloomy day – not decent splashy April rain but the sideways low-cloud mizzle Wales is so good at. Doesn't the spirit lift with the light! I hope your spirits are rising – I'm so sorry you've been down recently. We hope for all sentient beings to be free from suffering, yet we have to accept that human-kind is born to suffering as well as joy. My dad used to say 'man is born to trouble as sure as sparks fly upwards' and I never understood what he meant. I hope, Polly, that you're affording yourself as much attention as you do others. You must look after yourself, conserve your energy and stop worrying. I was a bit disappointed this week, feeling weak and woolly and wanting to be better now. Why can't I just get the energy? But we have to be patient, I suppose. The doctor gave me antibiotics yesterday which are helping already. So I shouldn't give myself a hard time for over-firing my kiln and flopping about and being generally useless. I'll get stronger, and so will you. Radiotherapy they say is very exhausting and I'm hoping I'll sail through it – can't be worse than chemo but the doctor says it's a different kind of tiredness and I won't be able to drive for six weeks. The doom and gloom these doctors spread! I thought it was all up from here and that radiotherapy was painless and simple. Still, forewarned is forearmed, so I'll maybe have to be a more patient patient and surrender to the human *being* in me and stop being frustrated at not managing the human *doing*. So much pain, Polly, for so long you will be debilitated, and it must wear you down terribly, so I wish you strength and patience and remember to be good to yourself and that the lambs will be springing for a long while yet. They're all so tiny here still, and white, not like the big putty-coloured ones we saw in Derbyshire. In time you'll be springing too.

Well, Polly – suddenly evening's here, and it's stunningly lovely and the blackbirds are in full flow. Last year we had the most amazing blackbird with a very long song – must have been quite old – and he was doing his usual round of the tallest trees and seemed to be practising a last verse that we'd not heard before. Then he went to the large post on the end of the barn and went through the repertoire again. Jim and I were laughing at him as we listened outside the caravan. There was something quite comical about it, and very sweet but unusual. I can't really explain. Next morning we found him dead. It must have been his swan song and we'd been laughing. Jim buried him

under a cherry tree we bought. He did look peaceful.
No more room now – hand is so tingly still – so sorry
for scrawl – lots of love, Jac x

We celebrated our second wedding anniversary. Tacitly,
this year we had not booked the Roundhouse at Druidstone
for a May week. The young female greater spotted woodpecker from last year was back at the feeders in the larch trees
behind the caravan with crimson-capped young of her own.
On the fourth of May, I drove Jac into Chester for one of her
regular cancer clinics. All across a south-facing hillside at Bryn
Eglwys bluebells were shimmering in the sun. We stopped, for
her to look at and to smell them, the hyacinth fragrance so
sweet on the air. At the hospital I waited in the canteen as she
went to her clinic. An hour later she came back, telling me they
were admitting her for tests and observation. It was a Wednesday. She sent me out to a nearby supermarket for things she
needed: toothbrush and toothpaste, mouthwash, chocolate,
cans of Guinness, rolling tobacco and cigarette papers for her
'sundowner'.

'It will only be a day they'll keep me in – two days at
most, they say. They just want to check something out that's
puzzling them.'

I came back and found her in a little single room, quiet at
the end of a ward. She smiled at me conspiratorially and
stowed the provisions away in her bedside cupboard, safe
from prying nurses' eyes. She was undisturbed after eight
o'clock. 'Make love to me,' she murmured, and quietly we did
so, for the last time, on the high metal bed that squeaked and
rolled. Nobody arrived to tell me to leave. I crept quietly away

in the dawn before the routines of the hospital began, came back later bringing her things from home. She was not let out that day, or the next. By the weekend she had been put on a morphine drip, was to have a scan on Monday. On the Saturday as she appeared to be descending into sleep I went quietly out of the door, and a moment later heard a commotion behind as Jac launched out, drip on its wheels preceding her, in pursuit. We sat for a long time in the corridor. Finally I saw her back on to the ward and left, drove to Derbyshire instead of going back to the caravan, and stayed with the Beattys. John and I sat outside the Barrel Inn at Bretton on Sunday before I drove back to the hospital. He told me of Jodie's impression of Jac from a fortnight before, that she seemed 'almost translucent', her touch like the brush of a butterfly's wing. I hurried back to her side, stayed till the small hours when she had slipped into sleep, was back next afternoon, knew immediately that something was drastically amiss. She could barely speak, her mind drifting. I stayed very late again, holding her hand. By the following afternoon she was scarcely coherent and the morphine pump had been turned up. Though she could not – and this was typical of Jac, who would never impose sadness – tell me, the Monday scan had shown the cancer to have metastasized. It was now in her liver and lungs. She sent me out into Chester to buy a nightdress, I came back with it and she tried to put it on over her hospital gown. I helped her out of the latter and saw the livid yellow flush of liver failure across her shoulders. A young doctor came in to drain the ascites. More comfortable now, she ordered me peremptorily on to the bed to cuddle her, and holding her I whispered how dearly I loved her as she sank into her last sleep. Her vital signs were fading away. Next morning at about eleven a last gentle exhalation of breath and she was gone.

Her face in death was lemon-hued and of a taut, grave beauty. People soon began to fill the room. A Buddhist placed ritual objects around her pillow, yelped loudly 'to drive the spirit out of the body', and lectured to those present with dogmatic assurance – there is nothing more ludicrous than pompous certainty in the face of what cannot be known – according to his beliefs on her present state of consciousness. After a while I left, came back alone the following day to bid her farewell. The staff nurse on the ward gave me her wedding ring in an envelope, directed me to the mortuary and chapel of rest. Jac's corpse was wheeled in on a gurney, a white sheet covering her that the attendant folded down from her face. A gingery fuzz of hair was growing back across her smooth skull. I sat with her for an hour, my hand on her cold one, her features marmoreal now, rigid and expressionless, the life and spirit wholly departed. I thanked the attendant and the nurses on the ward and shambled away barefoot down the corridors. At some point that day I remember being in Oswestry, going into a barber's to have my hair cropped, walking into Frances Denby in Sainsbury's and being barely able to speak, tears streaming down my face. I called Mavis Nicholson and we went to a pub together. Back at the house and caravan when I returned, the dismantling and appropriation had begun. Even from the shrine in the caravan things had disappeared. (Six months beyond Jac's going, in Canada for the mountain festival at Banff, I was talking to the writer Maria Coffey about losing a loved one in that phase when you are still 'in love' –

which can last, of course, but almost invariably modulates, if the relationship endures, into a more eirenic state. She told of how, after the disappearance on the north-east ridge of Everest in 1982 of her companion Joe Tasker, the locks on the home they had shared were changed to exclude her, and their joint belongings were pillaged.)

Jac's funeral – eventually held at Bangor Crematorium nine months after Will's had taken place there – was delayed by almost a fortnight so that a party could be organized. Bewildered, I talked to a friend, Jan Levi, whose simple comment was that 'my lot like to get us in the ground in two days at most'. The delay at some primitive level felt horribly wrong. I remembered back to the two boys I'd seen carried up past the hotel where I was staying on Assi Ghat in Varanasi eight years before, limbs lolling, having drowned in the Ganges. Within two hours their funeral pyres were burning. I remembered too witnessing the whole ritual on another occasion at Manikarnika Ghat. When the pyre at this funeral had burned quite down and only smoking ash and fragments of bone remained, the chief mourner filled a brass bowl from the river, circumambulated the pyre one last time, cast the water on to it over his left shoulder and walked away without looking back.

I waited out the time at the caravan until the funeral was over, using it to move things into storage, debating whether to torch it as I left in the gypsy style of which Jac would have approved, and only deciding against because of the damage it would do to the larches alongside. On one of my last mornings, as I lay in bed in the caravan in daylight after a night without sleep, suddenly alongside me, my arm around her and her eyes looking into mine with an imploring expression, there was Jac. We held each other's gaze, neither of us speaking, through timeless time until eventually, briefly, I slept. When I awoke, she was gone.

> Occasionally hypnagogic (half-waking) hallucinations occur. One widow was resting in her chair on a Sunday afternoon when she saw her husband, quite clearly, digging in the garden with only his trousers on; another saw her husband coming in through the garden gate; a third saw her dead father standing by her bed at night.[42]

It had not felt like a dream, was too intensely realized for that, would be categorized more precisely as psychotropic experience, its perceptual intensity and confusion compounded by the empty bed on my awakening being suffused with the scent of Rive Gauche.

One time each for Will and for Jac. 'I once told a Lady, the reason why I did not believe in the existence of Ghosts etc. was that I had seen too many of them myself,' Coleridge wrote in his *Notebooks*.[43] If these were their leave-takings – and I will believe no one who asserts them as such – I am glad for the experiences.

But not so glad as I was to leave that dreadful place in the dip of the moors, to which I never returned.

BOOK FIVE

Hidden Lord of the
Crooked Path

13

Searching

In his account of the period of his life following the death of his daughter in a road accident, and of his wife ten months later from cancer, Neil Peart – drummer and lyricist with the Canadian rock band Rush – poses the following question: 'How does anyone survive something like this? And if they do, what comes out the other end?'[1]

Peart's answer was to take off on his motorbike and keep on keeping on from Canada down to Mexico because to stand still was to be swallowed and consumed by grief. The Scottish writer Christopher Rush, after his wife died of breast cancer in 1993, arrested his own emotional disintegration and set out on the path to recovery by retracing the journey through the Cévennes that Stevenson described in his *Travels with a Donkey* of 1879, and later writing about it in a moving and finely-wrought book.[2] Dannie Abse, doctor and distinguished octogenarian Welsh poet and writer, whose wife Joan was killed in a car crash on the M5 in 2005, kept a meticulous journal for a year in which he recorded the fluctuation of his feelings and recalled their long years together: 'I'm OK. I'm coping. I'm limping along. I miss Joan...'[3]

Iris Murdoch's widower John Bayley memorialized her in three light and affectionate best-selling volumes, the last of them published in 2001. The American writer Joan Didion, famously, recorded her novelist husband John Gregory Dunne's fatal heart attack in December 2003 and the coincident serious illness of her daughter Quintana. In her forensic style Didion salved her grief by applying journalistic acumen to medical detail, immersing herself in this as she described the events and her own reactions to them in *The Year of Magical Thinking* – around the time of the publication of which Quintana died.[4] Sharon Olds in *The Father*, Douglas Dunn memorializing his wife Lesley in *Elegies*, Ted Hughes rejecting 'the white noise of the elegy' and instead powerfully recalling his life with Sylvia Plath in *Birthday Letters*[5] are three among many who approach the subject of bereavement from poets' perspectives.[6] These are no more than a few recent examples of writing on grief. Scan the centuries and the examples proliferate: Milton, Arnold and Shelley, of course, in *Lycidas*, *Thyrsis* and *Adonais*; Henry King's exquisite and passionate *Exequy* for his dead wife; Tennyson speculating on mortality in his masterpiece, *In Memoriam*, published in 1850 but inspired by the death of his dearest friend Arthur Hallam seventeen years earlier; Montaigne celebrating throughout his great essays the ardent friendship and intellectual companionship with his fellow lawyer Étienne de la Boétie; the novelist Flora Mayor more privately in her *Grief Journal*[7] communicating for ten years with her dead fiancé Ernest Shepherd; in the world's oldest written literature, the Sumerian-Babylonian *Epic of*

Gilgamesh, the eponymous king grieves for his dead warrior-companion Enkidu, keeps his corpse by him till a maggot falls from its nose, and then embarks on a quest for the means to bring him immortality. Mourning becomes its own literature. In its sharing of the universal human experience of loss, it can bring a kind of comfort.

What helped me most to navigate the compounding grief that had overwhelmed me in the months after Jacquetta's death were not these literary props, but a considered comment by the Scottish Gaelic poet Aonghas MacNeacail – a white-haired patriarch whose calm presence belies the wide-ranging passion of his work. I met Aonghas in the tent that served as green room in Charlotte Square Gardens before a gig at the Edinburgh Book Festival. It was three months after Jac had died, and the first anniversary of Will's funeral. Aonghas came up to the table where I was sitting, took a chair and began to talk about the piece that had just appeared in the *Observer* magazine on which chapter two of this present book is based. He mused for a while in the soft intonatory accent of Uig in the north of Skye – the harbour from which ferries sail west for the small ports of the Outer Isles – that makes his readings and broadcasts so pleasurable to hear; and then he delivered the following extraordinary and challenging comment: 'The thing that people don't generally realize is that in profound grief there is profound joy.'

Looking back, I feel extremely grateful to Aonghas for that gift; and perhaps a little ashamed also at having been so absorbed in my own grief that I gave no recognition to the obvious – that his wisdom surely came from tragic personal experience.

There is no riddle or religiose consolation in his paradox. It is perfectly simple. The greater the shared joy, the greater the subsequent grief, which grief is itself to some degree alleviated by memory of the joy's intensities. The wild fluctuations between the two states – awareness of loss, recollection of joy – I'm sure are experienced by most who have lost their loved ones. So that the fluctuation becomes a defining characteristic of the bereaved state.

I put on my performance in Edinburgh that afternoon, complete with bare feet and toenail varnish, to a warm and generous capacity audience. An exceptionally pretty woman on the front row heckled me gently as I was discussing issues of masculinity with my interviewer Jamie Jauncey, children's author, musician and the festival's founder. She and I compared notes on the semiotics of toenail varnish and flirted mildly until Jamie administered a figurative knuckle-rap and hauled me back to the subject: 'Do you mind! That's my *wife…*'

A north-east wind off the Forth was scuttering among the leaves that evening, chilling the air. People left early. I spent a desolate night of remembering in a vast hotel bed. On the far side of it, snoring gently through the dark hours, was a publicity assistant who had, in her woman's kindness, felt obliged to keep me company there, and who did not, mercifully, expect to be fucked in return for the favour.[8] In the bright forenoon I slipped away from the city on the road south towards Berwick, intent on returning to Fast Castle.

Searching is a restless activity in which one moves towards possible locations of a lost object. The person

who is searching has to select places in which to look,
move towards them, and scan them; he must also
select what to see.[9]

At Dowlaw Farm there was no sign of Ian Russell, and
though at one level I'd have welcomed his amiable presence, I
was living perpetually on the brink of tears, every reminder
reducing me to sobbing constriction of breath and streaming
eyes. I climbed up the bank, through the boundary wall of the
in-bye land, and took the slant, descending path through
blooming heather with the sun high and the castle on its
dramatic promontory in view against rippling indigo of the
sea. Aonghas's gift and spell was working. The sensual joy of
the time Jac and I had spent here was a shimmering presence
in my mind.

The rough path led me down to the isthmus again; to the
scramble up the polished slab with the rusty chain and kitti-
wakes careening through the arch beneath; to the grassy ward
of the old fortress. Thrift-spangled turf was just as I had remembered. The remnants of the old tower still hung over the
drop, enclosing the hidden bower where Jac and I had lain in
the sun two years before. I rounded the abutment to enter it
and a brief glimpse as I did so stopped me in my tracks. Two
middle-aged women in a tangle of limbs lay top-to-tail and
quite naked, clothes strewn around, lapping away enthusiastically between each other's thighs, oblivious and ecstatic on the
greensward where Jac and I had made love before them. A
handsome sheepdog looked on morosely, raised no alarm,
and, as I beat a silent and rapid retreat behind the abutment,
decided I offered better prospects of entertainment and lunch.

So he followed me for a mile back through the heather as I made myself scarce, leaned heavily against me when I sat down and started to fish around in my rucksack, and shared what I brought out to eat with mild appraisal and complacency. All the while I was convulsed by fits of fond laughter and he was smiling at me in a complicit way as only a collie can. After he and I had dozed together stretched out in the heather for an hour, his providers tramped by, clothed now, hand-in-hand, giving me a happy good day, calling off their dog and apologizing if he'd been a nuisance.

'Not at all,' I responded, 'I've enjoyed his company.'

He trotted away ahead of them as they set their sturdy haunches to the hill. The sight of them in that place had seemed more blessing than sad reminder: 'Morag, Sheenagh; Morag, Sheenagh,' I mouthed, laughing, to the rhythmic wash of the waves, thinking what a proper thing it is discreetly to make love in the open air, and drove on to the bend in the River Till to light a fire and sleep the night in the withies on the bank, kingfishers lapidary and whirring along above the water as I arrived, rising trout dimpling the smooth flow of the water, footprints of an otter in the gravelly shore, a gentle breeze drawing at the flames. As I drifted into sleep, fading down with the embers and all the sweet ache of memory, I was listening to the ripple of the river, and in the softness of it, in that place, something embodied:

> ...I'd say it's you who are speaking
> when my wish is
> to hear your voice
> who speaks is *you in my memory*

>   and in my memory when it was time for
>   speaking you seldom said much.[10]

Grief is a strange and wandering journey, continually returning to the same points in its maze of memory and loss. If this narrative at times confuses with its backtrackings and leaps forward, it does so in an attempt to represent the bewilderments of the time. When, soon after Jacquetta's death, I left the caravan among the moors it was to move to another caravan behind a house in a valley west of Snowdon. John Beatty had made the contact, and accompanied me to see it. The woman who opened the door of the house was the one who had paid such close attention to Jacquetta and myself each night in the restaurant at Valle Gran Rey on La Gomera eighteen months before. The recognition between us was immediate. There was a further connection, too – a photograph John had taken of her shimmering reflection in water had been the frontispiece to a short book I'd written and he'd illustrated a few years previously in which I'd first explored for myself the device of writing about landscape as objective correlative in a sustained way. Delphine was her name. She was an artist, with an intensely vivid, striking grasp of colour. In her mid-sixties, she was in poor health, kind-hearted, tempestuous, most difficult when in her cups, at which times she'd mount the steps into the caravan, scout out and drain any liquor I had there, berate me in fiercest terms late into the night, and eventually have to be helped back staggering to her own door, from which she'd creep out next afternoon with contrite postcards to slip under my door and promises redeemable only in the shortest of terms to mend her ways. I came to be very fond of

Del, grateful too for the few months I stayed in her caravan and set out on the path to recovery. She gave Serafina and myself a place of sanctuary, where I could go out in the darkness of the mountains and howl out my black grief to indifferent stars. The tears would come at a word, at a fleeting instant of memory, and demolish me. My eyes were continually puffy and red-rimmed, my cheeks sore with the salt of weeping.

'How does anyone survive something like this?'

I had no interest in seeing people, kept to my private place, made a shrine to Will and Jac in the caravan, each night would pour out a glass of wine and place it there for her, and each morning would pour it away on the grass, ritually, a libation to the tutelary spirits. Sometimes, when I had the energy – and mostly I rose late, sat in silence, remembered and wept – I would drive around to Llanberis and up to Dinorwig where Will and I had lived, walk into the huge, abandoned quarries, splash through two wet tunnels and climb a slope of loose scree in the hole beyond to the high terrace where his climbing friends had planted a rowan tree for him and made a simple slate bench among the birch and sycamore already growing there. Throughout his adolescence this had been an habitual place, hidden away, Gothically wild. The feral goats, magnificent and stinking creatures, had started gnawing at his tree so I carried a plastic sapling protector up there and fastened it firmly around. On the first anniversary of his death I took the urn that held his ashes from the caravan shrine, filled a large container with water, drove around to Dinorwig and climbed to the heather terrace. Choughs were squealing from the lower tunnels where they nest. I lifted the moss around the base of the rowan and spread the ashes around its roots, watering them into the soil before patting the moss gently back into place. A leaf in the early colours of autumn had fallen on to the bench beneath, its delicate serrations sharply outlined against the rock. Tiny green spots among its carmine picked up on the tone of duck's-egg markings in the slate. I heard a clatter from the slope below as stone settled on stone. A kestrel took off from a rock tower opposite to glide into sunlight pouring through a gap, its plumage a sudden brilliance in all the shadows and the greys, like a freed and playful soul on wings of flame. In these ritual moments of locating him here, I felt so close to my son, have never needed to search for him. If I held to any belief, that he had come back as one of these wild creatures in a place where he loved to be might define it – rather that fine fancy than imagining for him false heavens: 'Believing there is a better world elsewhere now looks like a way of not seeing the sufficiencies of this one.'[11]

Somehow, too, the element of volition in his going made the notion of searching for Will seem almost an act of impropriety. The only way I could come to terms with his decision was by respecting it – just as in his youth to let him go his own way as far as it was concomitant with safety and reasonable behaviour, and to keep the communication open between us, had been the vague principles of my fathering him. The rowan growing in his precious place gave my grief for him a location and a salve. In Jac's death, conversely, she had been re-appropriated by her family, her ashes scattered and dispersed out on the waves in a place that, if it had meaning in her history, had little in the one we had shared. No one had seemed to weep for her; the funeral in Bangor focused elsewhere than on her; sightseers came up and photographed her coffin – the same wickerwork as Will's had been – with their mobile phones; a sense of the essentially-uncaring and the inappropriate was all-pervading. The undertaker who had served so well at Will's funeral caught my eye. He shook his head, walked over, linked his arm in mine and took me to the lectern, showed me the button that opens the curtains and slides the coffin from sight. No one was left in the chapel to watch it go.

Having thus so completely lost her, she became the initial object in the searching phase of my grief – that instinctive and universal phenomenon so perfectly expressive of our mystification about where the dead go. Anne Karpf, writing in the *Guardian* after the death of her mother, a concert pianist and Auschwitz survivor, at the age of ninety-six, with a degree of passion and angry eloquence seldom to be found in the press, confronted the fatuous modern notion of closure:

> Shortly after my mother's death (how absurd those words still sound) someone asked one of my children if seeing her body had helped her achieve closure. Thankfully they didn't ask me, as if they had I'd have given them what for. Closure? Closure an hour after a beloved grandmother had died? Where did this pernicious piece of psychobabble come from, and how could anyone with a glint of understanding utter it? Perhaps it seemed a helpful idea, a reminder that for most of us mourning doesn't remain at the same intensity – a jumped-up way of saying 'you'll get over it'.

Yet even at this level it sucks because, in the most intense stages of grieving, it's no consolation to focus on the end of an ending. In fact, closure is the last thing that most bereaved people want; it's what they dread.[12]

In the first weeks after Jac's death, I drove to Wasdale for a few days for no other reason than that she had given me a photograph of herself taken there that I always carried. I stayed at Burnthwaite, the dale's topmost farm, hard under Great Gable, which was to remain resolutely hidden in cloud. I had not been to Wasdale in decades. In the bedroom to which I was shown I opened a book that had belonged to Jac by my old friend Harry Griffin, *In Mountain Lakeland*, and for its frontispiece there was a black-and-white photograph of two people walking hand-in-hand through the gateway to Burnthwaite, Gable clear of cloud beyond it, which moved me yet again to sudden, scalding tears. Driving in from Santon Bridge it had been a June afternoon of torrential downpours that bowed the drenched heads of yellow Welsh poppies in every verge and skeined a film of grey across all the blossomed fields. Suddenly, beyond the fork for Nether Wasdale, bare rock-ribs of mountain Lakeland gleamed all around dark, spray-streamered waters of Wastwater, a westerly tempest chasing the waves along its surface, the screes opposite stippled into the thinnings of the cloud. At Galesyke I had stopped the car and stepped out into the fresh of it, the lash of rain washing the salt from my cheeks and a small thrill of joy rising in response from behind a sigh.

Over breakfast ('Full cooked English?' asked Mrs Race

conspiratorially, in the curious, clipped code of proprietors of such establishments) I had idled and pecked at my food and let my gaze dwell on the glorious peach-colouring of an azalea, luminous even in lacklustre daylight, that thrashed in the wind outside the window; had watched the heavy stir of the vapours across Lingmell opposite and wondered what could be worthwhile about venturing into so inhospitable and dreary a season; had warmed myself by a fire lit early against its miseries and wandered up to my room and studied the map, and, having memorized the terrain, had put it and my spectacles away as being inconsultable and useless on such a day as this, and had clad myself in fleece top and trousers and full waterproofs and hat and scarf and all the paraphernalia that British hills can demand in the weeks so shortly before mid-summer, and had put hot chocolate laced with whiskey in a flask and packed a minimal rucksack and had gone downstairs and laced up my boots, unscrewed and adjusted to length trekking poles, stepped out into the rain, let myself out of the garden by a wicket gate, and set out along a stony track for a destination I could not see under a hill that was all but invisible to me, obscured, extinguished at this distance from every sense.

The previous evening I had walked down to drink a pint and get food in Ritson's Bar at the Wasdale Head Hotel; on the way I'd wandered through the burial ground of the little, low church among the fields, looked around at thick, buttressed walls that delineate the cleared fields with their characterful, surviving Herdwick sheep.[13] The evening was now very still, 'quiet as a nun', mist down almost to the tops of the few trees and the old inn gaunt and a little apart as focus of the place.

The stable door where Owen Glynne Jones[14] spreadeagled himself across his famous traverse still bore the painted legend, 'coach horses', the bar walls inside were patched in fading sepia with prints and postcards of early mountain activity around the dale.

This following morning had supplanted the calm hour of evening with a buffeting wind at my back. In the meadows before the path crossed on its high wooden bridge the flooding stream that tumbles down from between the paps of Kirk Fell, dapper pairs of wheatears were flitting, pausing on stones to regard my slow progress, calling out their lively discords and dancing away on the gale, their subtle colourings muted to plain monochrome in the sodden atmosphere. I had intended to take the path veering away after the footbridge to climb the spur leading straight to Westmorland's Cairn, and find the Napes Traverse from that, but missed it somehow in the fog, stumbling on with my attention distracted here and there by yellow-starred tormentil, and small violets sheltered by boulders, nestling and sprouting from their seams and cracks. 'The violets in the mountains have broken the rocks,' wrote Tennessee Williams. Had the great allegorist and symbolist of American drama trodden a path like this to Sty Head, seen this break and tumble all around of the earth's skin, and had that sense from it – of the quiet, salving, renewing force of life?

At Sty Head, among the maze of converging paths and by the coffin-like Mountain Rescue box, I crouched away from the wind and saw the nearby tarn as a mercury glimmer quickly shrouded again from view. The steep crags of Kern Knotts I knew lay just above, no more than ten minutes away, and I made my way there. From the foot of the crags I found the

Napes Traverse path easily, and where I had been struggling without rhythm before, now across all the interlinking paths and scree gullies and scrambly rounds of rock spurs, there came a flow and an eagerness in questing after route, an absorption; and an absorption too in tint and shade and texture of the matrix, of the rock itself: its mauves, purples, ochres and umbers, its cleave and form. The Sphinx Rock reared out of the obscuring mist, and rain flurried a trickling gleam across it as I negotiated a gully, then the toe of a buttress, and looking back saw the familiar form of the Napes Needle.

Running down scree from the end of the traverse, suddenly a brightness suffused all the surrounding grey and I descended into the valley again, Lingmell Beck roaring in front, shocking in its braided white among this subdued landscape. I feasted my gaze on the startle of it until it grew into an image replete with life; sat against a cold rock and thought of the woman I had cherished in my heart throughout my adult life; and knew then both the privilege that had been given me to be with her through her time of dying, and the goodness of her that enabled me to go on:

> Whoever has done good in the main has spirit-energy that is pure and clear when death comes... The pure and light energy rises upward and floats up to heaven, and becomes the fivefold present shadow-genius or shadow-spirit.[15]

I don't know what that means. Its terminology is both vague and alien to me. Yet its generality seems to me ultimately no more frustrating or inconclusive, and a good deal less pleased with itself, than the specific arguments on consciousness in which – another aspect of the searching – I read extensively after Jac's and Will's deaths. From Crick, Dennett, Damásio, Penrose, Searle, Greenfield, Blackmore, the Churchlands, Chalmers and Koch came suggestion, possibility, the sum of relevant physiological knowledge; and little of more summary and specific certainty than the undefined glimmer from that twelve-centuries-old Chinese text quoted above, *The Secret of the Golden Flower*. Coleridge, predictably, encapsulated the problem in one of his habitually brilliant phrases: '...that stubborn rock, the fact of *Consciousness*, or rather its dependence on the body.'[16]

How can we believe in the continuing existence of our loved ones, in a life for them beyond death, when our human perception is so overwhelmingly predicated on the evidence of the senses? What we might wish, and that which we can logically deduce, are entirely at odds in this. Freud defines the conundrum exactly in the passage from *Mourning and Melancholia* already quoted earlier in Beach of Bones:

> Each individual memory and expectation in which the libido was connected to the object is adjusted and hyper-invested, leading to its detachment from the libido. Why this compromise enforcement of the reality commandment, which is carried out piece by piece, should be so extraordinarily painful is not at all easy to explain.

Grief forces us into confrontation with transience, and fails to remind us that we do not expect the violets, the wood anemones, the bluebells to be any other than gloriously thus. Today, lying in bed with the morning sun streaming through the window, gold sheen on a filament of gossamer against the azure reminds me of Jacquetta. A shadow of cloud passes across, extinguishes the gleam. She is four years dead. Sometimes I cry for her still, but less often now. The blackbird in my garden takes food back to fledglings who will soon sing in his place. As I wish my son could have done in mine. Surely to believe in eternal love, in eternal life, is to condemn yourself to the inevitability of disappointment? There is enough that is good and beautiful in the world, aside from unreasoned expectations such as these.

In hardly any other sphere has our thinking and feeling changed so little since primitive times or the old been so well preserved, under a thin veneer, as in our relation to death. Two factors account for this lack of movement: the strength of our original emotional reactions and the uncertainty of our scientific knowledge. Biology has so far been unable to decide whether death is the necessary fate of every living creature or simply a regular, but perhaps avoidable, contingency within life itself. It is true that in all the textbooks on logic the statement that 'all men must die' passes for an exemplary general proposition, but it is obvious to no one; our unconscious is still as unreceptive as ever to the idea of our own mortality. Religions continue to dispute the significance of the undeniable fact of individual death and to posit an afterlife. The state authorities think they cannot sustain moral order among the living if they abandon the notion that life on earth will be 'corrected' by a better life hereafter.[17]

After Will's and Jac's deaths, I felt I would have died, as indeed I wanted to, thus to inhabit whatever dimension had received my loved ones, even though the most likely one was oblivion. Only slowly did I come around to the notion that 'life was about what could be done with what was left, with what still happened to be there.'[18] Three things saw me through the first two years of grieving, and convinced belief in any form of immortality was not among them. The redeeming factors were these.

First was Aonghas's gift: at the times when grief was overwhelming, it held out the possibility of slipping it by invoking memory of past joys. The second was work, its necessity and regular disciplines giving structure and purpose to days that might otherwise have passed in a welter of self-absorbed miseries. The last was perhaps the most important. Grief and depression are not the same thing, though similarities exist between them and strategies for counteracting the one also work with the other. My recourse when faced with what Coleridge calls 'the smothering weight'[19] of sorrow was to the easing rhythm of legs set in motion, taking me into the natural world, where process itself could only be seen as sad through anthropomorphic projection. One morning, whilst out walking by Llyn Dinas, I came across a verse typed on heavy, waterproof, lavender-coloured paper, pinned with rusting drawing pins to the trunk of a rowan:

Listen to the footfall in your heart.
I am not gone but merely walk within you.

It's a sentimental lie, of course. Will and Jac *were* gone, and did not 'merely' walk within me. But memory of them did, and the world went on. This particular day I remember looking at tint and texture of weed in the outfall from the lake, wavy russet and vivid, mottled green. The quality of Jac's perception was crucial to the delight it brought me. Her imparted qualities lived on, and I share them now with you, the reader. I trudged over into Cwm Bychan, idled across Pont Aberglaslyn, sought out the old way, moss-walled on either side, that leads through woods of birch, beech and Scots pine up to Oerddwr, one of the prime and quiet places in the Welsh hills, and here, after splashing through a quaking morass in quest of the lost path, I stretched out my limbs to rest in the sun on the sweet grass, and lapsed into reciting stanzas from a poem on the place by T. H. Parry-Williams:

Nid daear mo'r ddaear yno, nid haen o bridd;
Mae ansylweddoldeb dan donnen pob cae a ffridd...
O feudy'r Cwm hyd at feudy'r Hendre draw
Y mae llwybrau'n arwain i leoedd a fu neu ddaw.[20]

(Earth is not earth there, no mere crust of soil;
There is insubstantiality under each calloused field and
   sheepwalk...
From the cowshed at Cwm to Hendre beyond
Paths lead to places past or unborn.)

There were cows grazing across the slopes above the old farmstead, and the few fields below the *ffridd*, smoothed from stony acres, were summer-green, the blackthorn leafy around old grey barn and house. As if emanating from the ground itself, there was the feeling to which Parry-Williams had attuned; of the not-quite-real, of a small region apart from the physical world, of a *cantref* of the otherworld where the fairies and the former inhabitants still throng. The sense of a way of life departed but yet apprehended by the 'shaping spirit of imagination' was intense. And comforting – an assertion that we find our rightful place in natural process. I hurried on, eager to re-enter the valley, which is still, mysteriously, my sole and spiritual *cynefin*[21] in this physical world, and to me the most beautiful of all landscapes – the place to which 'the hidden lord of the crooked path' always leads me back.

In 1973, shortly after parting from Jacquetta the first time around, I went to live in an isolated cottage, Brithdir Mawr, a mile or so from the head of Cwm Pennant. The four years I spent here were the most formative of my life, held in compensatory balance now with the four years of my grieving. The surrounding circuit of hills, from Moel Hebog over Moel yr Ogof and Moel Lefn, then crossing Bwlch-y-Ddwy-elor – the pass of the two biers – to gain the 'Ridge of the Red Cairns' that stretches from Y Garn above Rhyd Ddu to Mynydd Craig Goch by Nebo, is arguably the finest hill walk in Snowdonia. Throughout the years I lived here, I walked some part of this circuit, in the course of the shepherding by which in part I was earning my keep, almost every day. To have that closeness with a natural landscape is a life-changing experience, taking you into dimensions previously unsuspected, initiating you into the earth's mysteries, reinstating the old human senses that urban civilization has atrophied. It was a time of gifts, and – in its way, though perhaps more in retrospect than when in process – of spiritual discipline. In all weathers, in all lights or no light, at all seasons, these hills became my intimates, disclosing, confiding. I slipped among them in the company of chough, raven and peregrine; of fox, polecat and hare. I came to know: where, in the moonlight, the hares would race and box; by what paths badger and stoat would cross the twilight fields below the mountain wall; or on what rocks the rose-root and the burnet rose, within what streamside spray the hay-scented buckler fern might grow. What the walking did, then and now, was to establish what I cannot but see as the most crucial, fulfilling and redemptive relationship of my life – the one on which all others depend and from which they have taken their contexts. Thoreau – incomparably the greatest of writers on nature and the wild[22] – puts the view to which I hold most succinctly:

> To insure health, a man's relation to Nature must come very near to a personal one; he must be conscious of a friendliness in her; when human friends fail or die, she must stand in the gap. I cannot conceive of any life which deserves the name, unless there is a certain tender relation to Nature.[23]

On this bright summer's afternoon I turned up into Cwm Llefrith from just above Cwrt-Isaf. The little farm where my nearest neighbours and friends the Owen brothers – *hogiau Cwrt Isaf*[24] – had lived with their mother, who had no words of

English, and which once would have been busy and thriving with animals and activity and children, was deserted, silent, tidy. But high among the rock bluffs of Cwm Llefrith and alongside the splashing stream bright heather and gorse were in bloom and the rarer plants too. I remade their acquaintance as if seeking out old friends. At Bwlch Meillionen I left my sack behind a rock and raced up to the summit of Moel Hebog to see the peninsula curving out west into the lowering sun, Mynydd Enlli offshore at its end, Ireland's coast faintly beyond and Pembrokeshire's hills far away to the south. I remembered coming up here with Will in a baby-carrier on my back when he was two years old, waving his arms around and tugging at my hair. So long ago now.

On the descent a bright, crescent moon glided out from behind Hebog, and I slipped back by riverside paths in the dew of evening to the caravan under Snowdon with a Daoist sense on me of the oneness of the Way, however wandering. A few weeks later I was coming down from Caer Caradog in the Shropshire hill country that Jac and I loved. The light of evening was filmy, moisture-laden. It was streaming through Lightspout Hollow and Ashes Hollow and Devilsmouth Hollow on the prime bracken hill of the Long Mynd opposite:

Ah! well I know my tumultuous days now at their
    prime
Will be brief as the bracken too in their stay
Yet in them as the flowers of the hills 'mid the bracken
All that I treasure is needs hidden away.[25]

I was reciting MacDiarmid's verse as I reached the lower

woods; thinking of Will and his love of solitary hill-wandering; of Jacquetta and her passion for the quiet times and the infusing light. There was an ancient, decrepit hawthorn across the slope to my left, leafless, stark. Suddenly the flooding sun reached it. Its lichened angles glowed emerald, the sparse haws on its branches brilliant as garnets. 'Blood of the hosts' these stones are called in Gaelic, their gift in folkloric tradition the mystical communion, the moment of knowledge that the unity of life can only be forged by love. To love the world, to notice its quick and startling beauties; to have loved my son; to have loved my woman – all these are aspects of a whole that I was moving on through grief towards the stage of being able to relate back and apprehend: '...a sense of being taken not out of myself but back *in*, of nature entering me, firing up the wild bits of my imagination' is how Richard Mabey describes this emotional experience of close natural rapport in his moving account of recovery from nervous breakdown, *Nature Cure.*[26]

The process would be long, but already, even before the darkest time of bereavement – which is the second year, when the stark finality of death emerges from all the shimmer of surrounding superstition, hope and wonderings – nature was busily asserting its endless process of renewal, its interrelating cosmic connotation; and from time to time, from among its gifts of moments, I was able to pay heed.

14

Solace

The last and most radical act in searching for my dead was to move back to Llanrhaeadr. My Whillans book had sold well in hardback, new contracts and advances were forthcoming, and back in the village Claire's house, unsold since her death, was still on the market and its price was down. Heavy poles used to hang curtains around a downstairs bed in her last illness were still in place. The dead flies were inches deep on window ledges and faded walls craved a fresh coat of paint. I moved in on the first anniversary of Jac's funeral. It soon glowed with new colour. On the surface the village had not changed much in the two-and-a-half years I'd been away, though the Health and Safety Executive had banned the young farmers' monthly dance on grounds of the village hall's decrepitude. The four big windows at the front of the house looked towards the churchyard down the little square. That of the room in which I chose to work faced on to the gable of Manchester House, in its old stone wall the ghost of a doorway, different stone intruded into the patchwork of masonry, the former entrance blocked off.

Beyond the roof-tree of Manchester House, larches where the ravens roost danced along the crest of the ridge and late May-blossom was puffed across the hills that rise from the farther bank of the river. It is place that is most redolent of histories – time is merely incidental. In the brief span of years since I had first come to live in Llanrhaeadr someone died from every house around this square apart from one (and that had the reputation of being haunted). I came to refer to it, sardonically, as *Sgwar y Meirwon* – the square of the dead – and could vividly recall the appearances, the conversations, of those who had gone, as well as every detail of the passages of my own life here involving Will and Jac.

Though memory attaches to place and not time, even in the place where events were enacted it has no property, no tangible presence, remains only memory, time hastening it away. I still thought of the house where I had come to live as Claire's house, though in its side wall, hidden behind a climbing rose and ten feet above the ground, was a mysterious slate plaque that said 'Mary-Ann's house'. No one in the village had an explanation for that, even among the very old people. Whether Claire's or Mary-Ann's or whoever had occupied it in the years between, it was certainly not *my* house in any other than the strict legal sense in which, as mortgagee, I had possession of it.

Above the elaborate wooden porch was another plaque, this time fully in view and dating to 1845. It carried a Welsh text from William Morgan's translation of The Bible. The verse was from Judges, and read *'Trefna dy dŷ/Canys marw a fyddi'*

– 'Put your house in order, because you're going to die.'

Die there I would have done had I stayed. With a stable residence at last after this time of the tragic and the temporary and the vagrant, and hence relieved of the necessity to maintain a front and hold things together if only for Serafina's sake, I became ill. The kindly women of the village who remained from my previous time here – Mavis, Frances, Glenda – insisted that I head for the doctors and after that embark on a round of tests and examinations and probing instrumental interferences – laryngoscopies, bronchoscopies (the latter notably unpleasant), biopsies – that had, within a few months, faltered from one provisional diagnosis to another and finally settled on a firmly-expressed view. It was delivered by a woman GP – my usual doctor, an amiable chap of amusing conjectures, having eloped with a receptionist from another surgery – in the medical centre at Llanrhaeadr. She had called me on my mobile phone whilst I was away in the Pyrenees asking me urgently to return the call, with which request I had naturally not complied. When I came back home I made the appointment to see her. She had me sit down, lowered her voice half an octave, punted her swivel-chair across to position herself between my knees – thus displaying at closest quarters her low-cut blouse and extravagant cleavage, from which I deduced she was working on my will to live – and pronounced the verdict: upper lobe carcinoma, metastases in both lungs. Even I, though I'm no Joan Didion, knew what that meant. I made it clear that I was not going to submit to treatment and consequent medicalized death. With the connivance of a wise old general chest physician on the brink of retirement whom I was also seeing, I refused the curious proffered option of right pneumonectomy, chemotherapy and radiotherapy – the combination of which would assuredly have dispatched me in short order.

'Those boys at the hospital are a bit knife-happy,' mused my white-haired medical oracle, 'I wouldn't have thought much harm would be done if we just wait and see for a while.'

So I sold the house, and with survival instinct on red alert, at my last gasp in the old black Citroën, left the country and headed south to a place where I might breathe again. It is not that I know better than doctors, but I know myself better than they do. With Gillian Rose, I could say that 'medicine and I have dismissed each other.'[27] Time and again I had come across anecdotes and examples from the literature of somatic manifestation of grief. I kept thinking of Hermann Castorp in Thomas Mann's *The Magic Mountain*, in the sanatorium after his wife's death, having 'got inflammation of the lungs'. The phrase of Coleridge's about grief's 'smothering weight' summed it up.[28] Certainly I was becoming more and more ill – but that illness at a level deeply subconscious was of my own creation. My dead were not to be found, however long I might search, and I needed more than anything to get away from the place that so continually invoked memories of them.

Also, news of my condition leaking out, and of the determination to evade suggested treatment, I needed to escape the ravening hordes of the well-meaning with their earth-wisdom and unconditional love and infinite modes of alternative healing and syrupy-shallow hieraticalism, to all of which newage religiose blandishments my tacit response was 'shut the fuck up!' The iatrogenic megalomania of the doctors was almost preferable. As far as I was concerned, there was no time to be wasted on the healers, whatever their sect or persuasion: 'Life was about what could be done with what was left, with what still happened to be there.'[29]

Before I left the country and the village that were – and remain – to me the most precious, and before I became so ill, if that was to be the course of things, that I would be incapable of doing so, there was a ritual act to perform. And so, for my sixtieth birthday, with a small group of friends, I headed north for the Orkneys.

15

Landscape of Loss

The end of March two years ago. It is my sixtieth birthday. Up on Cuilags, Ward Hill and the Knap of Trowieglen – heights of barrenland sheltering the great natural harbour of Scapa from the south-westerlies, seen hulking across Clestrain Sound and the Bring Deeps from Stromness – on the stony slopes, ground thawed billowy and spring-soft, their surface litter of stone graded into parallel or polygonal abstractions, a pair of snow buntings scurry past. Minimal low plants crouch beneath a dry wind – saxifrages and sedums here and there in sheltered crevices. The bog cotton ever-moving will soon flower above Berriedale Wood in the Glens of Kinnaird. By the Dwarfie Stane – the strangest prehistoric tomb in Britain – on the way to the Old Man of Hoy I glimpse movement across the moor, watch enthralled as a male hen harrier – the most ethereal, lovely and rare of all our raptors – ghosts out of the Red Glen and over the heather in pursuit of meadow pipits. Minutes later he's joined by the female – darker and larger – and together the pair of them ride the soft easterly blusters around the spur of Burandie.

We walk over a moor of gleaming stones from the exquisite bay of Rackwick, past the Geo of the Light and the Loch of Stourdale and Flingi Geo. I fall to wondering about the powerful, continuing appeal of these wild places, and the immense variety of activity, meaning and mood that they render to us when we come to them. This wonder-filled day of my sixtieth birthday seems to encompass all that's drawn me into the outdoors through the greater part of my life. There is the continuing potency of rock climbing within that attraction – the adventure and technicality of the climb, the intense companionship of the rope, the insouciance and discalculation that conspires to leave you facing a joyful exigent – moonlit abseils, the dark scramble out, all devolving to laughter. But I would be self-deceiving if I were to think this any other than a fading shadow of former adventures. The elastic strength and resilience of youth goes. Our capacity for enacted experience lessens, though the intensity of felt experience remains and grows. I've long admired the sound model of those lines uttered by the old warrior-chief Byrhtwold in the Anglo-Saxon poem *The Battle of Maldon* – a text peculiarly apt for this Orcadian setting:

> Thought shall be the harder, heart the keener,
> Courage the greater as our strength grows less.[30]

We slip over the rim of the cliff, descend the wet and slithery gully that cuts through the last steep tier of sandstone and take the long traverse by a path barely marked across exposed and plunging slopes to where a last rock scramble drops us into a grassy bay before the isthmus leading across to the Old Man. On tidal slabs around the great stack are twenty grey seals. Sighting us, they roll and flail and slither towards the water. I set to singing, which stops them in their pell-mell tracks and has them craning their heads around, raising flippers in our direction. But then they plunge on wavewards again. Once back in their abler element, they bob in a row to peer at our antics – quaint enough to attract any sensible creature's curiosity. The 450-foot-high top of the Old Man is the most inaccessible summit in Britain, the highest of our true stacks[31] but also the most imposing and difficult – jamming cracks and mantelshelves, traverses and overhangs, a magnificent rock climb, one of the great classics in the British repertoire. The base is narrower than the top, and the long crack of the second pitch in particular is far beyond the vertical. I look up the soaring south-east arête, see the livid scar left from the block pulled off by Will. Fulmars peer at us with amiable interest. I feel grateful for being here before their nesting, when their defensive gambit of projectile-vomiting a stream of stinking, yellow, oily liquid can render you unfit for human company and your clothes evermore unwearable. Their curiosity and lack of fear is distinctly endearing. You can understand why these 'mallies', as they're known in Orcadian dialect, were held to be ghosts of drowned sailors come back to seek contact with humankind.

We start the climb. I'm out of shape, I feel my age, the wind's cold, it's already well into the afternoon, the days of March are not long here in the north and this is a big, serious climb at a grade of extremely severe. It's filthy after the winter.

No one has yet climbed it this year, the holds are all banked out with fine silt and have to be cleaned as we go, the grit blown back in your eyes.

And yet I want to climb it.

I doubt if that ever occurred to me in my childhood, when I first saw my father's pictures. It was just something mysterious then, barely explained – an object of wonderment. And for God's sake, this great prick of a thing – what can you say about a sexagenarian's desire, far beyond the seasons of his strength, for this ascent?

Except, it's not like that. You can be reductive if you so wish, but view it through that lens and no more than a fraction of the picture comes through. Sure, you can think of this climb in terms of all the wan assertions of depleted testosterone and fading masculinity. But to me, achievement anyway is beside the point. The climbing is less physical sequence than symbol: a sunset thing, a rage against the dying of the light, a last waltz. The stack's presence for me transcribes the bass note of inconsolable grief that underscores every waking hour. The idea of it has gathered force in my mind through generations, and because I have survived this far, I come here as if by proxy – I come on this day in pilgrimage. Some indefinable sense of the life-journey is caught in the mesh of this great and tottering rock.

You know what I'm doing here is editorializing, talking at a remove, attempting to extrapolate meaning from experience; and experience isn't like that when you're living it through. Climbing especially isn't like that – it's immediate and in the moment, entirely absorbing to the senses. You think on rock, initially; but then you act. It becomes mindless, a kind of ecstasy, a dance in three-quarter-time to the stilled rhythms of geology. The birds wheel around you in the different dimension of air, and the roosting birds watch curiously and speak in tongues, and the void's beneath and the sun's circling westerly and the ferry back to the world of human concerns passes far beneath, butting a brief reminder of those into your consciousness.

When you climb in an elemental place, you go beyond all that fiddle of the everyday. Time's insistence is put aside. Each step you take is to a different rhythm, and potentially mortal.

Look here at this old man on the rock – he struggles to remember how to tie into his harness or make the moves, has to use his hand to hoist a foot to the starting hold. Then the old knowledge begins to ease back – the precise footwork, the deliberate adjustments, the fulcrums and pivots and levers creaking rustily back into use, and with them all the long delight. I have practised these impromptus all my life. I knew the silken ease when my body was strong; and saw that gift in my son's climbing too.

My father was a dancer – polished shoes, the woman in her sequins pressed against him, her back arched, that elegant style of things. For me, for my boy, instead these rough, high places where the world is tactile and at your fingertips. Where the world is natural.

Do you know how it smells, this stack, this pinnacle?

It reeks of sex. That salt, piquant musk when you have slipped detumescent from inside your lover lingers on its every ledge, fishy and strong. The tides swirl around its base and the seals sing from the boulder beach, their bodies slick and round. All this, and all the while the sun is westering, shining now through the last cleft before we come to the top, the rock corrugated as weathered flesh, the mounting urgency. The old Jacobean coupling, love and death – it belongs here. West is the landscape of loss. West is where the light dies.

At last, the summit, isolated, and beyond it the gathering dark. On the same latitude here as Cape Farewell in Greenland, we huddle briefly – Ed, Martin, Ray and myself – in a heathery hollow on top, our breath ghosting out, to shelter from an icy crystal wind. The sun dips into the sea, a bright moon near the full has risen to sail through the eastern sky. Those who do not climb might think as do those who cannot love, in terms of conquest – but for us, up here, it is not thus:

> O chestnut-tree, great-rooted blossomer,
> Are you the leaf, the blossom, or the bole?
> O body swayed to music, O brightening glance,
> How can we know the dancer from the dance?[32]

My father, my son, my woman – memories now. The stars are coming out and the waves surge far beneath. We rope down into the night below, and the moon casts our spinning shadows soft and silvered on the stack as the seals wail and moan. This too is a moment of ecstasy, a journey westering through the passages of joy. Love and death, light and dark, grief and joy…

Unseeing at the end of the day, we climb back by perilous paths to the top of the black cliff behind, turn our faces towards a sun that will rise, and walk away over the moor, where every solid boulder shimmers and all that haunt us there are the wild birds' cries.

Acknowledgements

'*No man is an island...*' To put this book out and not acknowledge the warmth and support received over the years it describes would be the most churlish omission. The outdoor community and the literary community of Wales in their understated and caring ways have seen me through. I thank them from the heart. As I do individual friends, who knew the importance of quiet sympathy and patient presence, and who proved what instinct had long sensed, by which I was drawn to them. So, variously, to Al Alvarez, Elizabeth Ashworth, Desmond Barry, Sally Baker, John, Jan, Robin and Jodie Beatty, Polly Biven, Martin and Maggie Boysen, Bill and Honor Bowker, Joe and Val Brown, David and Helen of Browsers' Bookshop of Porthmadog, Colleen Campbell – the original Rocky Mountain Hippy Chick, Martin Crook, Sian Melangell Dafydd, Mrs. Frances Denby, Ed Douglas, Paul Evans, Grant Gee, Jon Gower, Sarah and Conor Gregory, Professor Ian Gregson, Niall and Deborah Griffiths, Roger Hubank, Jamie Jauncey, Nigel Jenkins, Aled Jones of the BBC in Bangor, Stephanie Kerstein, Catherine Lockerbie, Jan Levi, Celia Locks, Robert Macfarlane, Isobel MacLeod, Jane MacNamee, Aonghas MacNeacail, Andrew MacNeillie, Cameron and Gina MacNeish, Bernadette McDonald, Professor Patrick McGuinness, Robert Minhinnick, Jan and Elizabeth Morris, Mavis

Acknowledgements

Nicholson, Sian Northey, Shannon O'Donoghue, Tom Perrin, Angharad Price, Hannah and Jan Rawlinson, Medwen Roberts, Keith Robertson, Harry Rothman, Scouse Bob in Llanrhaeadr, Tony Shaw, George Smith, Luke Stephenson, Professor Gwyn Thomas, Amanda Townend, Doug and Ann Verity, Tony and Martha Whittome, Robert Wilkinson, Glenda Williams, Ken and Gloria Wilson, Neil Wilson, Ray Wood, and to all those I have inadvertently omitted, again, thank you. Without you, there would have been no book.

I would also like to thank the staff at the Mountain Culture department within the Banff Centre, Alberta, for extraordinary warmth and support on repeated visits, for the invigorating opportunity to teach there and for the award of a Fleck Fellowship in 2006 that enabled me to ponder many of the themes considered in the text in the most stimulating and magnificent of environments. Closer to home, *Academi*, the excellent representative body for writers in Wales, is a boon to all who are of this small jewel of a nation.

I owe an enormous debt of gratitude and affection to Jessica Woollard of the Marsh Agency – a tigress on behalf of all her authors, and the most empathic and sensitive of editors – for her enduring faith in the project and sharp and timely application of the occasional boot; as I do also to my skilful and amiable editor, Sarah Norman, and publisher, Toby Mundy, at Atlantic Books for faith beyond the call of reason and very good lunches. I feel, as a writer must, that these friends are the true authors of a book for which I have been simply the channel of expression. Again, thank you, all of you, from the heart: *Diolch I bawb o galon…*

Ariege, April 2010

Notes

Book One: The Aftermath

1   Henry David Thoreau, 'Walking', in Carl Bode (ed.), *The Portable Thoreau* (Penguin 1982) pp. 602–3.

2   Antonio Damasio, *The Feeling of What Happens* (Vintage 2000), p. 16.

3   John Bayley, *The Widower's House* (Duckworth 2001), p. 100.

4   cf Joan Didion, *The White Album* (Penguin 1981), p. 11: 'We tell ourselves stories in order to live'.

5   Published in the *Observer* magazine (14 August 2005).

6   R. L. Stevenson, *Travels with a Donkey in the Cévennes* (Dent 1925), p. 158.

7   *Waincrat* – a Cumbrian dialect word according to Jacquetta (who was from Kendal), which she told me was synonymous with 'wanderer'.

8   A mawn pool – the term is peculiar to Radnorshire – is a shallow moorland pool, the name deriving from the Welsh word *fawnog* – a quagmire.

9   Shakespeare, *Sonnets* 60.

10   The fifteen-year-old Joan Abbott Parry, daughter of Judge Parry of

Manchester, who drowned here in September 1904. Her grave is on the right as you go into Aberdaron churchyard. There is an essay about her in my *Spirits of Place* (Gwasg Gomer 1997).

11   Patrick Kavanagh, 'On Raglan Road', in *Collected Poems* (Martin Brian & O'Keeffe 1972), p. 186.

12   Wallace Stevens, 'The Rock', in *Collected Poems of Wallace Stevens* (Faber 1955), p. 525.

13   Sigmund Freud, 'Mourning and Melancholia', in *On Murder, Mourning and Melancholia*, tr. Shaun Whiteside (Penguin 2005), pp. 204–5.

14   William Hazlitt, 'On the Love of the Country', in *Hazlitt: Selected Essays* (Nonesuch 1930), p. 5.

15   Sigmund Freud, *The Uncanny*, tr. David McLintock (Penguin 2003), p. 144. As a pointer to the ease with which I still succumb to magical thinking, the passage following the one quoted in the text treats of numerology, the inclination 'to accord a secret significance to the persistent recurrence of [a] number – to see it as a pointer to his allotted life-span.' (*ibid* p. 145). The number Freud cites here – and it gave me a distinct shudder to read it – was 62, my own age as I read it.

16   B. S. Johnson, *Poems* (Constable 1964).

17   Albert Camus, *The Myth of Sisyphus*, tr. Justin O'Brien (Hamish Hamilton 1955), p. 12.

18   *Ibid*. p. 13.

Book Two: Pre-histories

1   Keidrych Rhys, *The Van Pool & other poems* (Routledge 1942), p. 32.

2   Walt Whitman, 'Crossing Brooklyn Ferry', line 90, in *Leaves of Grass* (Norton 2002), p. 139.

3   C. S. Lewis, *A Grief Observed* (Faber 1961), p. 6.

4   Shorthand, this, for an academic consensus that dates a cycle of poems the transcription of which is of much later date back to perhaps as early as the ninth century. For more information, the introduction to the volume cited in the following note is seminal.

5   Ifor Williams (ed.), 'Stafell Gynddylan', in *Canu Llywarch Hen* (Cardiff 1970), p. 35.

6   Gillian Rose, *Mourning Becomes the Law: Philosophy and Representation* (Cambridge University Press 1996), p. 10.

7   Elizabeth Gaskell, *Mary Barton*, Stephen Gill (ed.) (Penguin 1970),
p. 75 – the first half of this novel is one of the high-water marks of
Victorian fiction – its quality the more striking by contrast with the
ghastly sentimentality of its conclusion.

8   *Nain* means grandmother in Welsh.

9   Iain Sinclair, *Lights Out for the Territory* (Granta 1997), p. 4.

10   Anthony Burgess, *Little Wilson and Big God* (Vintage 2002), p. 74.

11   Gwyn Thomas, *Y pethau diwethaf a phethau eraill* (Gwasg Gee 1975),
p. 20.

12   Flora Finching – the childhood sweetheart of Arthur Clennam in
Dickens' *Little Dorrit*, re-encountered in his middle years and
become matronly, affected and florid.

13   Penelope Shuttle & Peter Redgrove, *The Wise Wound: Menstruation
& Everywoman* (Gollancz 1978, revised edition with a foreword by
Margaret Drabble, Paladin 1986).

14   Detective Chief Superintendent Dennis Greenslade, head of
Operation Julie, quoted in 'Operation Julie', *New Musical Express*
(18 March 1978).

15   It might be noted here that LSD, having been extensively used
both by government departments and psychiatrists prior to that
date, was criminalized – and some years later categorized as a
Class A drug along with heroin and cocaine – late in 1966, without
proper medical trials to establish its dangers, after a more-than-
usually flippant and puerile debate in parliament, and in response
to an ill-informed and demonizing scare campaign in the gutter
press, which sputters on indignantly to this day. By contrast, an
exhaustive two-year study commissioned by the Royal Society of
Arts and published in March 2007 assessed twenty drugs on their
capacity to cause harm, ability to induce dependency and criminal
or anti-social behaviour, and impact on society, communities and
families. LSD came fourteenth on the list – well below either
alcohol or tobacco. One of the authors of the study, Professor Colin
Blakemore, commented that its object had been 'to bring a dispas-
sionate approach to a very passionate issue... Some conclusions
might appear to be liberal in stance, but that was not our starting
position. We intended to reach conclusions that were evidence

based.' But then, as the police would no doubt hasten to point out, the Professor is one of the intelligentsia.

16 R. D. Laing, *The Politics of Experience and the Bird of Paradise* (Penguin 1967), p. 156.

17 Sandoz – for an excellent account of the impact of LSD on British popular culture, see Andy Roberts, *Albion Dreaming* (Marshall Cavendish 2008).

18 Jim Perrin, 'Venues', in *On and Off the Rocks* (Gollancz 1986), p. 177.

19 Samuel Taylor Coleridge, 'Sonnet to a friend who asked, how I felt when the nurse first presented my infant to me', lines 13–14, in *Coleridge: Poetical Works* (Oxford University Press 1967), p. 154.

20 'Frost at Midnight', *ibid*. p. 242.

21 William Blake, 'Poems from the Notebook III', in *Blake: The Complete Poems* W.H. Stevenson (ed.), (Longman 1971), p. 145.

22 *Ibid.*

23 Nia Wyn, *Blue Sky July* (Seren Books 2007), p. 173.

24 Bruno Bettelheim, *The Uses of Enchantment* (Penguin 1991), p. 63.

25 Robert Graves, 'Rocky Acres' in *Collected Poems 1965* (Cassell 1965), p. 7.

26 T. H. Parry-Williams, 'Hon' in *Detholiad o Gerddi* (Gwasg Gomer 1972), p. 89.

27 Samuel Taylor Coleridge, 'Frost at Midnight', *op. cit.* p. 242.

28 Edward Abbey, *Desert Solitaire* (Touchstone 1990), p. 247.

29 Jim Perrin, *The Climbing Essays* (NWP Ltd 2006), p. 13.

> Other times we acquire cars, race them down to Wales, build up a collection behind his house at Bigil, and then play the chicken game. The drivers' doors come off, we get into our bike leathers. A mile up the road is the quarry at Allt Ddu, 80 feet down to 200 feet of water. We've snipped through the chain-link fencing. Now we loop it back to give a six-foot gap at which you can get a hundred-yard run. The doors get thrown in first. Then the game. Gun the engine, aim for the gap, at the very last second jump so that you hit the fence in mid-air, bounce off and the car continues on its trajectory into black and midnight water; the plume of spray, the bubbles hissing

to the surface, the returning silence. If the lights and sirens come up the hill, we melt away down the paths into the dark. Years later, after Al's death, there is a European Community environmental reclamation initiative. It fills in the quarry – it's now called Bus Stop, is a popular venue for climbers. Before that happened they sent the police divers down to check it out. They found a pyramid of cars reaching to twenty feet below the surface, had to crane them all back up and check them out. Al's memorial…

30   The last fight I ever had – and I hope it remains so – took place on the late train from Euston to Holyhead some time in the 1990s, by which time I was getting far too old for such play. It was a Friday night, not many people in the carriage beyond Rugby, and I was talking across the aisle to a young Irish medical student on his way home to Greystones in Co. Wicklow. A big, heavy Irishman with a bottle of cheap whisky in a brown paper bag and another on the luggage rack was swaying continually up and down between his seat and the buffet. He took a dislike to the medical student – a very mild and inoffensive young man – and the drunker he became, the more objectionable the comments passed. Somewhere before Crewe he rose from his seat and began swaying down the aisle again, eyes on the medical student and a knife in his hand. I went for him, smashed his wrist down on the edge of a seat, and snatched up the knife from where it fell. The big Irishman grabbed the blade as I pulled it away. I stepped back, tossed the knife on a seat, caught him with a perfectly weighted punch on the side of the jaw, his head snapped back and he crumpled in the aisle. The medical student, a little nonplussed by this turn of events, helped me drag him to his seat, bound up his hand – which was bleeding profusely – with a handkerchief, and when I suggested he go back to his own place and keep his head down gladly did so. I pocketed the knife, hid the whisky, and sat by the Irishman as he stirred back into consciousness. When he realized what had happened he was abject in his apologies, pleaded for the knife and whisky, both of which I refused, tried to thrust £50 notes on me for the young Irishman and myself, then slumped into snoring slumber. I stayed on the train beyond Bangor to Holyhead, saw them both on the boat and told the student to keep a very low profile and stay well clear. The main and extraordinary thing that still strikes me about

this incident was the way in which every other passenger in that carriage maintained perfectly oblivious, calm behind their *Evening Standards*. When I recounted the story to an Irish friend from Co. Roscommon, the writer and mountaineer Dermot Somers, he confided knowingly, 'That would either have been a BIFFO or a BUFFALO.' 'Meaning?' I quizzed. 'A big idiotic fucker from Offaly, or a big ugly fucker from Athlone, Laoise or Offaly', came the clarification. Enough said!

31 J. G. Frazer, *The Golden Bough* (Macmillan 1922), p. 267.

32 i.e. cannabis in resin form – freely available in the community we lived in.

33 The opioid analgesics with which this painful and debilitating condition was treated, and the insidious direness of their effect, convinced me of something I was later to witness in my friend Annette Mortlock's and in Jacquetta's final illnesses, and be at pains to avoid in the onset of my own supposedly terminal cancer – which is that pain is best combated intellectually by viewing it as neurological illusion, and that the price of dulling it, along with your intellectual faculties, through the use of drugs is too high a one to pay. I could point, as well, to the medical profession's complicity in the wholesale despatch of terminal patients approaching the end through the simple expedient of turning up the morphine pump. The usual comments on power are applicable here. My view is that I will make my own bargains and choose my own time to go with a clear mind, and steer well clear of the habitual disregards of those arrogant bastards, the doctors. Joke: 'What's the difference between God and a doctor?' 'God knows she's God – a doctor just thinks she is.'

34 This rings very true – Will was scabrously dismissive of older generations and their abilities. His pet name for me at the time was 'the crippled old bastard'. About others, he was rather less delicate.

35 'Runner' – a running belay – a protection device that can lessen the distance and consequences of a fall.

36 Yes, my car was robbed too – but it was open, so no great harm was done.

37 The top grade of climbing, extremely severe, was subdivided in the mid-1970s at the time of one of the sport's periodical revolutionary surges in achieved difficulty by the use of numbers – E1

upwards, the current highest standard in 2009 standing at about E11. The term 'on sight' refers to the manner and style of ascent – done without any prior acquaintance or inspection, on or from a rope, both of which have the effect of substantially easing a climb's difficulty. There are still very few ascents made 'on sight' of climbs of E7 or above.

Book Three: Chiaroscuro

1   Described in Jim Perrin, *Travels with The Flea* (NWP Ltd 2002).

2   A remarkable man, too little known outside his native Wales. A pupil of the gifted and odious Eric Gill, Jonah's stone-carving and lettering grace many public buildings in Wales. His novel *Zorn* (Heinemann 1986) is elliptically one of the most powerful on the subject of the Second World War, and the essays collected in *The Gallipoli Diary* (Seren 1989) are on a par with those of David Jones in *Epoch and Artist* (Faber 1959), with which they share many preoccupations. Jonah was married to the Hebrew novelist Judit Maro, and died in 2006.

3   i.e. disciples of the writings of the American anthropologist and peyote-head Carlos Castaneda – writings I suspect of being every bit as fictively inclined as those of George Borrow.

4   W. G. Sebald, *The Rings of Saturn* (Vintage 2002), p. 4. The book is, of course, far more than simply a description of a walking tour in East Anglia, and is certainly one of the most potent and resonant post-modern statements on melancholia and the twenty-first century human condition. I have to admit that I find its unremitting pessimism about human nature both bracing and accurate. Or as Nick Cave puts it, rather more succinctly, 'People just ain't no good'.

5   R. S. Thomas, 'The Moor', in *Collected Poems 1945–1990* (Dent 1993), p. 166.

6   *Plygain* – from the Latin *pulli cantio* – 'cock crow': it was originally a service of carols held between three and six on Christmas morning. In its rare surviving form in the complex border country of Denbighshire and Montgomeryshire, it is held in the evenings between mid-December and mid-January.

7   Gwenallt, 'Rhydcymerau', in *Eples* (Gwasg Gomer 1951), p. 20. This is one of the great Welsh poems of the last century, published

in the same year as an infamous pronouncement by a government spokesman that 'We intend to plant 800,000 acres in Wales. We intend to change the face of Wales. We know there will be opposition but we intend to force this thing through'. For conifers, today read wind-turbines – the Welsh landscape has long been an abused hostage to the whims of English government policy. The collection *Eples* ('Ferment') by Gwenallt, the bardic name of the poet David James Jones [1899–1968], is as accomplished and significant in twentieth-century Welsh literature as those of any major contemporaneous poet in English. He was a cousin of the great Welsh prose writer D. J. Williams, one whose family, like many others, moved from rural Carmarthenshire to the industrial towns of south-west Wales. Gwenallt's father was incinerated by molten metal spilt in an accident at the steel mill where he worked. Gwenallt himself rebelled against the Calvinism and industrial brutalization of his background, was imprisoned in Dartmoor for his pacifism, faltered his way through Christian Socialism and Marxism, on a visit to the Irish *Gaeltacht* encountered the idea of nationhood, and emerged to a reconciliation between Christianity and social justice as radical as it is rare. A profoundly interesting writer in many genres, his organic perception of the nation as cultural entity – not properly subservient to the requirements of the state but often, and most particularly in its stress on individual human creativity, superior to the latter's mechanical uniformity – strikes me as being of crucial importance. The poem 'Rhydcymerau', on its most obvious level, is about the effect on a small rural Welsh community of that 1951 government spokesman's infamous edict. I was in Hungary several years ago, lecturing at the university in Budapest on the tradition of political dissent in Britain, and read this poem to the audience – both in Welsh, where the language builds from grave, calm, humorous recall to spitting, apocalyptic ferocity – and in English. The response to it, from students in a country conquered and subject throughout much of its recent history that has yet managed stubbornly to practise the forms of cultural resistance and maintain cultural identity, was heartening, overwhelming. The full text of the poem, in my own translation, runs thus:

They have planted saplings for the third war
On the land of Esgeir-ceir and the fields of Tir-bach

By Rhydcymerau.
I remember my grandmother in Esgeir-ceir,
Pleating her apron as she sat by the fire,
 Skin of her face yellowy-dry as a Peniarth manuscript
And on her old lips the Welsh of Pantycelyn.
A piece of last century's puritan Wales she was.
My grandfather, though I never saw him,
Was a character – small, vital, tough, lame,
Fond of his pint;
He'd wandered in from the eighteenth century.
They brought up nine children,
Poets, deacons, Sunday School teachers,
Leaders each of them in their little sphere.

My Uncle Dafydd farmed Tir-bach,
A country poet, a local rhymester,
His song to the bantam cockerel famous around:
'The bantam cock goes scratching
Round and round the garden…'
I went to him each summer holiday
Of shepherding and sketching lines of cynghanedd,
Englynion and eight-line stanzas in 8–7 measure.
He too brought up eight children,
The oldest son a Calvinist minister
Who also wrote poetry –
In our family a nestful of bards.

And now there is nothing there but trees,
And their insolent roots sucking the ancient earth –
Conifers where once was community,
Forest in place of farms,
Corrupt whine of the southern English where once was
     poetry, divinity;
A barking of foxes where lambs and children cried,
And in the central darkness
Is the den of the English Minotaur,
And on the branches, as on crosses,
Corpses of poets, deacons, ministers, Sunday School
     teachers,
Bleaching, rain-washed, desiccated in the wind.

8   Gwenallt, 'Yr Eglwysi', in *Gwreiddiau* (Gwasg Aberystwyth 1959),
     p. 99.

9   See Richard Dawkins, *The God Delusion* (Random House 2006). Whilst not necessarily disagreeing with some of Dawkins's conclusions, and admiring the brio with which he pursues his arguments, the easy and obvious targets he chooses to attack, and the limitations to his knowledge of subject, do not impress.

10   'The Cattle Raid of Cúchulainn' – centrepiece of the eighth-century Ulster cycle of heroic tales – is an early-medieval Irish tale of epic proportions, rich in folk-tale motifs. A translation by Thomas Kinsella, *The Táin*, is published by Oxford University Press.

11   Anne Ross, *Pagan Celtic Britain* (Constable 1993), p. 304.

12   John Donne, *Elegies*, 9, 'The Autumnal', in A. J. Smith (ed.), *The Complete English Poems* (Penguin 1971), p. 105.

13   Alwyn D. Rees's classic study of the nearby parish of Llanfihangel yng Gwynfa (*Life in a Welsh Countryside*, University of Wales Press 1950) describes in some detail the forms of courtship from a period sixty years before my time in Llanrhaeadr. Whilst modern contraception had an obvious enabling effect on the rituals I witnessed in Llanrhaeadr, those Rees describes are still strikingly liberal.

14   Jim Perrin, *On and Off the Rocks* (Gollancz 1986).

15   W. G. Sebald, *The Rings of Saturn* (Vintage 2002), p. 182.

16   A. E. Housman, *A Shropshire Lad* (Harrap 1953), p. 60. These two phrases are from lyric XL, 'Into my heart an air that kills'.

17   W. G. Sebald, *op.cit.* p. 177.

18   *The Secret of the Golden Flower*, tr. Richard Wilhelm, foreword and commentary by C. G. Jung (Routledge 1931), p. 49.

19   W. G. Sebald, *op.cit.* p. 255.

20   Thomas Hardy, 'In Tenebris – II', in *Collected Poems of Thomas Hardy, New Wessex Edition* (Macmillan 1976), p. 168.

21   Albert Camus, 'Helen's Exile', in Philip Thody (ed.), *Selected Essays and Notebooks* (Penguin 1979), p. 136.

22   William Cobbett, *The Woodlands* (1825), quoted in Richard Mabey's enchanting and magisterial *Flora Britannica* (Sinclair-Stevenson 1998), p. 198.

23   Bill Condry was for many years the *Guardian* Country Diarist for Wales (a mantle I later inherited, thanks in large measure to his tutelage and patronage). He was the finest field naturalist I ever

met, one of the best writers on natural history in English, and a wholly endearing and delightful man. He died at the age of 80 in 1998, and his widow Penny still lives in their old house near Eglwysfach.

24 John Donne, 'The Good Morrow', *op. cit.* p. 60.

25 Bertrand Russell, 'Prologue: What I have lived for', in *The Autobiography of Bertrand Russell*, Volume 1 (George Allen and Unwin 1967).

26 Michael Mott, *The Seven Mountains of Thomas Merton* (Houghton Mifflin 1984), p. 535.

27 R. L. Stevenson, 'A Night Among the Pines', from *Travels With a Donkey in the Cévennes* (Dent 1925), p. 157.

28 Gerard Manley Hopkins, 'Spring and Fall', in *The Poems of Gerard Manley Hopkins* (Fourth edition, revised, Oxford 1970), p. 89. The 'Goldengrove unleaving' reference in the next paragraph is to the second line of this poem.

29 R. L. Stevenson, *op. cit.* p. 156.

30 John Berger, 'The White Bird', in Geoff Dyer (ed.), *John Berger: Selected Essays* (Bloomsbury 2001), p. 363.

Book Four: Life, dismantled

1 Kitchen roll and a hot iron, since you ask – quite infallible.

2 Several poor women from the vicinity of Barley, under Pendle Hill in Lancashire, were accused of witchcraft, tortured, tried and hanged at Lancaster in August 1612. The outbreak of vicious superstition and paranoia was dramatized by the popular writer William Harrison Ainsworth in his lurid novel of 1848, *The Lancashire Witches*. A more interesting and judicious analysis of the early-modern period witch pogroms throughout Europe is given in Shuttle & Redgrove's *The Wise Wound*, *op. cit.* Ch. VI.

3 This wonderful old village pub had featured in a film starring Hugh Grant, *The Englishman Who Went Up a Hill But Came Down a Mountain*, and had recently reopened after a period of closure.

4 John Rothenstein and Martin Butlin, *Turner* (Heinemann 1965), p. 74.

5 Thomas Hardy, 'At Rushy-Pond', *op. cit.* p. 713.

6   Albert Camus, 'Helen's Exile', *op. cit.* p. 147.

7   Homer, *The Odyssey of Homer*, tr. Richmond Lattimore (Harper & Row 1965), Book X, pp. 333–5.

8   Jim Perrrin, *The Villain* (Hutchinson 2005). I still have an early design for the dust jacket of this on which the subtitle reads 'Don Whillans – Bad Boy of the mountains'. And am thankful it wasn't used – the book brought me quite enough trouble anyway.

9   W. B. Yeats, 'The Fisherman', *Collected Poems* (Macmillan 1967), p. 167.

10   Thomas Hood, 'No!', in John Clubbe (ed.), *Selected Poems of Thomas Hood* (Harvard 1970), p. 122.

11   John Keats, 'The Eve of St Agnes', lines 370–371, in John Barnard (ed.), *John Keats: The Complete Poems*, Second Edition (Penguin 1976).

12   Thomas Traherne, *The Centuries of Meditations*, I, 31, in F. C. Happold, *Mysticism: A Study and an Anthology* (Penguin 1963), p. 341.

13   *Ibid.*

14   Jiddu Krishnamurti, *Meeting Life* (Penguin 1991), p. 44.

15   For an entertaining riff around this point from a knowledgeable indigenous perspective, read Gita Mehta, *Karma Cola: Marketing the Mystic East* (Penguin 1993).

16   R. S. Thomas, 'The Moon in Lleyn', in *R. S. Thomas, Collected Poems 1945–1990* (Phoenix 1995), p. 282.

17   Bede pithily summarizes the situation thus: 'Augustine then declared: "There are many points on which your customs conflict with ours, or rather with those of the universal Church. Nevertheless, if you will agree with me on three points, I am ready to countenance all your other customs..." [But] ... if they refused to preach to the English the way of life, they would eventually suffer at their hands the penalty of death. And, by divine judgement, all these things happened as Augustine foretold.' Bede, *A History of the English Church and People*, tr. Leo Sherley-Price (Penguin 1968), pp. 102–3.

18   Jiddu Krishnamurti, *op. cit.* p. 89, cf. 'Truth is not something to be attained, to be experienced, to be held. It is there for those who can see it. But most of us are everlastingly seeking, moving from one

fad to another...'.

19 Gillian Rose, *Mourning Becomes the Law* (Cambridge University Press 1996), p. 137.

20 Thomas Traherne, *loc. cit.*

21 Cathal O'Searcaigh, 'An Tobar' ('The Well'), in *An Bealach na Bhaile: Rogha Danta* (Homecoming: Selected Poems) (Clo Iar-Chonnachta Teo 1993), p. 45. (The translation from the Irish is by Gabriel Fitzmaurice).

22 W. G. Sebald, *The Emigrants*, tr. Michael Hulse (Vintage 2002), p. 230.

23 Lama Anagarika Govinda, *The Way of the White Clouds* (Hutchinson 1966), p. 60.

24 i.e. one accomplished without the use of any artificial aids such as pitons, slings for assistance, tension from the rope, etc.

25 The list of mountaineering accounts from Victorian times right down to the present day where the imaginative has played at least as large a part as the actual is both long and amusing, and would appear to include even one of the best-known of modern mountain stories of 'heroism' and survival.

26 There is a clear division in the modern sport between 'adventure climbing', in which as the name implies the risk factor remains traditionally high, and 'sport climbing', which is highly technical, gymnastic and completely safe. Will's distinction, which left his preference in no doubt, was terse: 'One's for if you've got balls. The other's for bullshitters and human yo-yos.'

27 Fyodor Dostoyevsky, *The Gambler, Bobok, A Nasty Story*, tr. Jessie Coulson (Penguin 1966), p. 167.

28 Lawrie Holliwell, who died when the belay of his abseil rope gave way whilst he was inspecting a potential climb on Craig yr Ysfa in September 1973, was one of the most significant and gifted figures from the time when I was most active in the sport of climbing. He and his brother Les, with whom he mostly climbed, were garrulous and entertaining East-enders. At the time of his death, Lawrie was just getting back in to the activity after a long absence following his marriage. His companion on the day he died, John Kingston, later maried Lawrie's widow Liz. He too died, in a car accident on an icy road in the 1970s, widowing Liz for a second time.

29 Jim Perrin, 'A Valediction' (1972), in *The Climbing Essays* (NWP Ltd 2006), pp. 257–9.

30 Every pitch – the sections into which a climb is broken up, each of them separated by a stance and belay – is given a technical grade (e.g. 4a, 5c, 6b, etc.) within the British grading system as well as the overall adjectival grade of the climb – VS, E1 or whatever. At that time, 6a was getting towards the higher end of the system.

31 Alison Wertheimer, *A Special Scar*, (Second edition, Routledge 2001), p. 217.

32 Primo Levi, *The Drowned and the Saved*, tr. Raymond Rosenthal (Abacus 1988), pp. 52–3.

33 Al Alvarez, *The Savage God: A Study of Suicide* (Weidenfeld & Nicolson 1971), p. 227.

34 Edward Thomas, *The Collected Poems of Edward Thomas*, R. George Thomas (ed.) (Oxford 1981), p. 41.

35 T. H. Parry-Williams, *Detholiad o Gerddi* (Gwasg Gomer 1972), p. 39 (my translation).

36 i.e. trying and failing to do it.

37 A Manchester institution – the Wilmslow Road, three miles south from the city centre, is lined with curry houses and Indian sweet-shops.

38 Elisabeth Kübler-Ross and David Kessler, *On Grief and Grieving* (Scribner 2007), p. 108.

39 Gillian Rose, *Paradiso* (Menard Press 1999), p. 46.

40 Mitchell's Fold is a Bronze Age stone circle of fifteen uprights, the largest of them the height of a tall man. The associated story runs thus: 'In bad times long ago, the people hereabouts were hungry. All they had was a fairy cow who came night and morning to be milked, gave enough for all so long as everyone only took one pail. But a witch came and milked the cow into a sieve until she ran dry, went away, and was never seen again. A giant had owned the cow, and when he found out what had happened, he imprisoned the witch within a stockade of stone from which she could never escape. And there the stones stand to this day.'

41 Friedrich Hölderlin, 'Erntezeit' ('Harvest-time'), in Leonard Forster (ed.), *The Penguin Book of German Verse* (Penguin 1957), p. 292.

42 Colin Murray Parkes, *Bereavement: Studies of Grief in Adult Life*

(Pelican 1975), p. 79. The sane, intelligent balance of Parkes's writings on the experience of bereavement is wholly refreshing after the sugary mendacities of the school of Kübler-Ross.

43 Samuel Taylor Coleridge, *The Notebooks of Samuel Taylor Coleridge*, Kathleen Coburn (ed.) (Routledge 1957–1990), II, p. 2583.

Book Five: Hidden Lord of the Crooked Path

1 Neil Peart, *Ghost Rider* (ECW Press 2002), pp. 87–8.

2 Christopher Rush, *To Travel Hopefully: Journal of a Death Not Foretold* (Profile Books 2005).

3 Dannie Abse, *The Presence* (Hutchinson 2007), p. 56.

4 Joan Didion, *The Year of Magical Thinking* (Fourth Estate 2005).

5 Ted Hughes, 'Caryatids (2)' in *Birthday Letters* (Faber 1998) p. 6.

6 Hardy's *Poems of 1912–13* spring to mind here, and fine though they are, the reason for consigning mention of them to an endnote is that they have always seemed to me a lament for the passing and the failure of love ('Summer gave us sweets, but autumn wrought division?/Things were not lastly as firstly well' – 'After a Journey'), rather than for the loved woman herself. ('...I shall traverse old love's domain/Never again.' – 'At Castle Boterel'. He did, of course, with his second wife Florence Emily, and rather promptly at that.)

7 The *Grief Journal*, which is unpublished, is among the papers of Flora Mayor in the possession of her niece Teresa, Lady Rothschild. Substantial extracts are quoted in Sybil Oldfield's admirable and fascinating *Spinsters of this Parish* (Virago 1984). Flora Mayor's novels include *The Rector's Daughter*, published by Leonard and Virginia Woolf's Hogarth Press in 1924 – one of the underrated masterpieces of early twentieth-century fiction.

8 'The widowers imagined, poor creatures, that women were always running after them. They misunderstood the kindness women bestowed on them in their trouble. They became inordinately vain, as if with an occupational disease. Pathetic really.' John Bayley, *op. cit.* pp. 48–9.

9 Colin Murray Parkes, *op. cit.* p. 64.

10 Aonghas MacNeacail, 'I saw you among the apples' in *hymn to a*

young demon (Polygon 2007), p. 5.

11   Adam Phillips, *Darwin's Worms* (Faber 1999), p. 118. Taken together, the four essays that make up Phillips's book are an extraordinary post-modern accommodation to mortality, and written with an elegance of expression and intelligence that are often breathtaking. Curiously, in my journey through grief the other book that was of most help was the bracingly provocative and beautiful memoir *Love's Work* (Vintage 1997) by the philosopher Gillian Rose – Phillips's sister-in-law.

12   Anne Karpf, 'If you offered me closure on my mother's death, I'd throw it back in your face', (*Guardian* 11 August 2007).

13   Most Herdwick sheep were slaughtered by government edict during the foot and mouth epidemic in Britain of 2001 – a policy in response to a catastrophe of its own creating that still fills me with disgust. I'm not sure I wouldn't rather see 'honourable' members of parliament slaughtered wholesale than innocent sheep and cattle. Though perhaps, populist though it may be, that's rather too extreme a view.

14   The leading British rock climber at the end of the nineteenth century, his 'Stable Door Traverse' was a favourite valley entertainment at Wasdale Head. A photograph by the Abraham Brothers of Keswick exists of Jones demonstrating the problem. He was killed on the Dent Blanche in 1899.

15   *The Secret of the Golden Flower*, *op. cit.* p. 29.

16   Samuel Taylor Coleridge, *op. cit.* III, 4087n.

17   Sigmund Freud, *The Uncanny*, *op. cit.* p. 148.

18   Adam Phillips, *op. cit.* p. 117.

19   Samuel Taylor Coleridge, 'Dejection: An Ode', line 41, *op. cit.* p. 365.

20   T. H. Parry-Williams, 'Oerddwr', *op. cit.* p. 91.

21   Literally habitat or home region – usually applied to the territorial sense of Welsh mountain sheep.

22   I might express my mystification here about the modern preference for the verbose and sententious John Muir, who as a writer is as manifestly Thoreau's inferior as Barbara Cartland is Jane Austen's.

23   Henry David Thoreau, 'Journal, January 1858', *op. cit.* p. 590.

24 Tr. 'The lads of Cwrt Isaf'.

25 Hugh MacDiarmid, 'Bracken Hills in Autumn', in Michael Grieve & William Russell Aitken (eds.), *The Complete Poems of Hugh MacDiarmid*, (Penguin 1985), II. p. 1152.

26 Richard Mabey, *Nature Cure* (Chatto & Windus 2005), p. 224.

27 Gillian Rose, *Love's Work*, *op. cit.* p. 95.

28 Samuel Taylor Coleridge, 'Dejection: An Ode', *loc. cit.*

29 Adam Phillips, *op. cit.* p. 117.

30 E. V. Gordon (ed.), *The Battle of Maldon* (Methuen Old English Library 1937), p. 61, lines 312–13.

31 Stac Lee and Stac an Armin in the St Kilda group are both higher, but are really rocky islets rather than the detached pillar that is a stack in climbing parlance.

32 W. B. Yeats, 'Among School Children', *op. cit.* p. 245.

© Ray Wood

JIM PERRIN is one of Britain's most highly regarded writers on travel, nature and the outdoors and in his youth was one of the country's most notable rock-climbers. He is a regular contributor to the *Daily Telegraph*, *Guardian*, *Climber* and *The Great Outdoors*. Among many other awards he has twice won the Boardman Tasker Prize for mountain literature and was voted Scottish Columnist of the Year 2009. He has written twelve books to date, including *Menlove*, *The Villain: A Life of Don Whillans*, *River Map*, *The Climbing Essays* and *Travels with The Flea*. He is a Fellow of the Welsh Academy, an Honorary Fellow of Bangor University and the *Guardian*'s Country Diarist for Wales.